De Minimis

De Minimis

LAW, HUMOR, AGING AND OTHER LITTLE THINGS

• • •

Thomas Avery Brown

Dedication

• • •

To my family.

About De Minimis

• • •

It's not surprising to hear that the law is full of heavy, goofy sayings. We've all survived "ex officio" or "non compos mentis" or "nolo contenere" – not even really knowing what the hell they even mean.

One famous saying in the law is "de minimis non curat lex." This is famous mostly to first year law students, who love that it means: "The law does not concern itself with little things or trifles." So, the phrase "...de minimis..." means "...about little things.

In early 2008, I was enjoying one of the greatest little monthly, fun community newspapers on the planet – the SENIORS SUNSET TIMES out of the Olympic Peninsula in Washington. It was truly a sprawling, light, eclectic monthly that catered to the grey-haired set. (I argued then...and I argue now that a publication for Seniors shouldn't have the word "sunset" in its name...but it's too late for picky, lawyer accuracy.)

I liked the newspaper and felt that it needed an article or two about the effect of the law on senior citizens and how we golden agers could cope better with "the system." ...so I contacted Lora Messenger, the brilliant mother of this publication and offered to submit a column that might interest the readership...that was 84 columns and seven years ago...and happily, Lora and I continued our monthly dance.

The ripple effect has been amazing for me. Too many comments to count. Too many stories. Too many real-life impacts to believe.

What we produced is collected there and (now here!) for your enjoyment. There are high spots and low spots; but all the articles strive to touch some question or prejudice or ideal about the American legal system, and perhaps shine some light there.

I apologize for the concentration on Washington and Northwest issues and law...but that is the nature of the deal. I hope you enjoy these insights into the law and into lawyers and into their clients and into the Pacific Northwest.

About Me

• • •

Thomas A. Brown
Brown Lewis Janhunen & Spencer

I ATTENDED COLLEGE AND LAW school at Creighton University in my hometown of Omaha, Nebraska, which is also where I met the love of my life...my wife Beverly.

After law school, I served in the Government's Office of Economic Opportunity, in the Legal Services program, providing legal assistance to people and programs that needed help in coping with poverty and its consequences. One of those stops was with the Pierce CoAssistance Foundation in Tacoma, which brought us to the beautiful State of Washington.

I ended up accepting a job with a small firm in Aberdeen, Washington in 1972, where we raised our three amazing kids.

I have been with that same law firm for nearly 43 years, serving clients in Southwestern Washington. We've grown to as many as six lawyers at one time; but the four survivors continue our traditions and imprint on the community.

I've been handling complex business and personal litigation for most of my professional career, representing both defendants and plaintiffs. The emphasis of the firm has always been litigation, highlighting a sophisticated insurance defense practice mixed with a busy and successful plaintiff litigation practice. Our firm also handles business litigation, real estate disputes and probate litigation. Our firm prides itself on being the "family law firm" for many of the good folks and hometown businesses in Grays Harbor and Pacific Counties.

I have consistently received the highest possible professional rating (A-V) from Martindale-Hubbell, the most well known attorney rating system in the country.

I am responsible for one of the few million-dollar plaintiff jury verdicts in the history of Grays Harbor County. Our firm was also among the early pioneers in presenting computer-generated graphics and animation in a Grays Harbor County courtroom back in the late 1980s.

Proud of my early roots in the Legal Aid movement in America, I was honored to be the State Bar Association's appointee to the Washington State Office of Civil Legal Aid Oversight Committee, where I served beginning in 2005, including a term as Chair of the Committee.

I return nearly every year to serve as a volunteer in the Youth and Government Mock Trial Program in Olympia, where -- each time --the kids invariably show me how to be a better lawyer.

I am admitted to the Washington State Bar, the Nebraska State Bar, and the Federal District Courts for Nebraska and Washington. I am also admitted to the Bar of the Ninth Circuit Court of Appeals and to the Bar of the Supreme Court of the United States. I am also admitted to the Bar of the Quinault Tribal Court.

Practice Areas:

Litigation; Insurance Defense Law; Insurance Coverage; Plaintiffs Personal Injury; Personal Injury Defense; Business Litigation; Alternate Dispute Resolution, Business & Corporations.

Admitted:

1970, Nebraska and U.S. District Court, Nebraska; 1972, Washington and U.S. District Court, Western District of Washington; 1980, U.S. Supreme Court; 1982, U.S. Court of Appeals, Ninth Circuit; 1983, U.S. District Court, Eastern District of Washington; Quinault Indian Nation Tribal Court

Law School:

Creighton University, J.D.

Member:

Grays Harbor County Bar Association (President, 1975-1976), Washington State (Member: Office of Civil Legal Aid Oversight Committee; Mediation Panel) and Nebraska State Bar Associations; Washington Defense Trial Lawyers Association; Association of Insurance Attorneys; Defense Research and Trial Lawyers Association.

Born:

Des Moines, Iowa

About Senior Sunset Times

• • •

WITH A REALLY UNIQUE APPROACH to publishing, this monthly newspaper is all about encouraging a freedom of expression with a light hearted approach and share life experiences with a minimum of editing while maintaining content focusing on History, Humor, Art, Health, Senior Assistance, Community Events, while weaving community and local business together with every issue. The community members write the paper for the Washington coastal community. All writers are volunteers. All submissions are welcome, as long as they do not have political content or overtly religious content. Our goal is to bring good news and uplifting moment to your day. We appreciate any comments, feel free to use the contact form on the subscription page, email us at sunsettimes@centurytel.net or like us on Facebook! *It is a locally owned and family operated business.*

Table of Contents

Hey, I've Got A Power of Attorney!

• • •

IT'S ALMOST SOME KIND OF American ritual: Aunt Flossy starts to forget where her checkbook is, so her niece-- on the suggestion of the boss's secretary -- goes to some office supply store and pays $2.50 for a form called "Power of Attorney" (usually titled in some sort of Old English script, like "Power of Attorney").

After persuading Flossy that this is something she has to do, the niece has Flossy sign the form at the bank, because they have a notary. Flossy's niece then leaves the bank a copy of the Power of Attorney, and starts taking care of Flossy's checking account. Perfect, huh? Maybe not.

It is true that there are probably millions of Powers of Attorney out there, motoring along very nicely, with no problems. It is also true that there are untold thousands of horror stories about the abuses of this ancient document.

Let's take a look at this crazy legal document, learn what it does, learn what it won't do, learn how it causes problems, and figure out how it fits into your life.

A Power of Attorney is a simple, straightforward document. When Aunt Flossy signs a power of attorney appointing her niece, she is giving the niece the power to do anything legally that Flossy can do. The operative word in the name of this document is POWER. Flossy's niece can now clean out Flossy's bank accounts, sell Flossy's house and car, cash out Flossy's time certificates of deposit, order the stockbroker to transfer the stock to the niece, change the beneficiaries on the life insurance, give the jewelry away, and...well, you get the idea. Of course, the law doesn't say that a person holding a power of attorney has the right to steal Flossy's assets, she just has the power to steal it all.

The Power of Attorney is a document based on trust. Flossy believes that her niece will do the right thing with the power that is being handed to her. And, fortunately, most people do the right thing and use the power in the right way, helping the person who trusted them. Obviously, it is very handy to have someone you trust doing your banking, paying your bills, and generally helping you cope with a life that maybe is starting to become overwhelming. When it works, it works beautifully.

How long does this thing last? The easy answer is that it lasts until Flossy dies or cancels it. It's actually a little more complicated than that (surprise!). Flossy's Power of Attorney is in force until one of these things happens:

1. Flossy cancels it in writing.
2. Flossy dies.
3. Flossy goes into a coma or otherwise becomes incompetent.
4. A Court takes over the handling of Flossy's affairs.
5. The world ends.

Looking at the list above, perhaps the most interesting situation is situation #3 -- Flossy's incompetence. In Washington (and in most states), you can eliminate that part of the puzzle by making the Power of Attorney durable. Yes, you probably have heard of it: a Durable Power of Attorney.

The concept is simple and effective. The Durable Power of Attorney says that if Flossy goes into a coma or loses her marbles or just can't function, the Power of Attorney doesn't stop. It goes on as if nothing happened, and the niece can continue to handle her affairs for her as long as Flossy is alive. This is a very handy arrangement on a short-term basis; but if Flossy goes on living in a coma for years, it can become a burdensome and unworkable arrangement.

That brings us to a point that people need to get fixed in their minds about the infamous Power of Attorney. I can't tell you how many times over the years people have asked me how to use the power of attorney after Flossy dies. They want to know if they can pay for her funeral; they want to know how to transfer the stocks, they want to know how to sell the house, etc. The answer is simple: A POWER OF ATTORNEY HAS NOTHING TO DO WITH DEAD PEOPLE.

When Flossy dies, the Power of Attorney dies. Her niece cannot do anything, even though she had the power to do everything the day before. When Flossy dies, it's time to see the lawyer about starting an estate...more about that in a future column.

OK, let's get a little more sophisticated: What if Flossy hasn't given a Power of Attorney; but she wants her niece to sign all the papers on the sale of the house while Flossy is in Dubai for the golf tournament. Hey, no problem. The law recognizes the magical Special (or Limited) Power of Attorney, which only gives a very special, limited authority to do one thing (or a small group of things), but nothing else! Flossy's niece can sign away on the house sale, but no dice on the bank accounts, or car, or CDs. The trick is that a Special (or Limited) Power of Attorney has to be very specific and very clear on what is covered and what is not. A lawyer should be involved in this if the value of the property is significant. (Hey, $500.00 is very significant to me.)

The Power of Attorney is a wonderful, useful, powerful legal device. But remember that it is one of the most powerful documents known to the law and requires some thought and analysis before someone signs off on one of these blockbusters. What should you do? See a lawyer. This is a cheap, bargain-basement deal as lawyer visits go. You'll probably get charged less than $100.00 and you'll end up getting a lot of advice about estate planning and other things while you're visiting the lawyer. The lawyer will be able to guide you on what to do after a few simple questions.

Only give a Power of Attorney to someone you trust completely. Money can be a scary motivator...it makes people do things they ordinarily wouldn't do. Remember what all of my clients have been told: if you sign this document, this person can empty your bank accounts and go to Brazil.

Is it OK to give the Power of Attorney to your spouse? Absolutely.

Is it OK to give the Power of Attorney to your child? Maybe.

Is it OK to give the Power of Attorney to your favorite cocktail waitress? No.

Make sure your Power of Attorney is durable.

Unless it's an emergency, combine the Power of Attorney with a comprehensive approach to your personal estate planning. You probably need a will, or a community property agreement, or a living will (pull the plug), and some other things your lawyer can suggest. This whole package will probably cost you less than $250.00 or so. (No guarantees!!)

Don't be talked into something called a Living Trust, unless you have some really concentrated, in-depth legal advice. That will be fodder for a future column.

Now, here comes the crazy part. 99.9% of the people reading this column are balanced, thoughtful people who know that every word of this column doesn't necessarily apply to every single person on the planet. They know that they need to take this with a 5 pound grain of salt, until they find out if it applies to their situation. They know that these are general guidelines. But, to that one person who doesn't get the concept of general guidelines...you need to be told: This isn't legal advice for you. This is a general discussion of legal topics. Don't make life-changing decisions based on what you read in a newspaper. Don't be an idiot...see a lawyer if you are going to do anything big.

Tom Brown

Basic Real Estate Documents 101

• • •

Sign right here, Mr. Noclue, and the deal will be complete. Don't worry, all the papers are in order, and you just need to sign and initial in seven places. A lawyer? You don't need a lawyer for this. Don't waste your money. Besides, we have got to get these signed today, or the world will end.

Have you ever heard this? What in the world are you signing? A deed? A mortgage? A lease? A security interest? What do these words even mean? HELP!

The world of real estate is full of surprises and trapdoors…and it's a good idea to have a basic understanding of what is involved.

Let's start with the basic rule: never ever, ever, ever sign a real estate document unless a lawyer that owes allegiance to you has reviewed it and says it's OK. Does that sound a little extreme? Think about this: you've agreed to sell your house for $350,000.00. The realtor is going to charge you $24,500.00 for the commission. The Title Company is going to charge you $722.30 for the Title Insurance Policy. The state is going to charge you $5,300.00 for the excise tax. The buyers' bank is going to charge you 1% ($3,500.00) because they can. You'll have to pay $850.00 for the appraisal. You'll probably have to pay $500.00 to $1,000.00 for an inspection of the premises. Did ever occur to you that this might be worth a couple of hundred bucks to see if you are about to shoot yourself in the foot? When you buy or sell real estate, a lawyer is the biggest bargain you can find. For a relatively small amount of money, the lawyer can save you hundreds of thousands of dollars and years of grief.

I'll have to admit that 9 times out of 10 (or even more), the lawyer will say that the papers look good, no problems. And here's a bill for $150.00 or $250.00. I have always been surprised at how people can sign off -- without a whimper -- on the substantial expenses (like the ones above) involved in a real estate transaction, but then flip out at having to pay a $200.00 bill for the lawyer to review and bless everything.

OK, the sermon's over...let's talk about those pesky real estate documents.

Real estate documents fall into three basic categories:

1. documents to transfer property to someone else;
2. documents to put a lien or mortgage on property; and
3. documents to define rights in property.

TRANSFER

The basic transfer document is a deed, but deeds come in a variety of names and purposes, just to confuse us. But, they all do the same thing: they transfer the property described on the deed from the owner to the new owner. You probably got your house with a Statutory Warranty Deed. That is the gold standard of all deeds...it not only transfers the property, it promises you that the previous owner had perfect title to the property (and makes some other promises). If you are buying a substantial piece of property...like a house or a condo or a building site...you should be getting a Statutory Warranty Deed. If you're not, ask questions or see an attorney.

Perhaps the commonest deed is the Quitclaim Deed. (I have had many people over the years tell me that they have perfect title because they have a "quick claim deed." Congratulations.) Simply put, a Quitclaim Deed transfers every scrap of ownership that the person signing the deed has, but there are no promises involved...if the person doesn't own the property, you get nothing. If there are mortgages and liens against the property, you are behind those. You basically have no recourse against the person that signed the Quitclaim Deed. Never do anything important on the strength of a Quitclaim Deed, without talking to your favorite lawyer.

Mortgages/Liens

Most of us can't pay cash for something as expensive as a house or a condo or a building site. So we borrow money from a bank or we promise to make payments to the seller or we borrow from our rich brother-in-law. In those cases, we are required to sign a document that gives the lender the right to take the property if we don't pay. In Washington, this might be a Mortgage, or a Deed of Trust or a Real Estate Contract... whatever the document, it "secures" the debt, by giving the lender the right to take the property in satisfaction of the debt. This is not pretty if it happens, and you need to talk to a lawyer ASAP. On the other hand, if the debt is paid as agreed, the mortgage is released at the time the debt is paid off and it's no problem. When you are considering signing a mortgage-type document, you are in deep legal water and you need to talk to an attorney.

Property Rights

Oh, Boy! This is the category where the lawyers roam. There is no end to the kinds of mischief that people get into when they mess around with their real estate. People sign easements, licenses, letters, right-of-way agreements, boundary line agreements, and all manner of other stuff that affects their use of property. Not happy where your neighbor's driveway is? Not liking the place where they put their fence? How about that shed that sits on the property line? In my career, I can honestly say that people get crazier about property issues than almost anything else. People get very territorial when people step on their property rights and the law's tools to deal with this are sometimes woefully inadequate.

What can you do if one of these situations arises? First of all, remember the rule...see a lawyer. This is no arena for amateurs...get help before a little problem turns into a lifetime nightmare crusade. Secondly, have a mind-set to get along. My neighbor's garage is clearly partially on my driveway at home and has been for over 35 years...I DON'T CARE! It's only a few feet and there's probably nothing I can do about it anyway. Now, after the December storm, their new spa roof extends over my driveway...again, I DON'T CARE, it's only a little and it doesn't interfere with my life. But, if it interferes with your life, or your use of your property, or your property value in the future, you may need to take a stand...if you don't, the law has a mechanism that can cut off your right to object after a certain number of years. Call your favorite lawyer.

SOME EASY REAL ESTATE RULES
Yes, you do need Title Insurance.

An Earnest Money Agreement is as powerful as any real estate document and can bind you forever to a deal. Don't believe the myth that it is just a formality that doesn't have any implications. Have a lawyer look at it.

Realtors are smart, nice people who want to make a sale. You want to call on their formidable skills in negotiating price and using tactics to consummate the sale. But you also need to remember that they are not lawyers, accountants, investment counselors, engineers, bankers, surveyors, septic engineers, water experts, architects, or any of the other professionals that you might need. Remember their very limited role in the transaction.

Is someone asking you to sign a real estate document RIGHT NOW, because it will be too late tomorrow or next week? Don't.

For every real estate transaction, get a file folder and put everything in it (letters, advertisements, copies of e-mails, documents, pictures, etc.) and keep it. Forever.

In negotiations and in disputes relating to real estate, remember that it is not personal. It is business. Don't make critical decisions with your gut; make them with your mind (and your lawyer).

If you won't take them to a lawyer, at least read the documents. You'll be surprised at what's in there!

See you next month!

Tom Brown

Do you need a will?

● ● ●

THAT IS A TOPIC THAT could take up every single page of this great little newspaper...but let's try to simplify it a little bit. Yes, you probably do need a will, but let's talk about some "estate planning" issues first.

COMMUNITY PROPERTY AGREEMENTS

Washington is one of the Community Property States. If you want to know what community property is, go to law school and then practice law for 30 years and you still won't know.

But, let me try a simple definition: Community Property is everything that you or your spouse earn during the marriage. Wages, dividends, interest on your community money, profits, lottery winnings, and salaries: all community property. But, if someone gives a gift of a million dollars to the wife or leaves a million to the husband in a will, it's not community property. That's "separate property." Also, what the couple brings to the marriage is not community property. That is also "separate property." However, the spouses can – and frequently do – convert some or all of their separate property to community property.

When they die, most spouses want to leave everything to the other spouse, whether it's community property or not. Fortunately, our law provides a magical, simple, effective way to do that ...the Community

Property Agreement. Most Community Property Agreements say three things:

1. We agree that everything we own is now community property.
2. We agree that everything we acquire in the future is community property.
3. Each of us gives all community property to our spouse if one dies.

The Community Property Agreement works without lawyers, without Courts, without any ceremony at all. After the death of a spouse, if you have a community property agreement, and a death certificate, you can change bank accounts, change vehicle titles, change investment accounts, change CD's, etc., etc. No will is necessary at this point... the Community Property Agreement takes care of everything in most cases.

It's a powerful document and every Washington couple with a simple estate under $1.5 Million should probably consider having one. But, as always, it's NOT a good idea to just get a Community Property Agreement form at the office supply store and just fill in the blanks. There are a lot of situations where a Community Property Agreement is a bad idea, and you might shoot yourself in the foot. See a lawyer!

TAXES

Taxes used to be the big bugaboo of the whole estate planning process. That has pretty much changed, since the Feds started dramatically raising the threshold on Federal Estate taxes. As things stand right now, the first $2 Million is disregarded, so no Federal Estate tax will be due on estates under that amount. Once you are over the threshold, the federal rates are dizzying.

The State of Washington has stubbornly held on to the concept of a death tax, and you also have to consider the effect of the Washington tax, as well as the Federal tax. The state tax also has a $2 million exemption right now, but the rates above that are pretty steep.

But watch out!!!…Both the state and federal exemptions are going to change in the future, so you have to plan carefully, if you have a substantial estate. Again, the only rational way to proceed is to talk to a lawyer and make a will based on the lawyer's advice. Also, if you have a really substantial estate (over three or four million dollars) you need some serious and sophisticated estate planning to deal with potential taxes and the other important areas of estate planning.

WHAT CAN A WILL DO?

The list is almost endless. A will can identify your heirs and state how much they are to receive.

A will states that will be in charge of making sure your will is followed. A will can direct how your funeral is to be handled. A will can set up trusts for your children or other heirs. A will can give specific items to specific people. A will can set up special care for a special needs member of your family. A will can explain why you favored one heir over the other. A will can execute your estate tax planning, if necessary. A will can be a platform for something you want to say to the world. A will can set up a way to keep an ongoing list (during your life) of who is to receive your personal property (dishes, furniture, heirlooms, etc.). A will can even fund a family foundation, if you want to create one! I had one client who vividly described the wake that he wanted after his death…he described it in language that would make Aunt Flossie blush!

In short, most of us like to exactly control who gets what and how much. The only way to guarantee that is by making a will in accordance with the strict rules the legislature and courts have set up to make sure the will is valid and effective.

WHAT ARE THESE RULES?

Well, first of all, the person making the will must be at least 18 years old and must be "of sound mind." Stripping away all the legal junk, this means that the person must know who he is, what he has, and who he is giving it to in his will. The will must be in writing. The person making the will must sign the will. Two independent competent persons must witness the signing and state in writing that they witnessed the signing of the will. Either at the time of making the will, or later when the will is presented to the Court, those witnesses must make an affidavit that they properly witnessed the signing of the will. There's no sense trying to cope with these rules by you. Lawyers know what is required and presumably do it the right way every day. If you do it yourself and screw it up, the law will probably treat your estate as if you had no will, and the property will be distributed as described below.

You will find that a simple estate plan is relatively inexpensive. If you are a husband and wife, with a modest estate, you will probably end up with a Community Property Agreement, two simple wills, two durable powers of attorney, a "directive to physicians" (living will), and some advice about gifts and other issues, all for well under $500.00. (Warning: this varies wildly from attorney to attorney.) These documents will cover most of the situations discussed here and to be discussed in the future, and will probably last for most of your life. However, if your estate is larger and more complex, and as your situations vary from the norm (whatever that is), you can expect the price tag to go up.

WARNINGS

Re-marriage. There is a law in Washington that says that your will can be changed or invalidated by a subsequent marriage. In other words, if you and your spouse made wills 25 years ago that left everything to each other and then to your children…and then your spouse died…or you got a divorce…and then you got re-married, …then be careful: your new spouse has rights created by law and is entitled to a portion of your estate, maybe even to the exclusion of your children. If this scenario applies to you, go see a lawyer as fast as your little legs will carry you.

No will. If you die without a will in Washington, the law takes over and decides who will receive your property. Most people are surprised to find out that the law distributes the property pretty much the way you would decide to do it if you were alive…to your wife and your kids. No wife or kids? Then to your parents. No living parents? Then to your living brothers and sisters. And so on. It gets complex, but the law's intention is to keep the assets in the family in an orderly way.

Property passing outside of probate. Most people are surprised to learn how much property passes outside of probate and without reference to a will. The most common examples of this are joint bank accounts with right of survivorship, "payable on death" accounts, IRAs or CDs with a beneficiary designation, insurance policies with a beneficiary designation, property governed by a community property agreement (as discussed above), and many other examples too numerous to list here. Most of these things transfer automatically by just showing the death certificate, and completing some minor paperwork. Sometimes these things are not taken into account at the time the will is made, and there ends up being a conflict between what the will says and what the actual situation at the bank is. Lawyer time.

Escheat to the State. The ads for living trusts and form wills always talk about losing your property to the State by "escheat." This doctrine says that if you have property, but don't have any heirs or children or parents or brothers or sisters or cousins, and didn't give it to anybody in a will, then the state can take it. This is unbelievably rare…I've never seen it happen in 38 years of practicing law.

Foreign Will. Washington law says that, if you die as a resident of Washington with a will made in another state, Washington will give that will full force and effect, as if it were executed in Washington. Obviously, there's no good reason to take chances on something like that...have your foreign will reviewed by a Washington lawyer.

Things we need to talk about. What about living trusts? What about living wills? Who should I select as my executor? Should I appoint a bank as executor? Should I be giving my property to my kids right now before I die? Should I "quitclaim" my house to my kids? What happens to my small business if I die? Where should I keep my will and other important documents? Can somebody contest my will if I leave him or her out? How expensive is probate? How long does probate take? All of this is very interesting stuff, and I promise to cover these questions in a future column.

REMEMBER THE RULE!!!

Everything you read in this column is generalized, so it will hopefully be of interest to a broad range of people. Don't rely on any of this as legal advice covering your individual situation. I just hope that we may have sparked an interest that motivates you to ask questions, see a lawyer, or at least recognize that you may have a situation that calls for a second look.

Tom Brown

What's under the hood of your car insurance?

• • •

SINCE I'VE SPENT A GOOD part of my lawyer life in litigation that involves insurance (one way or another), I like to tell (...or warn) people what is in their insurance policies. Usually, it turns out to be a surprise, sometimes a shock, once in while no surprise, but ALWAYS of interest. Let's face it...Most of us drive. Most of us drive every day. Most of us drive with insurance that costs us a lot of money. Why do we pay for this? What good does it do for us, if any?

First of all, let's ask why a lawyer is talking about insurance anyway. Isn't that the job of my insurance agent? The answer is definitely yes... you should be talking to your insurance agent about your coverage and limits. But remember that most insurance policies are the product of decades of experience by the insurance companies. That experience is not just about how many accidents there are, or about how many people over 70 get into accidents, or what kind of cars get in the most accidents. That experience is also heavily involved with court rulings and legislative changes in each state that the company serves. These policies have been hammered out over years and years by attorneys and claims people and actuaries at insurance companies, trying to figure out how to serve the customer and still make a profit. So...a lot of what is in your insurance policy is tied up with the law. Lawyers wrote that policy, lawyers interpret that policy, and lawyers are going to be standing before the judge when that policy is interpreted in a court of law. I'm not saying that lawyers are any better at explaining your insurance than your agent...it's just that we have a perspective that is worth hearing.

OK, let's go...

The most important kind of automobile insurance is the one that is required by law -- liability insurance. What is it? Well, it's fairly easy to state: The liability coverage of your auto policy says that if you get in an accident that hurts someone or damages their property, the insurance company makes two promises to you: (1) they will "defend" the claim to determine if it is legitimate; and (2) they will pay the claim, if it is legitimate. This coverage protects you from personal liability, meaning you don't have to empty your bank account or sell your house to pay for someone that you put in the hospital. OK, having stated the simplest outline of the issue, you have to know that this is one of the most heavily litigated areas of insurance law, and accounts for most of notoriety of lawyers and insurance companies. What does "defend" mean? It means a lot. First of all, it means that the "claims" people at the insurance company will deal with the injured person or their lawyer, and you won't even know or care what is going on. Most liability claims are resolved at this stage, and the insured never even realizes what happened.

However, it often happens that the claim can't be resolved because it's too big, or too complex, or the injured person is being ridiculous about how much money the injury is "worth." This when the lawyers take over and the injured person's lawyer file a lawsuit against YOU!! A deputy sheriff with legal papers that scare the horse feathers out of you serves you. What do you do???? Easy, you call your insurance company and tell them you got served. They immediately arrange for an attorney that they hired to take over the defense and defend you as well as it can be done. That attorney and his or her company stay with you for the rest of the case. The insurance company and the attorney continue to try to settle the case, but even if it can't be settled and has to go to a trial, they stay with you. All you have to do is cooperate with the attorney and the insurance company in handling the claim. Simple, right? Well, remember, this is the real world, so there are always asterisks. The main asterisk is the amount of your coverage. This figure tells us how much the insurance company will protect you for. The legal minimum is $25,000.00; but if you have anything to lose...house, savings, summer cabin, boat, RV, retirement money, etc., that is not nearly enough. Get as much liability insurance as you can afford...at least $100,000.00 for personal injury. (A terrible personal injury can eat up $100,000 in medical bills in nothing flat.) People with a lot to lose typically buy another extra policy (called an umbrella policy) to provide another million dollars (or more) in coverage. I recommend this if you can afford it and have something substantial to lose.

What if the accident wasn't really your fault, but the injured person says it was? Hey, this happens all the time. That's why it's great to have the insurance company and their lawyers on your side. What if the injured person says the injuries ruined his life, but you saw him re-roofing his house and dancing the Macarena at a nightclub? Again, it happens all too often; and it is the job of the insurance company and their lawyers to uncover the fake or inflated claims.

They're pretty good at it.

Another coverage that is critically important is UIM coverage. This coverage is optional, but the legislature has said that it is so important that the insurance company has to be able to prove that you were offered the coverage and turned it down. What is it? Well. UIM stands for Uninsured/Underinsured Motorist Coverage. That means that if someone gets in an accident with you and it's their fault and you are injured (or have property damage), AND THEY DON'T HAVE INSURANCE

OR THEY ONLY HAVE A SMALL POLICY, your UIM coverage will kick in and your own insurance company will put up the coverage on the person that caused the accident!!! In this day and age of many people running around without insurance (...oh, yes. Even thought it's illegal...it's very common), it is very important to make sure that you and your family are protected by this coverage. Remember, for a reasonable premium, it's like making sure that every car out there has enough insurance to cover your injuries. Sometimes, you can even tie your UIM coverage to your umbrella coverage and get really huge coverage to protect you from underinsured or uninsured motorists. I recommend it. I definitely recommend that you do not turn down the UIM coverage.

Now having told you to spend more money on your car insurance, here's how to spend less.

First of all, increase your deductibles if you can. You don't need your insurance company to pay the whole bill on the $250.00 dent in the parking lot. This is insurance, remember! Raise your deductible as high as you can stand. (If you follow this advice and get a $500 dent, you'll think I'm an idiot. If you don't get any dents, you'll think I'm a genius. See you at the Blackjack table.) Talk to your agent about your PIP coverage. This is the coverage that pays you and your passengers for medical costs and lost wages no matter whose fault the accident was. For somebody with a job and poor medical insurance, PIP coverage can be a godsend after an accident. To someone that's retired with full medical coverage...it might not make that much difference. Talk to your agent. Ask questions. How can you save here? Also be sure that you want or need all the "bells and whistles" that your agent is offering you. Can you eliminate towing or rental car insurance? If your car is a beater, do you really need "collision" or "comprehensive" insurance on that car? Did you get credit for all the possible discounts? (Good driving record, AAA, senior driver improvement courses, multiple cars insured, garage, low-crime area, etc.,

etc.) Be sure to ask about these. Are you getting the message that this is a process of weighing the "goods" and "bads"?

Finally, go with a good company. Ask your friends how they were treated when they had claims.

Read consumer reports on how insurance companies act. And then shop around among the best. And here we go with what I always say... it's not a bad idea to buy an hour of your attorney's time and review your whole insurance package with him. Include your homeowner's policy, your boat policy, your business policies, etc. And don't do this instead of talking it over with your insurance agent...do it in addition to talking it over with your insurance agent.

See you next month!

Tom Brown

Do-it-yourself Law

• • •

IN MY LAST FEW COLUMNS, you've heard me plead, beg, shout and otherwise make a fool out of myself to persuade people that it's no big deal to see a lawyer about the many important crossroads in life. Usually, you'll find the lawyer to be a lot less expensive than you expected, and it's relief to put your problem in the hands of a professional.

But this month, in a departure from form, I'd like to talk about the times that you don't really need a lawyer and about the non-"legal" resources you can use to sharpen your mental pencil about all things legal.

SMALL CLAIMS COURT

Everybody has heard about Small Claims Court, but nobody wants to try it, because it's too terrifying, too technical…too legal. Baloney! Small Claims Court is a user-friendly resource that can solve many of life's little problems.

What are the basics about Small Claims Court? Well, to begin with it's part of the "District Court" so there's a very competent, friendly staff to help you with your case. They have all the forms and can answer all the questions.

If you want to use Small Claims Court, it has to be a case that involves money...up to $4,000.00. That's a lot!!! So, it can't be a case about determining the property line with your neighbor, or getting a restraining order against the crazy lady next door, or getting a divorce. It has to be about getting a legal judgment against someone that owes you money, or caused you injury, or cheated you on a product they sold you.

So, if you bought a $3,000.00 hot tub from a neighbor, and he knew it had a leak the size of Conner Creek, but didn't tell you...let a judge decide. More important, if you bought a product from a local business that didn't perform as advertised, you can go to Small Claims Court and they CANNOT hire a lawyer. It's you and the local manager...one on one!! You have the right to bring in your wife, your friends, and your self to show how screwed up the product was. It's a level playing field, and you just tell the judge what happened. Remember the big, basic rule -- NO LAWYERS IN SMALL CLAIMS COURT!!! It's just the citizens...one on one.

But it's also important to remember that this is no place for crazies. If this is about the fact that your grandmother owes you 40 bucks for something stupid that happened at your senior prom...forget it. If it's a righteous claim for something real...go for it!

You can find your local Small Claims Court by looking up the County District Court and calling the clerk for directions to the location of the Small Claims Court, which is usually the same office.

Before you go to Small Claims Court, be sure to check out the free information about Small Claims Court cases and procedure at http://www.courts.wa.gov and at https://www.consumeraffairs.com/ and at http://www.lawforwa.org

Good luck!

Traffic Court

Some traffic tickets can't be messed with...get a lawyer. If you got a ticket for DWI or DUI or Reckless Driving or Failure to Appear on another ticket...GET A LAWYER!

But...if you're charged with 35 mph in a 25 mph zone or failure to signal a turn, think about trying out your lawyering/persuasion skills. Traffic court is an interesting human drama, and you'll never forget your brief stint on the legal stage. The judges in traffic court see an amazing variety of sullen, chip-on-the-shoulder, self-denial types, and it's a relief for them to see a normal, friendly, thoughtful human being who's never had a traffic ticket and just wants to explain what happened.

It's shocking what happens when you smile and act polite and don't accuse the police officer of unnatural acts. The police are human. The Judge generally has high regard for the police. The police want to do the right thing, even if they thought your ticket was righteous. If you've got anything to talk about on this ticket, take a shot...but be normal.

I have two personal instances where I challenged speeding tickets, but I didn't act like a lawyer...just like a citizen. It was fun and educational and scary. Do your homework, be normal, don't abuse the cops, and convince the judge that you are salt of the earth.

Besides, it's really too expensive to hire a lawyer for a small-time traffic ticket. But...as always...use your head. If there is any risk of jail time or loss of your license...you probably need the help of a lawyer. If this is your 17th traffic ticket in the last two years, think about the wonderful effects of having a trained professional looking over your shoulder or holding your hand in Court.

Product/Warranty Disputes

The individual consumer who is committed and diligent scares the hell out of corporate America. Don't just take what they tell you for gospel... fight back. All of us have had a "situation" where we were not satisfied with a product or service, and just gave up. Don't give up!!!

Find out who is on the Board of Directors of the corporation you are dealing with. Write to them.

Be normal. Be firm.

Don't threaten to hire or call a lawyer...that just makes them call their own lawyer. Keep communicating with the people who make the decisions. Your direct approach is powerful! Show them you know how to use Small Claims Court!! Show them you know how to handle a referral to a consumer protection agency! Don't give up.

Knowing The Landscape

You might be surprised to learn that lawyers actually like it when their clients come to them armed with knowledge about the issue involved. When people know a little bit (or a lot) about wills or welfare or dissolution law or landlord/tenant issues or other legal situations, it sometimes makes it a lot easier for the lawyer because you don't spend a lot of time chopping through the hairy legal issues that the client doesn't know anything about.

But where can you get the basics about simple or not-so-simple legal issues? As you might suspect, the answer is online...turn on your computer. I often begin with the basic tool that can't be beat: Google. Put in the crucial words and let Google lead you down the path of knowledge.

If Google doesn't help, try some of the helpful legal sites:
http://nolo.com/
www.freeadvice.com
http://www.lawguru.com/

Remember to use these sites wisely. Don't think that a little knowledge makes you a lawyer...use the gift of limited knowledge to make you a more savvy legal consumer when you do go to see your favorite lawyer. These sites can help you understand the issues and help you ask the right questions.

The website of the Washington State Bar Association is a rich source of all kinds of information about the law and about lawyers. http://www.wsba.org/

If nothing else, use it to see if your lawyer has been disciplined by the bar association (...or, God forbid, to see if your lawyer even has a license to practice law.)

In any event, be a pro-active legal consumer. Lawyers aren't all perfect...be prepared to deal with the system...warts and all.

CONCLUSION
Once in a while, it's OK to be your own lawyer. But when the stakes are huge, use common sense and let an expert take a look at your situation.

See you next month!

Tom Brown

Let's talk insurance...AGAIN

• • •

A COUPLE OF COLUMNS AGO, we talked about car insurance, and a lot of people told us they were surprised to learn some things they didn't know about their car insurance.

Well, since insurance is so woven into our daily lives, it bears a little more attention. It's also intimately connected with the legal system, so we lawyers bump into it all the time. Insurance is complex, interesting, surprising and full of twists and turns.

The most obvious place to start is with homeowner's insurance...it's something that most of us have, but we don't know what it is that we really have. The thing that many of us think about with our homeowner's insurance is...fire.

That -- of course -- is the basic coverage. The insurance company tells us that they will pay for damage to our home cause by a certain group of "perils" -- fire, windstorm, falling trees, things running into the house, vandalism, planes crashing into the roof, explosions, lightning, etc. It's a beautiful kind of coverage that protects us from losing our most valuable asset from the scariest things in life. It covers the house and the stuff inside the house.

They also tell us that if someone burglarizes the house or vandalizes the property, they will make it right. Again, it covers the house and the stuff inside the house.

But what's really important is what is not covered: the big three -- floods, earthquakes and landslides.

These exceptions cause great heartache during disasters. You might remember how much hatred there was for insurance companies after Hurricane Katrina...the houses that were flooded and destroyed were not covered and the people were very angry. Well, for a long time insurance companies have simply said: "Hey, these things are so quirky and so destructive that we can't make money by trying to insure against them." So they won't cover them or they will make the coverage "optional." The word "optional" in this context means prohibitively expensive. For example, earthquake insurance might be very expensive AND coverage probably won't even start until the damages exceed 15% of the value of the house...that's a huge deductible if your house is worth $300,000.00. You have to pay the first $45,000.00 of damage before the insurance even kicks in!!!

And flood insurance is even more confusing. The feds are getting involved and "National Flood Insurance" is the hot topic today. But, again, it's expensive. Spend a lot of time with a reliable insurance agent before you buy flood insurance.

One final point on what is not covered that most of us know. Insurance usually covers for events like a storm or a fire that produce damage. Rarely does a homeowner's policy provide any sort of coverage for long-term problems with your house, like termites, dry rot, infestation by critters, carpenter ants, erosion, etc. Even though the cost of these kinds of things can be a nasty, unexpected, expensive surprise... your insurance company is probably going to say: "Sorry, no coverage."

Be careful about your jewelry and electronic equipment or specialized stuff you have in your house. Some insurance policies exclude these things or limit the coverage severely. If you are burglarized, you will love your insurance, unless your policy excludes your jewelry and your electronic equipment and your husband's collection of exotic hardwood sculptures from Madagascar. All you have to do is check with your insurance agent and make sure this stuff is covered without a huge deductible. Be sure that you confirm your agreement with the insurance agent in writing after he promises to take care of it.

It's more fun to talk about the good stuff that's in your insurance policy that might surprise you.

For example, your homeowner's policy probably has something called "premises medical." This is like a sweet little policy for people that hurt themselves on your property. If they fall or trip and get hurt, your policy will pay for medical bills and lost wages for somebody visiting your property, no matter whose fault it is. It's a nice surprise in some cases.

But much more important is your liability coverage. This coverage protects you from lawsuits by people hurt on your property -- and away from your property! If you're shopping downtown and drop your packages and break someone's foot, or if you're horsing around at the park and fall into someone...there's a pretty good chance your homeowner's coverage will protect you from a lawsuit. Some policies are even broad enough to protect you from lawsuits for stuff like libel and slander, when you tell the world the gossip about your favorite co-worker or in-law.

For sure, if someone trips on your sidewalk or porch at home, or falls into your BBQ pit, or stumbles on your threshold, your insurance company will step in and protect you from a lawsuit from that person. In this area, the same advice as I gave on automobile insurance applies...

get the highest liability policy limits you can comfortably afford. If your surgeon friend gets his hand caught in your meat grinder because everybody got drunk at a party, I can tell you that a $50,000.00 liability limit is a joke. Get a $1M policy or an umbrella policy or both.

Always feel free to call your insurance agent and ask her if you have coverage for something.

Here's an example: we had a party at our cabin for my wife's birthday (she's young) and we rented a party boat to drive the guests around. We checked with our agent and found out that the insurance on our Sea-Doo extended to the rental boat and we didn't have to worry about getting some sort of temporary insurance on the rental boat.

Don't forget to buy insurance on your toys...scooters, Sea-Doos, boats, ATVs, and all the other things we play with. The injuries that can result from a thoughtless moment with a motorized toy can be devastating. When someone gets horribly injured at your summer party, you want a big insurance company by your side with a smart attorney in tow.

In a future column, we will discuss how to deal with insurance companies when you have a homeowner's claim or boat owner's claim or other similar claim...it's definitely different than the rules for auto claims...you're usually dealing with a different company altogether, with a different style and a different ethic.

Finally, for this month, remember the nauseating, incessant mantra that this column preaches.

Discuss these issues with your attorney. Tell him or her that you just want to come in and talk about different stuff...homeowner's insurance, car insurance, property lines, neighborhood disputes, child custody, DWI issues, small claims court, your drunken brother, buying a house, should you dump your wife, etc. Whatever is driving you crazy in life? Pay for an hour's time to get some of this stuff straight in your mind. Bring in your insurance policies and ask the attorney what they mean. Ask him if you need more insurance or less. Then do the same thing with your insurance agent. Knowledge is power.

See you next month!

Tom Brown

Whom do you trust?

● ● ●

I WOULD ESTIMATE THAT 75% or more of the people who come to see me about wills or probate end up asking some questions about trusts. They want to know if they should set up a trust, or why their neighbor decided to start a living trust, or if they should appoint the "trust department" of the bank as executor of their estate, or should they set up a trust for their grandson Alphonse, who always seems to end up in jail, and would never be able to handle money if he inherited it, etc., etc.

The first thing I always tell people about trusts is that they should be very, very careful before dipping their toe into the world of trusts. The reason I say this first is that I have watched so many people be victimized by the sellers and purveyors of "living trusts." Living trusts -- as they are marketed in America -- are dangerous and scary. I'm not saying that they should be eliminated.... but I am saying they are not the solution for most people. More about living trusts later in this article.

A trust is an arrangement where someone (the "trustor" or "settlor") creates a legal entity (sort of like a corporation) to hold money or other property and use it in a certain defined way. The person in charge of the trust (the trustee) MUST hold and use the money or property in the way set up by the person who created it. When the trust is set up, there is always a written document that describes the trust property and tells trustee how to administer it. The person who is getting the benefit of the money or who is being protected is called the "beneficiary." Some trusts can't be undone (irrevocable) and some can (revocable). Basically, all this means that the person with the money or the property entrusts it to someone else that they TRUST, to take care of another person who can't or won't take care of the money himself or herself.

The most basic and common kind of trust is where Uncle Marvin wants to leave some of his estate to his nephew Billy, but Billy is only 2 years old, and Marvin doesn't want him to get older and blow his inheritance on a new Camaro and a bunch of wild living. So, Marvin (the trustor) sets up a trust, which says that Billy's father (the trustee) is to hold the money and invest it conservatively for the benefit of Billy (the beneficiary). He also orders that the money is to be spent only for Billy's education, and health, and useful things -- like a house. So Billy's father has discretion to do the right thing with Billy's money. Usually, a trust like this finally lets the rest of the money go to Billy when he is an adult; but sometimes Uncle Marvin surprises us and says that after Billy grows up, the rest of the money goes to a good charity, like the home for old lawyers.

A trust can be created while the creator of the trust is alive. This is called a "living trust" or an "inter vivos trust." ("Inter vivos" means "among [or between] living people"). Or, it can be created in the will of the trustor, so it won't start until he dies, telling how part of his estate is to be used. This is called a testamentary trust. When I talk to people about testamentary trusts, I always remind them that the person who is being protected (the beneficiary) is probably going to end up wanting to get their hands on the money and resenting the trust arrangement. I tell them to think of a testamentary trust as being like a dead person's hand sticking out of the grave, wrapped around the money. (There's an image, huh?)

Trusts have many legitimate purposes, and can be very flexible depending on the situation. For people with a lot of money, the lawyers that are writing their wills often suggest wills containing trusts that help to avoid excess taxation on both the estates of the husband and the wife. If your combined assets are in the millions, you want to be sure that your tax planners/lawyers consider this kind of will. If you have a modest estate, you won't need trusts to minimize taxes, because you probably won't be paying any taxes to begin with! Hooray!

Trusts also have purposes that are not so legitimate. Some unscrupulous advisors recommend trusts that amount to tax "evasion" rather than tax "avoidance." Never be tempted by one of these arrangements... the IRS has seen it all, and is merciless in its pursuit of scammers.

The biggest scandal in the world of trusts -- and the one you are most likely to encounter -- is the marketing of "living trusts" as a way to avoid probate and save taxes. These "living trusts" are sold at "seminars" where slick salesmen tell people all the benefits of "living trusts" and then sell them to people for 5 to 10 times what they could ever hope to save in taxes or probate fees.

The poor victims end up transferring their bank accounts and houses and retirement accounts and real estate into a trust. I have had the unpleasant duty of undoing these ridiculous things for people who are crying because they feel like they've lost control of their "stuff." Never, never, never sign a living trust agreement without taking it to your lawyer (not their lawyer) and asking if it's a good idea or not. I'm not saying a living trust can't be a useful tool...I'm just saying don't buy one from a stranger without having your lawyer (or even accountant) bless it first. Even our friends at AARP warn you to be careful of these things.

www.aarpmagazine.org

One very interesting kind of trust is the "special needs trust" which is a wonderful innovation thought up by very smart lawyers and accountants. This trust is for people that are getting government benefits (like Social Security disability) and would become ineligible if windfall money went into their bank account. Instead, a trust is created to limit the money to very well defined, helpful things for the disabled person (housing, specially equipped car, medical devices), but not frivolous expenditures. So they can enjoy the benefit of their government benefits and still have some positive uses for the money that would otherwise be lost.

The uses of trusts are diverse. You probably don't need one. But if you think you do, be sure to have your legal advisor and accounting advisor check it out carefully. And you do your own homework...turn on that computer and check out trusts on AARP's website, on Wikipedia, on the government websites, on freeadvice.com, and dozens of other great websites. But even more important...use your head and your nose. If it doesn't make sense and it stinks...it's not for you.

See you next month!

Tom Brown

What's a Tort?

• • •

ONE OF THE MOST ACTIVE, busiest areas of the law in the United States is tort law. But it's almost invisible to most of us, unless we bump into it directly. Many of you might have never even heard the word "tort."

What in the World is a Tort? Let's think of a few examples...

1. You sent an e-mail to everybody you know calling your boss a thief.
2. You didn't maintain your sidewalk and it was dangerously broken up.
3. You got drunk and tried to pick a fight.
4. You accidentally ran a red light.
5. You threw a bag of rocks off the Space Needle.
6. You're a doctor and you accidentally prescribed the wrong medicine.
7. You own a bar and didn't stop serving someone who was grossly drunk.
8. You designed and built a faulty bridge.

We could make a 500-page list here, but you get the idea. A tort is any situation where a person or a corporation or a city or a state has a duty to do something that should be done. ...or doesn't do something that should have been done. It might also be a crime...but it's definitely a tort.

Just step back for a moment, and let's first divide the whole legal system into two big parts: criminal law and civil law. The civil law side includes contracts, divorce, property, labor, a lot of other things, and... you guessed it...torts. The criminal side does one thing...it punishes people for committing wrongs against society.

Tort law is about wrongs we do to another person that are civil, not criminal. But, just to keep things interesting, some torts are also crimes! And most crimes are also torts!! Is it getting crazy enough for you? Just remember...you don't go to jail for a tort, but you do for a crime.

Let's talk about some examples. O.J. Simpson was charged with the crime of murder. That is a crime against society, not just a tort against an individual. There is a very high burden of proof, because the penalty is so high. He was acquitted because that burden wasn't met. But -- on the civil side -- the families of the deceased people sued him for the civil tort of wrongful death, saying he did something that was wrong. The burden of proof is much, much less and the jury found that -- under that lesser burden of proof -- he was the perpetrator. They won a huge civil verdict for money (which is the only penalty that the civil law can award).

Here's another example: You get drunk, drive home from the bar, run a stop sign and cause an accident. The pregnant mother in the other car is killed. You are going to get charged with Negligent Homicide and probably go to jail because you committed a crime against society. But you are also going to get sued for driving while you were drunk (a tort!) and are going to be responsible for millions of dollars in damages (tort damages) to the woman's family.

Obviously, these are extreme examples. Most of us encounter the law of torts when we are in a less serious car accident. Somebody does something stupid or negligent with a car and hurts somebody else. The person that did something stupid is going to be sued and his insurance company is going to protect him up to the limits of the insurance policy. The insurance company pays for the defense of the lawsuit (including the lawyer!) and pays the judgment that is entered. Or somebody falls on your sidewalk at home, and claims that you should have taken better care of the sidewalk. Hopefully, you have homeowner's insurance and your insurance company defends the lawsuit and pays any judgment.

Most of the situations in the law of torts that could produce a lawsuit are likely to be covered by insurance. Your car insurance provides protection against torts connected with your car. Your homeowners insurance provides protection against torts around your house (broken sidewalks, slippery floors, accidental food poisoning of your dinner guests) and other stuff (libel, slander, fighting, etc., --even if it's not around your house). Your malpractice insurance provides protection against your mistakes if you're a professional (doctor, nurse, lawyer, accountant, etc.). Your marine insurance provides protection if you run your boat into a dockside restaurant and injure the people eating there.

Most torts are accidents, but the law of torts also includes deliberate, intentional acts. The interesting catch here is that insurance usually will not cover intentional acts. What does this mean? If you sexually molest a child or murder your business partner, no insurance policy in the world will protect you from the consequences of those torts. (Forget for a moment about the criminal liability...you're going to jail.) You can be sued for millions, but the insurance will not defend you and will not pay the damages, because their insurance policy says they do not cover intentional acts. You will be responsible for the money damages awarded and the injured people will seek to recover their damages against your vast fortune and real estate holdings. What if you have nothing? Then there's nothing to get...and you probably won't be sued, because it's not worth the bother.

No matter what the situation, the law requires the existence of "fault" in order for there to be tort liability. In order to be liable to someone else, you must have acted in a way that is negligent or reckless or criminal or in violation of legal standards or just plain stupid. (It is only in rare cases that the law imposes what we lawyers call "strict liability" for extremely dangerous activities, like transporting explosives or raising dangerous wild animals.) Virtually every tort lawsuit has two phases: liability and damages. In the liability portion of the case, the injured party has to prove that the defendant acted or failed to act in a way that was reasonable. If that hurdle is cleared, then the question is damages...how badly was the victim injured and what were the economic consequences?

Why do we even have this system? Why is this the law? Well, the law -- in its wisdom -- believes that the threat of financial responsibility will prevent people and corporations from committing torts. In other words, if a lawnmower manufacturer is going to be sued and forced to pay money for making dangerous lawn mowers that cut people's feet off, then they will make safer mowers that won't cut people's feet off. The law believes that if you can be sued for driving recklessly, you will be a safer driver to protect your money. The law believes that -- if you are a dentist -- you will be careful not to hurt or improperly treat your patients, so that you don't owe them a bag full of money when their teeth fall out or when they find out that they had cancer of the mouth that you didn't see. In legal lingo, the whole law of torts has a "prophylactic effect" -- it prevents people from doing stupid, negligent things by making it clear to them that they will have to pay for the consequences. Pretty basic stuff, huh?

How well does it all work? The reviews are mixed. The whole field is so permeated with insurance that the issue has become insurance rather than the viability of the tort system. We are in a rapidly changing environment where these disputes are no longer decided by juries of our neighbors, but are going to arbitration or mediation or some other form of less expensive dispute resolution. Personally, I think we are 5-10 years away from a settled system of dispute resolution and insurance claims handling.

In the meantime, keep buying all the insurance you can reasonably afford, and make sure that it covers all your potential "torts." Don't libel your boss, don't drive drunk, don't throw a bag of rocks off the Space Needle, don't build a dangerous bridge, and -- for cryin' out loud -- don't sue your lawyer for malpractice!

Tom Brown

The Law as Art

• • •

OK, IT'S TIME FOR A break. We've been studying the nuts and bolts of the law for eight months in this column and it's time to kick back and think about the law as art.

Art? Are you kidding me? What could be further from art than the law?

Actually, the law is so fascinating, so complex, and so human that it has been the subject of fiction and film for ages. Of course, the problem with literature and cinema is that there's a lot of garbage and a lot of unrealistic nonsense that makes its way to the screen and to the page; and most of it is not reflective of the reality of the law. But there is a body of work out there that is so real that it helps us understand law and shows us how the law really operates in life.

I thought it might interest you readers to get some advice on what books and what movies lawyers think give a realistic view of how the law operates...or maybe how it should operate. So, the rule for today (unless I arbitrarily change it) is that we will discuss art that teaches us how the law really works, or how it really should work, while being wildly entertaining. Fair enough?

LET'S BEGIN WITH MOVIES.

The absolute best movie to ever go into the jury room and look at the dynamics of wringing the truth out of a mass of conflicting evidence is "Twelve Angry Men." This is a black and white, 1957 movie that is based on a Broadway play. The cast is stunning (Lee J. Cobb, E.G. Marshall, Henry Fonda, Jack Klugman, Martin Balsam, etc.) and the dynamic of the jury's deliberation is a study of the meaning of "reasonable doubt." Be sure to rent the original black and white movie from 1957. There is a subsequent 1997, made-for-TV version which isn't bad, but not as compelling as the original. When you're done with this movie, you'll understand why our English ancestors fought for the jury system.

Moving out of the jury room into the actual courtroom, one of the most gripping movies to show the drama of a high stakes criminal trial is a 1959 movie entitled "Anatomy of a Murder." This movie was based on a real trial and the book was written by a real judge, so there is a fantastic load of authenticity to the plot and characters. All you need to say about the cast is: Jimmy Stewart, Ben Gazzara, Lee Remick, and George C. Scott. Wow, what a group! (By the way, the guy that plays the judge in this movie is a real lawyer...and he's the person who spoke those immortal words to Senator Joseph McCarthy during Senate hearings: "Have you no sense of decency, sir?") This is another movie that makes you feel good about how the law stumbles and trips its way to the correct result...or maybe not!

I'm going to talk about books later in this article, but don't miss both the book and the movie about class actions called "A Civil Action," by Jonathan Harr. The beauty of this book and this movie is that it take all the glamour and hype out of class actions and shows you what a tedious, back-breaking business it is to sue big, powerful interests. The book is absolutely fascinating, and the movie is pretty good too. It is a little tedious sometimes, and has a lot of details, but it is truly one of the greatest books about the law that I have ever read. It will change your view of "class actions" forever.

A nitty-gritty movie about the ugliness of divorce, how it works, and the impact on the people involved is "Kramer v. Kramer" -- a 1979 movie starring Dustin Hoffman and Meryl Streep, that won the Oscar for best picture. It's not fun to watch, but you get a close-up look at the reality and the business of divorce. The acting is superb and the messages are electric.

If you really want a dense, thoughtful movie about the criminal justice system, you have to see "Presumed Innocent" based on a book by Scott Turow (a real lawyer). You have to stay awake to enjoy this movie (and the book), but it's worth the effort. Lots of good, technical stuff about what lawyers in the criminal justice system do. A great movie and a great book.

Way too many of the movies about the law are concerned with criminal cases, because they are so exciting and so thrilling. But, the truth is, most of the law is in the civil arena, and that's where the real action is. One of my favorites, but not a "great" movie is "The Verdict" -- a 1982 movie starring Paul Newman as an alcoholic lawyer handling a big medical malpractice case. This has a load of realistic details about trying to pursue a case against people with a lot of money and a lot of big lawyers. One of my favorite Paul Newman movies, by the way. This little movie got a lot of Oscar nominations, including one for best picture.

OK, what if you're not in the mood for heavy thinking on a Friday night, but you want to see a movie that is fun and has a little something to do with the law? Here are my best bets: "My Cousin Vinnie" -- a laugh riot, you'll watch it twice! "Miracle on 34th Street" -- proving that Santa exists! "A Few Good Men" -- you can't handle the truth! "Adam's Rib" -- Spencer Tracy and Katherine Hepburn as lawyers and lovers. "To Kill a Mockingbird" -- not much law, but a few great courtroom scenes, and one of the great movies of all time.

Remember the power of Google to find reviews and lists of good legal movies.

WHAT ABOUT BOOKS?

I'll try to limit this part of the article to books that are readable, because so many have the great books about the law are dense and (God forbid!) boring. The best authors are those that can wade through the acres of pages of legal stuff and produce an interesting and readable synopsis of what happened.

Steven Brill, a well-known and scholarly legal type has written a readable and compelling collection of stories about leading civil and criminal cases, "Trial by Jury" (1989). This is a very interesting collection, which has the beauty of being by a true legal scholar, but still very, very interesting.

It's a little different, but one of my favorite books of all time is called "Helter Skelter." (1974). This book was written by the guy that prosecuted Charles Manson and his harem for the California murders. It is an amazing look inside the legal system, and remains one of the most compelling, yet strange books I've ever read in my life. For example, this book contains the story about the lawyer who objected to the question to the witness "What is your name?" on the ground that it was hearsay because the only way the witness could know his name was that someone told him what it was!!! Hilarious.

It's a little outdated now, but I really liked Bob Woodward's 1979 book about the Supreme Court, called "The Brethren." It's easy to read and gives you a good look at what goes on in the Supreme Court in those big cases you hear about. Recently, a new book was released which is along the same lines as "The Brethren" but I haven't had a chance to read it yet. It's called "The Nine" by Jeffrey Toobin, which I hear is pretty good and is certainly more up to date about what's going on at the Supreme Court. Toobin is a television lawyer, so I expect that his book would be pretty readable.

Almost everybody agrees that one of the great books about a Supreme Court case is "Gideon's Trumpet" by Anthony Lewis. This is the story about the famous case of Gideon v Wainwright, the case that established the right of all people, including the poor, to have the assistance of counsel in criminal cases. It's a little on the dense side, but a fabulous technical read about a very important case.

So, since I've been boring you about legal books, it's only fair to ask me what my favorite books (not necessarily legal) are. Here they are: "Catch 22" (Joseph Heller); "Mother Tongue" (Bill Bryson); "The Bonfire of the Vanities" (Tom Wolfe); and classic science fiction by Ray Bradbury, Isaac Asimov, and their ilk. Movies? "Doctor Strangelove" and "The Hunt for Red October" and "The Dish" and "October Sky."

See you next month! Thanks for reading my column!

Tom Brown

A Blind Date With A Lawyer...EEK!

● ● ●

IF YOU NEED A LAWYER, and the situation is serious, you are facing one of the most complicated selection processes known to modern society. Only a few selection jobs are scarier than finding and picking a lawyer. (Picking a wife, a proctologist or a nanny comes to mind.)

The entrepreneur that comes up with a smooth, accessible process that puts you in the hands of just the perfect lawyer match for your needs and personality is going to make a lot of money and a lot of friends.

This month, let's try to take some of the mystery out of this process...and I'll try to give you a look at the lawyer's thought process and issues in this unwieldy enterprise. If we're lucky, you'll find yourself in the hands of just the perfect match to your personality and needs. From my point of view, this is a three-step process:

Figure out the nature of your problem and identify it.

Get a small list of lawyers in your community who handle this kind of problem.

Check out the lawyers on the list is a systematic way.

The first step -- identifying your problem -- isn't as easy as it sounds. Most people are very confused about the law (with good reason), and don't know if their issue is civil or criminal, state or federal, serious or minor, needs a lawyer or a slap alongside the head, expensive or not, etc.

So, spend a little time doing your research on your problem. Google it. Look it up on Wikipedia on the Internet. Talk to your friends (if it's not too embarrassing). This process will help to define what it is you're dealing with and it will also help you get perspective on your problem.

Invariably, this tends to reduce the scare factor and will put you a little more at ease about your immediate future. (Incidentally, this kind of deliberate process is not intended for the situation where things are deteriorating fast. If you think the police are getting a search warrant for your house, don't be Googling or talking to your friends...hit the yellow pages or whatever and get on the phone to a criminal defense lawyer!)

The next step is to put together a small list of the lawyers who handle your type of problem.

Most lawyers have areas they prefer and areas they don't touch. (In my case, I don't do any divorce or criminal work.) Also, some areas are so exotic that you are not likely to find a lawyer at all outside of Seattle or Portland. (Good examples of this situation would be patent or copyright law, Federal pension litigation, or complicated maritime litigation.)

Anyway, there are a number of resources available to see who does what. First of all, check the yellow pages. It sounds simple...but it does give you the lay of the land on which lawyers handle what kind of cases. Don't rely on the yellow pages exclusively. Just use it as a tool. After you've narrowed it down to a manageable number, check out the firm's website. Again, this is advertising, but it is another tool to get an idea of what these lawyers do for a living.

Call a few lawyers and ask them if they handle your kind of case. This can often develop into a situation where the lawyer talks to you about the case and about your problem in a very honest way. I field calls like this all the time (because our office staff knows I'm a sucker for these calls and they can't get the other lawyers to take them). Good lawyers will tell you if your case is substantial and whom you should talk to. In these conversations, I try to fit the caller's personality to the lawyer or lawyers I know who handle this kind of case. Of course, if you have a friend or acquaintance who is a lawyer, give him or her a call...you'll get good insight. Good lawyers know who the screw-ups and idiots and superstars and winners are.

The most common calls I get are for employment law cases...maybe where someone has been illegally fired or harassed at work. There is a certain firm in Olympia I usually refer these cases to, because it is very specialized work and is not usually accepted readily by local lawyers.

All right, we're down to step #3. Presumably, you have a small list (under 10 names) of lawyers who handle your kind of case. You already have some sort of idea as to which of these lawyers are competent. Now what?

First of all, let's make sure that these lawyers have a license to practice law and that the Bar Association for conduct has not disciplined them that is not acceptable. To check this, go to the Washington State Bar Association and check out the lawyer. Go to http://www.wsba.org/ and then click on "Lawyer Directory." After you input the lawyer's name, you will get a summary of his information...you are looking for two things here: Does the lawyer have a license to practice law and has he (or she) been disciplined by the Bar Association?

If the lawyer is not licensed, run away. If the lawyer has been disciplined, your warning flags should go up, but read the summary to see what the discipline was all about. If he was disbarred for stealing from his clients, run away. If he was admonished for not getting his legal education credits in on time…maybe he deserves a second look. This website also contains information about what kind of work the lawyer does. (By the way, the WSBA website has a lot of useful legal information, and I recommend that you spend some time here and soak up some of that good ol' legal stuff that we lawyers love to talk about.)

Your next stop is a website that ranks most of the lawyers in America, based on what their peers (other lawyers) say about them. This website belongs to Martindale-Hubbell, which publishes a directory of all lawyers and spends a lot of time and money collecting information on lawyers. Go to http://martindale.com/ and then input the information about the lawyer. This will bring you to a "results" page with the lawyer's name. Click on the name and you will get another page with a lot of information. You are looking for this lawyer's "Peer Review Rating." The rating will begin with the letter A, B or a V should follow C or none and it. This tells you what other lawyers and judges have been saying about this lawyer. You are looking for a rating of AV or BV, which means that the lawyer has been rated highly by his or her peers for years. The website explains the rating system for you. This is the oldest, most understood, most predictable rating system for lawyers and most lawyers rely on it to some extent when looking for lawyers to refer good clients to.

There is also a new, upstart rating service of lawyers that is trying to perfect a more populist approach to identifying good and bad lawyers. It's called AVVO and can be found at http://www.avvo.com/ This service takes a much broader approach to evaluating lawyers, looking at their outside activities, their clients' opinions of them, and many other factors. This system is in its early stages, but it's worth a look if you're evaluating a lawyer. I think this is promising, but it is distorted by the fact that lawyers can purchase advertising on the site, which does tend to distort the findings somewhat.

All right, by now you should be down to two or three lawyers who handle your kind of case and who aren't disbarred or disciplined and whom other attorneys or clients have recommended. What do you do now? Simple...call him up. Give him the basics of your case. Tell him you'd like to talk to him...either by phone or in person...about your case. Make it clear that you are evaluating this lawyer and trying to pick the right person for the job.

When you actually talk to the lawyer, there are a few simple rules to remember, if you want to create a healthy relationship. First of all, get it locked in your head that money is not the center of the universe. If you've gotten this far with this lawyer, he probably has all the work he can handle and has a decent income. Of course, he wants your case to produce a fee, but he is probably long past the stage where his car payment depends on you putting down a retainer.

Talk about the case and why it is important to you. Emphasize why you are a "good guy" in the equation, and not a "crazy" who wants to teach somebody a lesson. Also, be willing to listen.

Despite all the research you have done, you are now speaking to someone who lives in the system and knows how it works. Let the attorney educate you about the pluses and minuses of your situation. Offer to drop the documents involved by the office, so he can get a look at them. Don't be a know-it-all, and don't be shrill about how you are the "rightest" person on earth.

Make it clear that you will be a "team" with the lawyer, and you are not sitting on the sidelines critiquing and second-guessing every move the lawyer makes.

If you've gotten this far, you have probably created a relationship with a decent lawyer who will probably send you a confirming letter, defining what the lawyer is expected to do and setting out the financial terms of the relationship. Don't be put off by this. The Bar Association requires them to commit your relationship to writing, so there's no misunderstanding later. If your relationship is a healthy one, you'll probably never look at the letter again. Now you're about to embark on an adventure that you will remember for the rest of your life.

A legal struggle is more than just a dispute, more than just lawyers hurling citations at each other -- it is the recognition of centuries of evolution in resolving disputes. No longer do we shoot each other, or torture each other to see who is right. Instead, we trust a system that has shown us how to be the greatest nation on earth. We lawyers are proud and happy to serve as the technicians of that system. Good luck!

See you next month! Thanks for reading my column!

Tom Brown

Your Home is Your Castle…Really!

• • •

THE NEWS OF THE LAST few months has led us to believe that foreclosures are rampant and people are being tossed out of their homes willy-nilly; landlords can't get any rent out of their tenants and are evicting them as fast as they can; mobile home parks are in chaos; even office buildings are echoing with empty offices and deserted hallways.

From a legal point of view, this chaos is interesting because it shines the spotlight on one of the basics of American law: the right to stay in our homes and workplaces without fear of interference.

As our legal system evolved, our forefathers recognized that one of the basics of a free, stable society was the sense of permanence and security that we derived from being safe and comfortable and…yes…immune…while we are securely in our homes and castles and workplaces. The protections of our homes are carved deeply into all aspects of our legal system.

A good example of the sanctity of our homes under the law can be found in our criminal laws, where entering someone's home illegally is one of the most serious crimes in the universe of offenses. Burglary, trespass, breaking & entering…the outrage and sense of violation inherent in these offenses has been permanently embedded in the law, and people who violate the sanctity of our homes face the most serious punishments. In our society, we don't take kindly to people busting into our homes!

Even when the government thinks we have committed a crime or there may be evidence of a crime in our home or workplace, they can't just march in and look. They have to convince an independent judge that there is good reason to support an entry and search of our home; and if the judge isn't convinced...no search warrant, no search, no entry into that castle!

But this column isn't about the criminal side...it's about the civil side...what does it take to be legally moved out of our homes? The answer is that it is very, very difficult to move someone out of his or her homes or businesses, even if there is a good reason.

If someone can't make the mortgage payment, the bank (or other mortgage holder) has a basic, underlying right to take the house back. But, in order to do that, they have to follow a very complicated and precise set of rules designed to give the homeowner and his family plenty of notice and plenty of time, not to mention plenty of opportunity to contest the foreclosure if it is not legal or right. Most banks use a kind of mortgage called a "Deed of Trust" which allows them to get the property back quicker, but it still takes months. Under the older, more traditional mortgages, a homeowner could stay in the home for as much as twelve months before having to leave after a foreclosure.

The important thing for the average citizen to know is that if you can't pay your mortgage, the law will provide you with a surprising amount of time to do what you need to do to solve the problem...but –ultimately – the sheriff can evict you and the house returned to the mortgage holder.

What if you don't own the property, and you're just a tenant? Well, again, the law has evolved in a way that protects you from a landlord just marching in and putting you out on the street.

Your rental home is your castle...but for very short periods of time. Again, there are strict, precise rules that must be followed before anyone is evicted. The landlord has to give you notice in writing in order to re-take the premises. If you haven't paid the rent, the notice is very, very short -- three days! If the landlord is throwing you out for other reasons, or just wants to end the relationship, the notice is longer, but nothing like a mortgage foreclosure. If you are on a month-to-month tenancy, you can be kicked out on 30 days' notice. But if you have a one-year lease, you get lots of notice unless you are in violation of the lease in some other way.

And...even after these notices are given, the landlord can't just physically move you out. The law requires the landlord to ask the Court to have the Sheriff move you out of the premises.

These rules are basically the same if the property in question is your workplace, rather than your home. If you are buying the property, you are going to have more time to work things out before you have to move out. If you are leasing, the amount of leeway will be dramatically less.

What can you do to protect yourself? If you are buying your house, it's obvious that you want to keep your payments current, your insurance current, and your taxes paid. If your world is disintegrating and you can't keep those things current, prioritize and communicate. Priority #1 is to keep the house insured. If it burns down, you still owe the money and you don't have the house! (This is so important that the bank usually pays the insurance if you don't...but, of course, you have to pay it back.) After the insurance is paid, talk to the bank or other mortgage holder. Everyone on the planet knows that the economic doo-doo has hit the fan and banks are going to be more reasonable than they would have been a year ago. They don't want your house (they are already holding a bunch of foreclosed properties that they can't peddle). Pay them a little, talk to them, show them that you are serious about keeping the house, call them every month and give them a progress report. In this climate, many banks and lenders will work with you. The lowest priority is taxes...you have a couple of years to deal with things before the County forecloses...but the interest and penalties are breathtaking. See if your County has a hardship program in these tough times.

If nothing else, while your credit rating is still above water, take a crack at re-financing. Rates are low, payments are low...who knows? You may hit on a fabulous deal.

If you are a tenant, your position is tougher. You are not the owner of the property, and your landlord wants you out, so the property can be rented. If you are not paying rent, the landlord can give you three days' notice, and then can start a lawsuit to evict you. This process moves fast, and you could be facing s Sheriff's eviction within 20 or 30 days. The best practice is to show good faith to the landlord. Make partial payments. Offer to do improvements to the property. Mow the grass. Paint the hallway. Bake a cake for the landlord. Don't just clam up and hope for the best. These people are humans, too. They don't want to go to court! Make their life simpler and they may make your life simpler.

It's a little off topic, but don't think that insurance is just for home OWNERS, it's also for home RENTERS. If you have a fire, or if you're burglarized, you'll wish you had renter's insurance.

And, of course, here comes the monthly lecture. When it comes to all things relating to your home or your castle, go talk to your lawyer. A half hour with your favorite lawyer may be the cheapest preventative medicine you've ever bought. If you're buying a house, see a lawyer. If you're being foreclosed or evicted, see a lawyer. If things seem out of control, see a lawyer. You may even want to consider talking to a bankruptcy lawyer (which we'll discuss in a future column).

As always, thanks for reading my column. I hope you have a wonderful, no-foreclosure, no-eviction New Year.

Tom Brown

Honey, let's drive over to the County Courthouse!

● ● ●

OK, IT'S TIME FOR A break. You all have been absorbing legal topics for eleven months in this column, and you deserving a diversion. So, I'm not going to stray totally from the safety of the law; but this month will be different. We're going on a legal tour.

In a lot of ways, the law is like a religion in this country, and it definitely has its temples. The buildings that house our legal institutions have always been amazing. There are obvious examples in the Supreme Court Building in Washington, D.C. and many of the baroque and grand Federal Courthouses scattered around this country.

But you may be surprised to learn that some of the most interesting, most beautiful temples of the law are right in your backyard, and are available for you to wander around in and inhale some of the beauty and history that throbs in their hallways. Let's go...

Your first stop has to be the Grays Harbor County Courthouse. This is one of the most beautiful, most storied courthouses of the Western United States. This building has it all...huge beautiful murals, grand courtrooms, acres of marble, history dripping from every parapet, a clock tower (that works,) and impeccably maintained grounds. It's located in the Grays Harbor County seat of Montesano, about 15 miles east of Aberdeen, and about 30+ miles west of Olympia. (By the way, the whole history of how Montesano ended up, as the county seat is a rich slice of history that you might like to read the town has been called the "Maid of the Wynoochee"…amazing story…but we're here to look at a building.)

Don't be bashful about going in and looking around…you are a taxpayer…you own the place! As you enter, you will see a huge mural to your right as you climb the first set of stairs. This depicts an early meeting with the native Indians. Gorgeous! But the real treats are on the third floor where the Courtrooms are. The rotunda outside the Courtrooms offers a magnificent view of the interior dome overhead. It is lush and colorful, depicting Industry and Agriculture and all kinds of beautiful stuff. The murals in the dome are gorgeous…and the very top of the dome even manages a small field of stained glass.

If you're really tuned in, you'll notice that the Courthouse has been dramatically altered…the stairs to the third floor didn't used to come up the middle, and there was a balcony all around.

Look at the differences in the marble where they made this big change sometime in the dim past. Now the stairs march right up the center…but it wasn't always that way.

But, now, it is time for the piece de resistance, the main event, the raison d'etre for going to this Courthouse: the Courtrooms and their murals. There are two courtrooms and they each proudly display brilliant, vibrant murals with very strict messages for you miscreants unlucky enough to be sitting accused before the bar of justice. Really, these Courtrooms are downright breathtaking. Murals, a wooden bench with a dark wooden proscenium behind the Judge, classic wooden pews for the public, giant windows, carpeting, ceilings and lights that are just perfect, etc., etc. These are the two most beautiful and majestic Courtrooms that you will ever lay your eyes on.

If you're lucky, you'll bump into one of the judges prowling the hallways, and he'll be happy to tell you some of the stories that echo in these hallways. Maybe he'll show you the dent in the metal doors where a bullet from a deputy sheriff's pistol chased an escaping prisoner, or tell you how this building was wracked in 1999 by the Satsop earthquake and then was beautifully restored by a public/private cooperation that saved a great landmark.

Bring your camera and drink it in.

HEADING SOUTH

But don't use up all the battery in that camera. You're next going to be headed south to see another unbelievable Courthouse, sitting improbably in one of the most sparsely populated counties of the State. South Bend is about a 35-minute drive south and west of Montesano. (As you make the drive, you will be amazed by the devastation still remaining from the windstorm of December 1997...shocking.) Anyway, push on through Raymond to South Bend. You will see the white Pacific County Courthouse on the hill to your left. Prepare yourself for a shock...this is an amazing, unexpected nugget of beauty and history.

As with all Courthouses and County seats, there is a rich, colorful history ready to be absorbed in connection with these beautiful buildings. In the case of Pacific County, the citizens spent nearly 50 years fighting over where the county seat was going to be located. One faction even "stole" the county records from one location, and took them by steamboat to South Bend in 1893. By 1909, things had settled down enough for the County to consider a proper Courthouse.

The result is a splendid, magical edifice that can take your breath away. This shining, white Courthouse sits on a hillside, watching silently over the city of South Bend and the Willapa Bay beyond. You park in the midst of impeccably groomed grounds and walk toward a grand entryway with strong architectural flourishes. As you enter, you will find yourself in a rotunda, with lots of wood and lots of stylistic devices; but, strangely, it is not overwhelming...it almost seems cozy. But your true mission is to get upstairs...a feat achieved by taking the twin circular wooden stairways at the rear of the building. (Notice that the staircases have marble newels and oak handrails.)

As you emerge on the second floor, there are two totally different aspects to be absorbed. The first is the overlook down to the rotunda from the balcony that circles the entire second floor, which gives you a feel of the whole Courthouse. But, as you stand at the rail, your eyes drift upward to the most stunning, most improbable feature of this rural courthouse. There looms above you a huge stained glass dome nearly 30 feet in diameter, and rising to a height of over 100 feet. The beautiful stained glass is fed by generous light openings under the dome that make the stained glass glow with its colored glass panels. The monogram of the County is nicely made part of the stained glass display. The result is memorable...you won't soon forget it.

While you are on the second floor, look across the well of the rotunda to one of the giant columns on the other side. Obviously, beautiful marble, right? Perhaps from the hills above Pietra Santa, Italy, where the marble for The David was mined, huh? No such luck. These columns are cement...but the same county jail inmate who painted the scenes of county life on the panels in the rotunda in the 1940s, also painted curvy lines on the columns on the second floor to make it look like marble from a distance. Walk up close and take a look...you'll get a laugh out of this.

Unfortunately, budgetary constraints conspired to eliminate marble and other costly materials during construction, but it does not detract from the essential beauty of this building, even with its home-town touches.

When I was a young lawyer, the dome was blackened with years of dirt and the light openings were blocked, so that you could bare-ly tell that there was a glass dome at all. Similarly, the courtroom was "modernized" with hanging industrial fluorescent lights and other crass touches. It was terrible. Fortunately, over the years, the County had the good sense and vision to realize that this Courthouse was an irreplace-able jewel, and undertook a terrific restoration that now captures the glory of the building.

While you're in the building, drift over to the Jury Room in the southwest quarter of the second floor. In there you will find about 15 of the grandest ancient chairs for the deliberating jurors that you will ever see. They are huge wooden and leather monoliths that have witnessed nearly a hundred years of judicial history in this grand building, includ-ing my very first civil jury trial some 36 years ago...which I lost! (If only that darned dome had been cleaned up earlier...I'm sure I would have won that trial.)

Be sure to drink in all the historical information on the main floor. Look at the paintings, read the plaques, admire the heavy, dark wooden doorways. It's been cleaned up over the years...the wall used to con-tain a copy of the Sheriff's invitation to a hanging on the lawn of the Courthouse. There's a lot of history here.

AND TO POINTS BEYOND

OK, back in the car! It's time to see the Jefferson County Courthouse in Port Townsend. This is quite a drive from Pacific or Grays Harbor County, so you might want to make an overnighter out of this visit. You couldn't spend a nicer day than one in Port Townsend...probably claim-ing the most beautiful, scenic setting in the state. You can't go wrong in

Port Townsend …great places to stay, great restaurants, lots of stuff to see, and the most beautiful natural setting you can imagine.

But how about the Courthouse? Every time I see or think of the Jefferson County Courthouse, I think of the Bates mansion in the Hitchcock movie "Psycho." The building absolutely looms over the city and over the bay.

The Courthouse was built in the early 1890s, and reminds the new-comer of an ornate castle perched on a hillside in Europe. It has stunning features, not the least of which is the 125 foot clock tower, housing a bell and mechanism that was manufactured in Boston and hauled across the continent to its home. Purportedly, the mechanism for the clock was also manufactured in Boston and shipped "around the horn."

To be honest, I'll have to say that the Jefferson County Courthouse has struggled over the years, and has not been as lovingly restored as others. But great strides have been made. The gorgeous entry, crowned with a beautiful stone arch has been restored to its original glory.

Some of the tower's clock hands are the original cedar hands, and others have been replaced. The interior of this Courthouse is not in the same league as the two others discussed earlier, but this massive edifice is well worth the visit. And, as previously mentioned, we are talking about Port Townsend…this is simply a great place to visit. Here's a great website to help you plan this part of your Courthouse tour. http://enjoypt.com/

To the west, the Clallam County Courthouse is a special case. The original Courthouse has been replaced with a new, modern Courthouse, which is usually a recipe for loss of character, loss of history, and loss of majesty. After all, our Courthouses are analogous to the medieval cathedrals of Europe...we want them to inspire, to generate awe, to make spirits soar, to make us feel that something very special is happening in these great edifices. I'm sorry, but the "modern" Courthouses of Thurston County, Cowlitz County, Lewis County, do not inspire. Sure, they are functional, wired, efficient, user-friendly, etc., etc. But they just don't make you feel the majesty and power of the law. I hate them.

Anyway, Clallam County had the good sense to preserve the old Courthouse and turn it into a museum that at least reminds us of the glory of traditional, turn-of-the-century legal palaces. What they built was somewhat different than the other counties that went "modern." The exterior of their new Courthouse is unfortunately modern (including solar panels!) but the interior is a wonderful surprise. Somehow, someway, the architects recognized the need for certain feelings and emotions in a Courthouse, and gave us an interior that is positively wonderful. It's spacious, grand, quiet, roomy, airy...I just love it, even though I remember fondly how the old Courthouse was.

Finally, try to catch the ultimate Washington Courthouse...the Temple of Justice in Olympia. This is where our Supreme Court sits and decides big issues that affect all of us in many ways. This building is one that we Washingtonians can all be proud of and has it all: majesty, tradition, purple velvet drapes, lots of wood and marble, and nine women and guys who are devoted to making the law work properly for all of us. If you can work it out to watch the Court in session, it would be worth your while. Go to the Court's website and figure out who to talk to. Then set it up to be there.

Remember, you own these places. You have a right to see them. Come on in, take pictures, do pencil drawings, write a book about what has happened in these hallways, make suggestions about what could be better, become a volunteer tour guide, research and write a book about the building of these palaces...these are your Courthouses. Enjoy them.

See you next month. Thanks for reading my column!

Tom Brown

Why do I have to serve on a jury?

• • •

I THINK I MENTIONED IN an earlier column that one of the curses/joys of being a lawyer is that people think I have the keys to the courthouse, and I have the ability to keep them from having to respond to the dreaded call for Jury Duty.

I won't annoy you by pointing out that the operative word here is "duty" and that it is one of the premier hallmarks of citizenship...the ability to sit in judgment in a Court of Law. Oops, I guess I did point it out!

Seriously, let's spend my time with you this week talking about jury duty...how it works, what it means, whether you should try to get out of it, what kind of cases are involved, etc.

JURY BASICS

Many of the people who call me about jury duty ask if they are being asked to serve on a "grand jury." The answer in Washington is almost always a resounding "No." Grand juries are something completely different from the typical, run-of-the-mill jury, and they have a completely different function. In my 37 years practicing law in Grays Harbor County, I don't think a grand jury has been convened.

So, we are talking about a petit (French for "small" or "little") jury. The word "jury" itself comes from the Latin root juris, meaning "law" or "jurisprudence." A petit jury in Superior Court in our state usually consists of 12 persons, but the parties can agree on 6. In the lower courts, which have jurisdiction over smaller cases, the jury will consist of six persons.

In our state (and in most states) the job of the jury is to figure out what the facts are in a trial.

This is true of both civil and criminal trials.

For example, in a criminal trial, a jury might be asked to decide if the defendant pulled the trigger or set the fire. Was it an accident or on purpose? Was it self-defense? Did the accused intend to do what happened? Was he carrying a gun or other deadly weapon at the time the crime was committed? Was the accused insane? Was a person acting in self-defense? Did the event happen inside the county line? How much money was embezzled?

In a civil trial, the jury's function is the same...what are the facts? Did the person run a red light? Did the person deliver the products as the contract specified? How much does the person owe to the other person? How fast was the car going? What was the weather like that day?

What did the one person say to the other person? Is the person's sore back attributable to the car accident, or was it there before?

In both civil and criminal trials, the juries listen to testimony and look at evidence. The jury decides if witnesses are telling the truth. The jury decides if the witnesses are biased. The jury decides if the testimony makes sense, in light of all the other evidence. Juries have full responsibility in evaluating the evidence, but sometimes "expert witnesses" testify to help them understand the facts involved. For example, an orthopedic surgeon might testify that a certain kind of car accident could or could not cause the type of injury the person is claiming. Or, a professional forester might testify about how many thousand board feet of wood were lost in a fire. Or, a highway design engineer might testify why a certain highway was dangerous.

So, you can see how important the jury is...they make the ultimate decision. The judge -- in addition to supervising the trial -- tells the jury what the law is and what issues they will have to decide. (Sometimes, the parties waive a jury, and the judge does it all. Also, in some cases, a jury is not allowed...divorce, child custody, juvenile criminal law, etc.) So, when there is a jury, the law puts the ball squarely in its hands.

A Little Bit About Jurors And Their Importance
Who are these jurors? Where do they come from? All you know is that you got a card in the mail...why you? Well, the names of jurors used to be taken exclusively from the voter registration lists. Over the years, it became clear that the voter lists didn't provide enough diversity, and the state added the driver's license list (and Identicards) to the mix. The names of potential jurors are drawn randomly from those lists, and you are then cordially invited to visit the Courthouse.

If a person who has been called to jury duty intentionally fails to appear, that person could be charged with a crime...but, as you can imagine, this is rare. The Courts are too busy and too under-funded to chase down errant prospective jurors.

Anyway, this is where we started. People call me all the time to find out how to "get out of" jury duty. I always respond by telling them several things:

1. It's the opportunity of a lifetime, that shouldn't be missed. Most of the people I know who have served on a jury, would not trade the experience for anything.
2. It's one of the cornerstones of our system...comparable to the right to vote or the right to seek election to public office, and should not be avoided.
3. If the most productive members of our society choose to opt out of jury selection, they will not leave a pool of jurors, which is representative of society... that is not fair to anybody.
4. If you are lucky enough to be selected, the commitment in time is usually only a few days in the smaller counties, like Grays Harbor, Pacific, Clallam, and Jefferson.

Most of my friends and acquaintances that have served on juries spend years afterwards recounting and raving about the experience. It truly is a life-changing event for many people, who not only are awed by the process itself, but also feel that they have truly touched the lives of other people, and have made the system better.

How Things Have Improved For Jurors

The most uncomfortable part of the trial for the jurors used to be the questioning to see if anyone has any prejudices about the issues in the case, or knows one of the lawyers, or is related to one of the parties, or knows anything about the case. It is true that this is a very sensitive part of the process; but it is important to remember that the lawyers are 10 times more nervous and concerned than the jurors are. Even this part of the process has been improved for the jurors. It used to be that the jurors were questioned one by one by the attorneys. Now, in something we call the "Phil Donahue Method," the lawyers ask questions of the whole group as they sit in the back of the Courtroom and then follow up with the individual persons. It's a lot less intrusive for the jurors, and the jurors enjoy a strong group sense among themselves, and they don't find the attorneys so intimidating.

In recent years, the Courts have become more sensitive to the demands that jury service makes on civilian lives, and Court personnel, especially the judges, treat the jurors with great respect. In fact, the judges are so protective of the jurors that it has changed the nature of trials. In the old days, the jurors used to be yanked in and out of the courtroom, while the lawyers argued arcane points of law. Now, the judges lean on the lawyers to get all the arguments and non-jury issues out of the way early or late so that the jury is not treated like cattle.

Many of the rules relating to jurors have changed in recent years. In the past, jurors were not allowed to take notes during the trial. The explanation for this archaic rule was that something that one juror wrote down might become a point of undue emphasis in the jury room later. The absurdity of that rule forced the State to change the rule, and now the jurors are encouraged to take notes and are provided with note-taking materials during the trial. The Court personnel take extreme measure to make sure that the individual notes of each juror remain private and are protected from intrusion. The notes are destroyed after the trial.

Perhaps the biggest change in recent years is that jurors are now allowed -- even encouraged -- to submit questions that can be presented to each witness. When each witness is done testifying, the judge asks if any of the jurors have questions. The jurors pass up their written questions and the Court reviews them with the lawyers to see if there any objections. (Usually none.) Then the Judge poses those questions to the witness and asks if it spawns any other questions by the lawyers. To the surprise of most lawyers, the system really works pretty well.

Old-timers like me were cringing at what the jurors would ask... but it has turned out to prove something that I've been saying for many years -- juries and jurors are smart.

One of the most important things to remember about the jury system is that it is a human system, administered and overseen by human beings. This means that typical human issues and problems like emergencies, sickness, tardiness, disabilities, dependent children (or adults) in the family are handled with understanding and genuine compassion. In my long experience with the jury system, I have never seen a problem presented by one of the jurors that couldn't be resolved in a humane and caring way without disrupting the trial completely.

FINAL THOUGHTS

Just as an aside, there was a case in Australia last year where the trial was a huge one that had lasted several months. The jury was busily taking notes throughout the case. One day, one of the defendants (who faced life in prison) noticed something odd about the jurors who were taking notes. He thought they were writing up and down as well as left to right and thought it was weird. He mentioned it to his attorney, who then saw the same thing. The attorney asked the Judge to look into it, and it turned out that 5 of the jurors were playing Sudoku (kind of like a crossword puzzle with numbers) every day, and in competition with each other!!! The judge had to declare a mistrial, and the whole sorry episode cost about a million dollars!!

The judge chastised the jurors involved, telling them they had let down their fellow jurors and let down everyone else in the case. Unbelievable!

Anyway, I encourage you to grab the opportunity to be a juror, if you are lucky enough to be selected. Sure, there are many ways to get out of it -- both responsible and stupid. All you have to do is go to Google and input "get out of jury duty" and you will find pages and pages of outrageous behavior, designed to make you look stupid or irresponsible, so the judge and the attorneys will toss you out. Better reading would be the Washington Courts website about jury service that will answer ALL of your questions. You can find that at:

http://www.courts.wa.gov/newsinfo/resources/?fa=newsinfo_jury.faq

http://www.courts.wa.gov/newsinfo/resources/?fa=newsinfo_jury.
jury_guide

And finally, here's a good quote about how it all works:

"What jurors say before or during their deliberations is unimport-
ant; it is what they conclude that is important. Different jurors start
from different positions, express themselves differently and may reach
different conclusions. But this process of discussion is a means of neu-
tralizing differences so that a fair verdict can be reached. The strength
of the jury system is that it causes jurors to engage in debate about the
evidence with their peers."

So, say yes when that little notice comes in the mail. You will be
helping to perpetuate a system that is the best the world has ever devised.
You will be enriching your own life. You will be able to tell your grandchildren about one of the proudest days of your life... when you served
as a juror in the American system of justice, and made a difference.

See you next month...thanks for reading my column!!

Tom Brown

May I have a word with you?

• • •

WE LAWYERS LOVE WORDS. WE love to quote them. We love to think about them. We love to throw them about. We love to twist them. We love to stretch them. We love to fit them into places they've never been before.

When you deal with laws and peoples' rights on a daily basis, you come to learn the power and majesty of how words are used...it's not the words themselves, it's how we handle them.

One of the most famous lawyers this country has ever produced, Oliver Wendell Holmes, Jr., said it this way:

"A word is not a crystal, transparent and unchanging; it is the skin of a living thought and may vary greatly in color and content according to the circumstances and time in which it is used."

Wow! That's powerful stuff! Words dazzle us with their meanings, their subtle differences, their power, and -- yes, sometimes -- even their inability to capture what we mean.

This month, I'd like to talk about the many foreign words that have made their way into our everyday legal lingo. Many of these are words that we take for granted, but even lawyers sometimes don't know what they really mean or where they came from!

But, the interesting question is: Why? Why do we choose to use foreign words or phrases rather than our good ol' Mother Tongue? Why is a regular jury called a petit jury, rather than a "little jury?" Why do we insist on calling something a writ of habeas corpus rather than "get this guy out of jail?" Why in the world do we still give somebody a subpoena duces tecum rather than an "order to appear with certain materials?"

Well, I believe the answer lies within our own nature. We like things to be certain, clear and free of doubt. This phenomenon has led us to use a lot of foreign phrases, not only in the law, but also in medicine and academics. We are used to doctors talking about delirium tremens (DTs), rigor mortis, placebos, etc. These words have a certain meaning that cannot be mistaken or misunderstood. When the doctor prescribes your medicine q.i.d., everybody knows exactly what that means...the nurse is not going to screw it up, the pharmacist is not going to screw it up, and the insurance company is not going to screw it up. It stands for the Latin quater in die, which means four times per day. The same is true of t.i.d. and b.i.d. You get the idea...these are constants that everybody can rely on. No mistakes.

In academics, people that are quoting masses of academic material need a system of identifying the material, which everyone will recognize, so they use common Latin phrases that tell us what the situation is without further explanation. If they say ibid, they are using the Latin abbreviation for ibidem, which means "...in the same place..." What they are saying to their fellow academics, without spelling it out, is: "Hey, you'll find the supporting information in the same place I told you about on the last page!"

Or, if a scholarly writer says "et seq" after a reference, he is really saying "...and the following ones," meaning that the information he's talking about was gleaned from the place he mentioned...and also from the places following that specific location. Again, it's kind of shorthand that is precise, understandable and universal.

But, I'll confess, we lawyers are the worst. We have a Latin phrase or a French phrase or a Swahili phrase (just kidding!) for everything.

But our motives are pure...we want certainty, understandability, and clarity.

If your lawyer talks to you about estoppel, he or she is talking about one of the most widely known legal principles of American law, but it only has a French name...it doesn't even have an English one-word equivalent! It literally means, "stopper plug" and refers to a body of law that prevents one side from taking unfair advantage of the other.

If you have a situation that is unique, and needs to be treated in its own special way, you would tell the judge that it is sui generis -- or, of its own kind and not subject to another set of rules. If you say sui generis in an American courtroom, the judge knows what he or she is dealing with, without a lot of blah-blahing from the lawyers.

It is very common to hear about the Supreme Court "granting cert" or receiving a writ of certiorari from a lower Court. Again, this is legal shorthand for asking the Supreme Court (or other appellate court) to "take a look" at the case and see if they want to tackle it, even if there's no right to appeal. Every lawyer, every judge, every clerk, and every person in the system knows what certiorari is, and they don't need a Berlitz travel book to translate it.

Here are some common foreign word legal phrases and what they really mean, with my own loose translations:

Pro se
"for yourself"…you are acting as your own lawyer…(usually a big mistake)

Voir Dire
"to speak the truth" questioning the prospective jurors about whether they can be fair -- should be called "crapshoot".

In camera
"in chambers" -- the judge hears something out of the presence of the jurors and the public, like the testimony of a child.

Inter vivos
"between living persons" something that happens between two adult, living persons, like a gift or a trust.

Res ipsa loquitur
"the thing itself speaks" or "the thing speaks for itself" a body of law that says that if you are killed by a runaway mower inside the Honda Lawnmower store, the storeowner is probably responsible.

Force Majeure
"superior force" -- a very common provision in contracts (that often carries this French name!) that means that if there is an act of God or a war, the parties are excused from performing the contract.

Per Stirpes
"by branch" -- a very common phrase used in wills to designate that the maker of the will wants certain property to go to a "branch" of the family, even if the named person didn't survive.

Per Capita
"by head" -- another very common phrase used in wills to designate that the maker of the will wants certain property to go to a particular person in the family, but not to that person's heirs and successors if that person doesn't survive the maker of the will.

Quantum Meruit
"the amount deserved" -- a common way of determining how much a person is entitled to under a contract, if the contract amount will not be used to set the compensation. For example, a person might get his hourly rate of pay rather than a percentage fee.

Trial de novo
"a new trial from the beginning" -- an order from an appellate court saying that the whole thing has to start over, brand-new. Sometimes a new trial can be part of a procedure where an arbitrator decides the case, but the parties are not satisfied and want to start over.

Caveat Emptor
"Let the buyer beware." Probably the most outmoded legal axiom known to man. The new slogan should be: "Let the seller/manufacturer beware of the greedy buyer."

En banc
"On a bench"...an appeal that is heard by the full Court of Appeals, rather than by a Commissioner or by a "panel" of the Court of Appeals composed of less than the full court.

Lis Pendens
"a suit is pending" This is a document filed in the same place deeds are filed to alert the world that there is litigation over a certain piece of property, and you may not want to buy it right now.

Res Judicata
"a matter already decided" This is something that the Court has already decided and is not going to address again.

Ex Parte
"from one party" A decision or order of the Court that is based on input from one party only. Very rare...usually involves a situation where the other side has simply not appeared or shown up in the lawsuit. Can be an important tool, but Judges are very reluctant to sign an ex parte order unless it is clear that the other side is in agreement or has some kind of notice.

Corpus delicti
"body of crime" A grossly misunderstood concept -- a lot of people think this refers to a physical body of a human being as in a murder case. Not so. This refers to the fact that there must be some independent, real evidence of a crime in order to prosecute. For example, someone usually can't be prosecuted if they come in and confess to a crime when there is no other evidence of a crime being committed. Or, more likely, it would be a situation where someone just suspects that a crime was committed without any proof.

Pro Bono
Actually short for pro bono publico, which means "for the public good." This describes the situation where a lawyer is not working for a fee, but is doing something because it helps society or helps a person that needs legal representation. Believe it or not, this is a very common situation!

Subpoena
"under penalty" A subpoena is a piece of paper that tells someone they must appear in court or at an office for a legal proceeding. If they don't appear...there's going to be a penalty!

In loco parentis
"in the place of the parents" This phrase describes the situation where a Court (or other agency) assumes the role of the parents to protect a child who is not being protected properly.

OK, that's enough for now...you get the idea. There are dozens and dozens...maybe hundreds...of phrases from other languages that we use in the law to give us a short, clear, concise phrase that is well understood by all the participants.

If you're involved in a legal proceeding and one of these pops up, don't sit around and wonder what it means or why it is being used. Ask your lawyer, Google it, look it up - do whatever it takes to make sure you understand the situation.

And, by all means don't forget our favorite...the name of this column, which is always explained at the end ...and as always, thanks for reading my column!!!

Tom Brown

Malpractice. Hello Doctor! Hello Lawyer! Hello Teacher!

● ● ●

FOR THE LAST 20 YEARS or so, you've heard people bellowing about Malpractice. "Malpractice is the reason that medical costs are so high!" "Malpractice is the reason that my medical insurance is so expensive!" "Malpractice is keeping all the good doctors out of the profession!" "Malpractice is just another way for fat-cat lawyers to make more money!"

This is what we have be hearing for many years, as doctors and insurance companies and politicians all jump into the swamp and try to dismantle your rights as a consumer of professional services who might have a legitimate malpractice claim.

Let's have a rational, quiet, reasonable talk about malpractice.

First of all...what is it? Well, malpractice is that part of the law that says that if a professional of any kind fails to perform with reasonable diligence, the professional must compensate you for any losses you suffered because he or she did not act competently.

If you trust a professional to do something within the normal, accepted boundaries of what all reasonable professionals would do under the same circumstances, you have a right to expect -- at the least -- a minimal competent handling of what you expected that professional to do. If he or she doesn't live up to that standard, and you are damaged as a result, you may have a claim. (The operative word is "may".)

For example, if your doctor was supposed to take a cyst off your left elbow but instead amputated your right arm, he is going to owe you some money for your medical expenses and for the trauma of losing your arm.

For another example, if your lawyer was supposed to sue General Electric for a million dollars for a business deal gone badly, but he missed the deadline, he may owe you some money for the loss you suffered because of his negligence.

For another example, if your surveyor made a 50-foot error on your property survey, and the 50-foot error ran for a quarter mile and involved some salt waterfront and caused you to lose $750,000.00, you would have a malpractice claim against your surveyor.

For another example, if your dentist failed to tell you that you had a bad case of periodontal disease, and your teeth fell out, you would have a claim against that dentist for not taking care of you.

WHO CAN COMMIT MALPRACTICE?

Virtually any "professional" can conceivably be guilty of malpractice. Doctors, lawyers, dentists, accountants, architects, engineers, stockbrokers, marriage counselors, teachers, chiropractors, nurses, ...the list goes on and on. One of the most famous cases in the state of Washington was about a soils engineer who got in an ugly fight with an engineering firm that ended up in a defamation fight! Crazy!

WHY DO WE EVEN HAVE MALPRACTICE?

The existence of the right to make a malpractice claim is part of our beautiful system of justice that says that everyone is equal and has a right to seek compensation for every wrong that is done in violation of legal standards.

I know many of these cases are close and make for late night arguments, but let's talk about the easy cases first.

If the Doctor in the operating room is drunk and amputates your left leg rather than your right arm, shouldn't he be responsible for your resulting medical bills, and pain and suffering, and lost income? Why is it against society's best interests to hold him responsible?

What if he wasn't drunk, but just careless...he didn't read the chart, he didn't listen to the nurses, and he just plunged in without being careful. Is it any different? He still cost you a leg and it was because he wasn't careful. If it were YOUR leg, wouldn't you think it was his responsibility?

Let's stretch it one more time...what if it happened because the operating room staff screwed up and put the wrong information on the chart and prepared the leg (rather than the arm) for amputation. Whose responsibility is that? Isn't the doctor still the "captain of the ship?" Maybe the hospital is a defendant also? In any event, a healthy leg got cut off and the patient didn't have a clue.

(Before you say that this is preposterous, let me tell you that my wife's nephew had a basic case of meningitis as a baby in the emergency room, but the doctor was drunk and sent him home without a simple shot that would have solved the problem. He lived as a dependent, helpless, brain-damaged child for 18 years.)

But all of that is really just personal responsibility...the real reason we want and like malpractice is because it has a -- get ready for this -- prophylactic effect!! (WHAT IN THE WORLD DOES THAT MEAN?) OK...this is important...one of the reasons we let people sue other people for mistakes is that it makes people be careful so they won't be sued. If lawnmower manufacturers will get sued for making dangerous lawnmowers, they will make safe lawnmowers. If people will get sued for driving too fast or driving drunk, they'll hopefully drive slower and not drive drunk. If doctors will get sued for making stupid mistakes that kill people, they will be less likely to make stupid mistakes.

This "prophylactic effect" has made enormous changes in medicine over the years. There are now many, many safeguards in effect to protect the patients, safeguards that never would have been dreamed of in our parents' and grandparents' days. Happily, this has improved medicine greatly in this country (and in others too.)

I am working on a case right now (not a malpractice case -- I don't do them) where I had occasion to read the operative report on a very serious back surgery. When the case was all ready to go, the patient was under anesthesia, the staff was ready, then the doctor called a mandatory "time out" and everything stopped. During that time out, they made sure they had the right patient, were going to do the right procedure, and all the preparatory matters were properly completed. Wow!

We can thank the malpractice system and the malpractice lawyers for procedures like that which provide just that extra layer of safety.

I have heard many funny (and not so funny) stories about patients and loved ones writing with Magic Markers on patients the night before surgery, stuff like "NO, IT'S THE OTHER ARM!" Or on their chest, "MY NAME IS JOHN JONES...I'M SUPPOSED TO HAVE MY APPENDIX OUT!"

AREN'T THE DOCTORS GETTING PUNISHED UNFAIRLY IN MALPRACTICE CASES?

Let's be honest. Most doctors are dedicated professionals who do their best to protect their patients from harm. They work hard to follow the procedures and practices that have been set up to keep the patients safe. They want their patients to get better and be healthy.

...But, they are also human. They make mistakes. One of the most stunning and interesting facts about malpractice cases against doctors and hospitals is this: the doctors and hospitals almost always win.

That is the deep, dark, dirty secret of malpractice cases against doctors and hospitals -- they almost always win the suit. Jurors love doctors and hospitals and nurses and they are reluctant to render a verdict against them, even if the jury thinks there was some problem.

So, if it works out so well for doctors and hospitals, why are they so "anti" about these lawsuits?

Oh, that's easy. These lawsuits are expensive, scary, unpredictable, time-consuming, etc., etc.

Doctors and hospitals want no part of these lawsuits...they get them dismissed, settle them, mediate them, arbitrate them...anything to avoid putting the decision in the hands of twelve jurors!

But the lawyers who handle medical malpractice suits -- on both sides -- will agree on one thing: it is very, very difficult to get a jury to find against a doctor. Most legitimate malpractice suits are settled for far less than what they are "worth" (whatever that is!)

I think the system is pretty much in balance. The system is very reluctant to penalize a doctor for a simple mistake, but juries can rise up and be very punitive if the facts are gross.

WHAT ABOUT NON-DOCTOR MALPRACTICE?

Malpractice lawsuits against professionals other than doctors are increasing dramatically.

Virtually all professionals carry malpractice insurance of some kind. Ironically, insurance brokers are a frequent target for failing to provide the right kind of insurance!

People who sit on Boards of Directors are vulnerable for not giving good advice or guidance to the Corporation. Insurance adjusters carry malpractice coverage for failing to properly figure out insurance claims. Veterinarians are commonly sued for not properly caring for animals.

This list could go on for pages, but you get the idea.

SUMMARY

If we are in a position of trust or authority, where people rely on us, we may be held responsible for giving negligent advice. The good news is that there's no liability for just making a human mistake in judgment... we all do that. Liability lies where the professional doesn't exercise the correct level of care in making that judgment.

So, what should we conclude from all this? Professionals do make mistakes and sometimes those mistakes are not reasonable. It seems to me that it's a good idea to have a system that tends to lessen those kinds of mistakes, and also compensates someone who was the victim of that kind of gross mistake.

Food for thought...and probably food for argument!

See you next month, and -- as always -- thanks for taking the time to read my column!

Tom Brown

Anatomy of a lawsuit

• • •

IT'S REALLY AMAZING TO ME how misunderstood and mysterious lawsuits are to the general public. Most of the people I encounter...clients, witnesses, potential jurors...either have no idea about what goes on in a lawsuit or have a grossly distorted idea of what a lawsuit involves.

I attribute this to several factors:

1. The huge, overwhelming percentage of people in our society have never been directly involved in a lawsuit. It is always a revelation to me, when interviewing jurors, or talking to community groups, or just dealing with friends and acquaintances... how few people have ever had occasion to come in contact with a lawsuit as a party or witness.

2. Lawsuits are such popular fodder for movies and television and books, that the fiction smothers the reality. The crazy courtroom antics of **Boston Legal** or the mid-trial breakdown confessions of **Perry Mason** eventually bend our collective minds and give us a skewed perception of what really goes on in those courtrooms and law offices.

3. Lawsuits have such negative vibrations, that we all tend to shy away from them. People basically hate conflict; and – let's face it – lawsuits are all about conflict.

So, just for today, let's put aside our preconceptions, negative vibes, and goofy ideas about litigation, and take an analytical look at what goes on in a "typical" lawsuit. For purposes of today's discussion, we'll leave aside criminal cases and bankruptcies and divorces, because they are so specialized. Today, we're talking about the ordinary, run-of-the-mill civil lawsuit, like ones over a car accident, a business dispute, or the malpractice case we discussed in an earlier column.

The Dispute

Every lawsuit starts with a dispute of some kind. You were hurt in a car accident and you can't agree with the responsible party's insurance company how much will compensate you. You and your partner in the hardware store business can't agree on how to end and divvy up the business. Your neighbor built his driveway on your property.

The good thing about disputes in America is that most of them get settled without a lawsuit.

There is just so much risk and expense in a lawsuit that most of us just swallow our pride and agree to some sort of resolution that is probably short of perfect, but close enough.

As we try to work out these disputes, we also begin to see the weak side of our own position. Perhaps the insurance company points out that maybe the terrible limp wasn't totally caused by the car accident, but might have something to do with the fact that you fell off the roof while painting the house a month before the accident. Or your hardware store partner shows you the hidden camera videos he has of you stealing money from the till and taking inventory home. Or your neighbor shows you a 100-year-old survey that puts the new driveway on his property rather than years.

The lawsuit is already working, even though it hasn't even been drafted or filed! We begin to see the other side's position. We begin to see the softness of our position. And we start to think how a judge or jury will react to what we are learning. The pressure mounts. Most disputes in America are resolved at this stage. The combatants are simply not ready to step on the floor of the arena.

THE SUMMONS AND COMPLAINT

If the nagging dispute won't go away under the threat of a lawsuit, the parties (or at least one of them) gets down to the grisly business of taking the big step. He visits with the lawyer, talks to his family and friends, weighs the negatives, gets told how much it will cost, and gives the lawyer the green light to plunge ahead.

The lawyer prepares a Complaint, which is the document that states who the parties are, what the dispute is all about and what the person who is suing (the "Plaintiff") wants. In the early days of the law, this document had to contain special words, special paragraphs, and all manner of specific things that could make or break a lawsuit. But, fortunately, this has changed dramatically in the last 50 years or so. Washington and most states and the Federal Courts have all adopted what we call "notice pleading" – which says that a Complaint only needs to be clear enough to give the other side notice of what the lawsuit is all about.

This document has to be "served" on the other party (the "Defendant") in a way that makes sure that the Defendant really gets the paper. Usually, it has to be handed directly to the Defendant, but there are many exceptions to that rule. For example, if you serve Jane Smith at home, you can also serve her husband John by handing her another copy when you serve her. For another example, you can sometimes serve a corporation by delivering the lawsuit to the Secretary of State. This whole area is governed by very strict rules to insure that notice is given to the other side. (This is an area where a lot of malpractice by lawyers is committed!)

When the Complaint is served, it must be accompanied by a "Summons" which is a two page document that tells the Defendant that a lawsuit is being brought against him, who the parties are, when he has to respond (usually 20 days after being served), and who the Plaintiff's lawyer is that they must respond to. If there's no correct summons, there's no service. (More fertile ground for lawyer malpractice!)

The Answer (and Counterclaim?)

When the defendant gets served with the Summons and Complaint, he usually is expecting it…rarely does a lawsuit come as a complete surprise. So he calls his attorney or insurance company and reports that he has been served.

If it is an insurance case (like a car accident), the insurance company will turn it over to one of their regular lawyers. If it doesn't involve insurance, the Defendant turns it over to his attorney or finds an attorney to represent him.

The first move of the attorney is to "appear" in the case. While it sounds somewhat mystical or ghostly, it simply means that the attorney files and sends to the other lawyer a piece of paper that tells everyone that the Defendant has a lawyer and who it is and how he/she can be contacted.

[By the way, you'll notice that I referred to the lawyer as "she" – there are many, many women in the law these days, and it has changed the face of the whole legal system. In my law school class – back in the second ice age – there was one woman. Nowadays, more than half of the law students in this country are women. In a future column, I'll try to tell you about the good and bad differences it has made without getting sued myself.]

At some point after the initial 20 days passes, the Plaintiff's lawyer will require the Defendant's lawyer to file a response to the Complaint, called the "Answer." The Answer explains who the Defendant is and sets out the Defendant's response to all the things claimed in the Complaint.

This is also the Defendant's opportunity to sue right back, by including a "Counterclaim" in the Answer. The Counterclaim can arise out of the same incident or dispute or it can be about something completely different (rare). This is also the Defendant's opportunity to list all the reasons why the Plaintiff's lawsuit should fail. These are called "affirmative defenses" and include concepts like: "You're too late." Or "We settled this." Or "You sued the wrong party."

Discovery
Now the fun begins.

The rules of all Courts in America allow each side to engage in "discovery" before the trial.

This is a wide open process, that lets each side find out what the other side has in the way of evidence, witnesses, theories, etc. The amazing thing about discovery is that you not only get to look at the evidence the other side has about this case...you also get to look at everything else they have that might impact the case. For example, if it's a car accident case and the plaintiff is claiming injuries, the Defendant not only has the right to look at the medical records from this case, but also has the right to look at all the Plaintiff's medical records, before and after the accident! If the Plaintiff is claiming lost income on the job, the Defendant not only gets to look at the employment records of the present job, but every job before and after the accident! The Defendant can look at the Plaintiff's diary, e-mails, correspondence, Facebook page, Social Security records, Workmen's Compensation records, etc., etc.

In what is called a "deposition," either attorney can take the testimony under oath of the other party, not to mention witnesses, doctors, fellow employees, friends, spouses, and anybody else that might have relevant testimony. What amazing power!

Wait – we're not done yet! The Defendant's attorney can ask that an independent doctor to evaluate the claimed injuries or symptoms examine the Plaintiff. If there's a question of mental stability, a party can be evaluated by an independent psychiatrist!

Are we beginning to understand why lawsuits are so scary and feared by the average person?

Alternate Dispute Resolution

In a major lawsuit, or even in a small one, the prospect of a trial is very forbidding, both to the parties and to the lawyers.

Everything is on the line, win or lose. Trials are prohibitively expensive. Trials are notoriously difficult to "put on" – arranging the witnesses, preparing them, organizing the exhibits, dealing with expert witnesses, making sure there is no "dead time" in the courtroom, preparing the reams of papers needed for the trial, the whole thing is like herding rabid squirrels.

As a result of this insanity, the system looks more and more to Alternate Dispute Resolution, meaning ways to resolve the case without the all-or-nothing, expensive approach. The two main ways are Arbitration and Mediation.

Arbitration is handing the case over to an arbitrator, usually a lawyer that practices in the subject area, and making an abbreviated presentation to the arbitrator (or panel of arbitrators), that might be one-tenth the cost of a full courtroom trial. One of the advantages of arbitration is that the chance of an extreme result in either direction is greatly reduced...particularly if your trial would have been to a jury.

Mediation – an extremely popular process these days – is the situation where a trained mediator is hired to listen to the parties and put together a settlement that they both can agree on.

Usually mediation lasts a full day, with the mediator shuttling back and forth between the two camps, discussing, cajoling, arguing, calculating, pushing, begging, encouraging, until the parties finally agree on some middle ground and settle the case. Mediation has become a mainstay of modern American litigation.

THE TRIAL

The ultimate test of the legal system in this country is the trial. It comes in two basic varieties...the jury trial and the bench trial. In the jury trial the judge decides the law and legal issues and the jury decides the facts. In a bench trial, the judge decides the law and the facts.

As pointed out in earlier paragraphs, it is expensive, risky, full of adrenaline, and just plain difficult. But the trial is also the symbol of why we prize the American Judicial System. When everything else fails, when the parties simply cannot agree, when the issues cannot be mediated or arbitrated, when the little guy needs to stand up to big government or big business, when the rules need to be changed, when society screams for right over might, when an injured party needs to force an insurance company to do the right thing, when a crazy, possessed Plaintiff just won't let go, when lots of people are being harmed by something that needs to be stopped...Americans can step into a Courtroom and place the difficult, thorny problem in the hands of a neutral judge or a jury of people just like us.

Of course there are thousands and thousands of trials every day in America, some fascinating, some dreary, some sad. But some are fantastic, and collectively they represent a critical part of the fabric of our amazing system. In a future column, we'll discuss a few of the great trials of all time and what they mean to us.

Hey, thanks for reading my column...I love writing it!

Tom Brown

Bankruptcy Stigma or Salvation

• • •

FOR THE LAST 18 MONTHS, the American financial crisis has caused us to be inundated with references to bankruptcy. Our next-door neighbors are going bankrupt, because they can't make their house payments. General Motors is filing bankruptcy to save itself. People are filing bankruptcy because they can't pay their credit card bills.

What is this thing called bankruptcy? Why do we have it? Is it good? Bad? Useful? A rip-off?

HISTORY
Let's begin this discussion by talking about some history.

People who get in over their heads have been around for centuries. Unfortunately for those people, society was not very tolerant. In the ancient world, debtors were sometimes executed, sometime tortured, sometimes sold into slavery. As a race, we were not very forgiving of debtors until the ancient Roman Empire, when Julius Caesar (who, ironically, owed a lot of money to various people) pushed through some progressive laws that said that a debtor could surrender all of his goods and let the creditors divvy it up. The debtor would then escape the terrible penalties like slavery or death or torture.

Even though this was more humane, things didn't seem to get all that much better for centuries. As late as the 1500's, the English were still mutilating debtors! Henry VIII, famous for killing his wives, decided that something had to be done, so he changed the laws to provide for debtors' prisons, but they filled up immediately! Henry's daughter -- Elizabeth I -- decided that more had to be done and she created comprehensive bankruptcy legislation that formed the loose framework for the American laws that would follow later in the century. It was crude, but her laws said that the creditors could simply grab everything the debtor had and split it up...they would even break into the home and grab anything they could sell!

BANKRUPTCY IN AMERICA

Enter America. Surely, we must have been more forgiving in our early days? Hah! We were almost as brutal as the early Greek and Romans. Colonial debtors were thrown into disgusting and terrible prisons. But, things got better. As the Revolutionary War wound down, lots of great patriots found that they had pledged their fortunes for real... they were underwater after financing the Revolutionary War against Britain.

This self-interest spawned two important results: the Federal Government took control of Bankruptcy, and the individual states abandoned their debtors' prisons and similar horrible punishments for chronic debt problems. Our early federal bankruptcy laws were modeled on the English laws that evolved from Elizabeth's reforms. The American laws evolved quickly from 1800 to the present.

Now, we have a highly evolved Bankruptcy system, which affords debtors a known, reliable system for reorganizing and/or shedding debt.

How Bankruptcy Works

How does it work? If you go bankrupt, you come to the court and say: "Here's what I own and here's what I owe." You list all your assets: bank accounts, real estate, cars, cash, investments, jewelry, lawsuits, corporations, etc...... and then you list all your debts: credit cards, mortgages, car loans, family loans, medical bills, etc. Some of your assets are protected (part of your home, your tools, some of your clothes, some insurance, some pensions, some insurance, etc.), but most of your assets will be taken to pay your debtors. Washington State has fairly generous laws that protect your personal assets in a bankruptcy. But don't be fooled...the boat is gone, the Sea-Doo is gone, the Motorhome is gone, the trail bikes are gone, the Swiss bank account is gone, your lake cabin is gone. This type of Bankruptcy is called a "Chapter 7" bankruptcy. Most Chapter 7 bankruptcies do not involve significant assets...it's usually just wiping away debt and the creditors get little or nothing.

If you file under Chapter 13, you can pay off your debts at a reduced rate under Court supervision. It protects you from your creditors, while you follow a strict plan set up by the Court. Ask your bankruptcy lawyer if it's a good idea for you.

(Chapter 11 is a separate category...that is the kind of bankruptcy that allows a corporation to be protected from its creditors, while it reorganizes and hopefully makes itself profitable again.)

One of the nice things about Bankruptcy is that the Bankruptcy Court stops all collection actions against you after you file. No more threatening letters, no collection agencies, no collection lawsuits, no phone calls...just silence while the Court and the lawyers and the Trustee (a court official) work out the solution to your particular problem.

How easy is it to file Bankruptcy? Not that easy. First of all, you have to see an attorney who knows what he or she is doing with respect to Bankruptcy. I'm not kidding you...it's going to be expensive. Figure around $1250 - $1500 including filing fees for the basic Chapter 7 with no problems. If there are problems and the lawyer has to spend more time, the price goes up. A Chapter 13 is more expensive...probably at least $1800.

If you do file Bankruptcy, don't be cute, don't withhold or try to hide anything. Everybody wants to keep back something they don't think the creditors should know about...forget it...confess and tell everything. Remember that you are dealing with the Federal Government here, and they have seen every scam or trick or diversion you can imagine. Plus, your lawyer will dump you if he or she finds out that you've been lying.

OPTIONS

Bankruptcy can be a useful tool if you have a huge debt that is threatening your financial security and your peace of mind. If you don't have anything else to lose, a bankruptcy can be a lifesaver. But if you have lots of money in the bank, and lots of property, and lots of investments, you need expert advice from a good bankruptcy attorney.

Never, ever, ever attempt a do-it-yourself bankruptcy. See a competent lawyer. Don't do something on-line. This is one of the most significant financial moves of your lifetime.

There are alternatives to bankruptcy. There are companies out there that negotiate with your creditors to reduce the amount that you have to pay. They usually do this by threatening bankruptcy. There are some responsible companies in this category as well as some really sleazy operators.

Another option is a Debt Counseling Service, which can be helpful if you're not too far underwater. Another option is to consolidate your debt, usually by borrowing against your home...the trick here is not to make your situation worse.

Is bankruptcy a stigma? Well, it is going to be on your credit report and your financial statements for years. But, let's face it; this is the era of terrible financial situations. You can explain a bankruptcy. You can provide information. You can fess up. Don't avoid the relief of bankruptcy because it seems like a life sentence. Talk to a good, savvy bankruptcy attorney. Ask him or her hard questions about the lasting effect of bankruptcy.

And then...when the storm has passed...sit on your deck or your porch and say to your partner: "Where will we be ten years from now?"

Make sure that's a happy place and then hold each other and say: "This is where we are going."

Thanks for reading my column. Come back and see me next month!

Tom Brown

What in the world is Legal Aid
and why should I care?

• • •

ONE OF THE BUILDING BLOCKS of our society is the notion that we all are entitled to "...equal justice under the law." As a nation, we have been touting that from the very beginning, as a fundamental part of our national DNA.

However, like most ideals, it has been a concept that needed careful tending and nurturing in order to grow into a robust and mature part of our daily national life. Unfortunately, in the early days of our beloved republic, our national leaders didn't really think that equal justice applied totally and universally. They certainly didn't see the need to protect slaves, criminals, debtors, the poor, etc.

For decades, we gave a casual wink to many of the concepts of our Constitution as they related to criminal law. The landmark cases that insured the right to counsel, the protection against self-incrimination, the need to be advised of our rights, and other rights we take for granted in criminal law didn't occur until the 50s and 60s, when the Supreme Court was forced to confront the fact that those rights were being routinely abused...and had been for as long as those rights existed.

But only a small percentage of our population gets involved with the criminal justice system, whereas most of us are involved in the civil justice system at some time in our lives. Divorce, landlord-tenant, mortgage foreclosures, property disputes, child custody, restraining orders, fights with the government over social security or other benefits, adoptions, wills, probates, unlawful firing from a job…all of these things are part and parcel of our daily lives whether we like it or not. The civil – as opposed to criminal – justice system is something that touches most of our lives at one time or another.

When we bump into one of these situations, we suck it up and bite our lip and go see our favorite attorney, who hopefully guides us through the shoals toward the best possible result under the circumstances. Sure, it costs money…but that's part of life…unless you are so poor that you can't afford food or housing, much less the cost of an attorney.

In the 60s, when we began to emerge from the dark ages of ignoring our fellow citizens who weren't able to just hire an attorney, our government recognized a simple truth: if every citizen can't take full advantage of our fabulous civil legal system because they can't afford it, then the dream of equal justice under the law is nothing more than a motto with no substance. In response to that realization, our government put its bureaucratic toe in the water as part of the "War on Poverty."

Inside the then newly -established Office of Economic Opportunity, the US government created a program to provide free, essential legal services in civil matters to people who couldn't afford a lawyer.

The result was a wonderful, happy dawning of an age when at least some of our impoverished citizens could raise their voices and be heard in a court of law, just like the big corporations, just like the rich, just like the government, and just like most of us. This spawned a new era of responsibility, where the privileged had to recognize and respect the rights of those people who had never been heard before.

The concept was so powerful, so sweeping, so effective, so right... that 35 years ago this last month, legislation was signed into law creating the Legal Services Corporation as an agency of the United States Government. For at least 5 years before that, President Nixon had been urging Congress to pass this law and make legal services for the poor "...immune to political pressures and make it a permanent part of our system of justice." What had been an experimental program in a government agency had blossomed into a fully enfranchised, independent Government Corporation that survives to this day as a centerpiece of civil legal aid in this country.

As you might imagine, the road before and after that historic event has been a rocky one indeed. While it's certainly nice to talk about poor people having rights and having a lawyer to enforce those rights, the people on "the other side" haven't felt so warm about the concept.

Slum landlords don't like to have to follow the rules to evict people. Collection agencies don't want to deal with lawyers, who question the validity of their claims. Government agencies don't like to have their unilateral actions challenged. Corporations don't want to spend money to make their products safer. To put it bluntly, it's been big pains in the ass for the privileged side of our society to have all these people has their rights! But...true to the dreams and wisdom of our founding fathers...it has also forever changed the lives and hopes of millions of people who became enfranchised members of society, with the same package of rights and privileges of the Bernie Madoffs and Washington Mutuals. Like everything else, change is hard...and controversial. And, of course, like all government programs, funding is always a problem. The states still bear the overwhelming responsibility for providing legal aid to their citizens...the federal Legal Services Corporation is only a part of the funding picture.

In Washington State, the need for legal services for the poor is critical. Several years ago, our Supreme Court, under the inspired leadership of Chief Justice Gerry Alexander, ordered a study on the access to justice for our underprivileged citizens. The results were truly shocking and sad. There is a huge "justice gap" for people who need legal help. Although the existing programs have struggled mightily to provide service, the tsunami of need is overwhelming.

Thanks to the work of the Supreme Court and the multiple agencies that are part of the "Equal Justice Community," the legislature has been educated and responded to the need.

Unfortunately, even with the positive response of the lawmakers, the need is still massive and the "justice gap" is really more of a canyon.

But our part of the State did benefit...we have new offices for legal aid lawyers (The Northwest Justice Project) in Aberdeen for Grays Harbor and Pacific counties, and in Port Angeles for Clallam and Jefferson counties. The attorneys in those offices are hard working, smart, savvy lawyers who are dedicated to making life better for the underprivileged of our society by giving them full access to the law. They help them through difficult domestic violence problems, they defend them against predatory collection agencies, they assist them in dealing with government bureaucracies, they protect them from unlawful evictions, and they help them avoid foreclosures the list goes on. Of course the clients have to qualify financially and the case has to be one of the types that is not prohibited for legal aid (like fee-generating cases, immigration matters, class actions, lobbying, etc.).

Legal aid is one of the most powerful and "hands-on" forces for equal justice in our society. If even our poorest, most downtrodden citizens don't have access to the law and its benefits, then the dream of our forefathers for a society that provides equal justice to all of its people will go unfulfilled. When we all have access to the law and its benefits, our great country can realize its promise of equal justice under the law.

As always, thank you for reading my column, and thank you for the many wonderful comments I have received about the column. Anything in particular you want to hear about? Let me know at tom.brown@lawbljs.com See you next month!

Tom Brown

Are you sick of hearing about symbols?

• • •

IF YOU'RE A FAN OF pop fiction, you know that "symbology" is all the rage. The Dan Brown books, *The DaVinci Code, Angels and Demons*, and now *The Lost Symbol* and all of the copycat books are filled with religious and historic and Masonic symbols that we didn't even realize surrounded us. We are being introduced to the dizzying array of symbols that are present in our government buildings and monuments, which are based on religious –and sometimes – Masonic influence.

But if religion and government are rich with symbols, certainly the law must have its share, huh?

Oh, yes…the law is swimming in symbols.

To understand the law's love for symbology, you first have to recognize and accept that the law is also steeped in history and religion and Masonic lore and Greek legends and all of the human quirks that make for a fascinating historical tour.

Let's start with our courthouses. If you haven't noticed already, the classic Courthouses look like temples, the same temples that the ancients used to build on high hills over Athens or in the forum in Rome. Go to Montesano or to the old Courthouse on Capitol Way in Olympia or to Port Townsend. These aren't mundane governmental buildings…these are temples to the law. The Courthouse in Montesano has murals in the courtrooms in classic roman style. Columns abound. Ceilings soar. Let's face it…we are confused about the relationship between the law and religion and mysticism. You could stand in the Montesano courthouse for hours and see the symbolism in the murals, the paintings in the dome, in the stained glass and in the architecture itself. Lots of angels flitting around the Courthouse in Monte!

But, to discuss this realistically, let's go to the main temple, the mother ship of the law, and the home of the Supreme Court of the United States. This building has it all. The scales of justice are everywhere. This is the most basic, clearest symbol of the law. It represents the weighing of both side of the argument and it can be found in the Courtroom, in three friezes of the exterior, on the front plaza…it just goes on…the scales are everywhere as one of the great symbols of our justice system. We weigh all the facts and evidence.

The Supreme Court Building is drenched in the symbolism of the "book" of the law. In this magnificent building, there are at least ten separate places where the book of the law is represented and glorified as our guiding light. From the pediments to the elevator doorframe, you will find the theme of reliance on the "book" of the law, even as held by Confucius and Muhammad and John Marshall. What a collection of lawgivers, eh?

Another enduring symbol of the law in our society is the Ten Commandments. The Supreme Court of the United States also honors the religious side of the equation by showing us Moses and the Ten Commandments in various contexts as a fundamental underpinning of modern law. At least eight or nine times in the Supreme Court Building, we find the lawgiver or the tablets or both. What an incredibly strong religious influence on our legal system! http://

www.supremecourtus.gov/about/courtbuilding.pdf   http://www.su-
premecourtus.gov/about/symbolsoflaw.pdf

Even the building itself is a symbol. Chief Justice William Howard
Taft worked with the architect Cass Gilbert to come up with a monu-
mental temple that itself symbolized the power and majesty and legiti-
macy of the Supreme Court, standing elbow to elbow with the homes of
the other institutions of government.

But, c'mon...we all know what the basic symbol of the law in our society is, right? Of course! It's a blindfolded woman, holding a sword and
a set of scales. She's supposed to be justice blindfolded to show that the
law doesn't pretend to understand each side until it "gels" in the courtroom. But here's the scary part...that woman is the ancient Goddess
Ma'at, the ancient Egyptian goddess of truth, balance and order.

Watch out, here it comes...that sacred goddess became a fundamental Masonic concept centuries ago and so remains to this day. We share
her with our Masonic friends. Some even say that the term "magistrate"
(a kind of judge) is derived from her name.

Anyway, this woman from ancient Egypt (who had an Ostrich feath-
er in her hair instead of scales), evolved into the Greek goddess Themis,
who was a seer of the future and was one of the oracles at Delphi, and
then she evolved into the goddess of divine justice. Surprisingly, the
Greek goddess Themis didn't need to be blindfolded (because she was
a prophet) and didn't hold a sword (because she represented agreement
and consent, not coercion.

Finally, along came the Roman goddess of justice -- Justitia. She had
the scales and the sword and the blindfold. Later, the Romans added
an ax for judicial authority and a flame for truth. The website of the

University of Washington Law School has some interesting information on this enduring symbol of the law. You can find it at http://lib.law.washington.edu/ref/themis.html

There's more. The judge's gavel pounding on the bench is a derivative of the famous-- or infamous -- Masonic hammer and block! It almost makes you want to read another Dan Brown novel!

But all of this should not make us feel like strangers to the law. To the contrary, the use of symbols is a very basic, human endeavor that strives to make the law more understandable, friendlier, more in touch with our humanity. It's very much like the warm, patriotic feeling we get when we see one our national symbols, like the flag, or Uncle Sam or the Statue of Liberty. We cling to our symbols, whether they are crosses or union bugs, peace signs, shamrocks, or whatever. Our legal system is one of the foundations of our freedom and leadership in the world…it's no wonder that it is rich in symbolism.

Are you loving symbols yet? I am.

Thanks for reading my column. If you have any ideas for columns in the future, just let me know at tom.brown@lawbljs.com

See you next month!

Tom Brown

Who is in charge you or your lawyer?

• • •

IF THERE'S ANYTHING IN THE world that drives me crazy, it's the idea that lawyers are inaccessible, distant, expensive, and just not part of our lives. Most of this feeling relates to money. We don't want to go see the lawyer and end up with a huge bill in our mailbox. We're afraid to talk to them because it's going to cost us a bundle. We just don't have control over the costs, like we do when we're shopping at Top Foods or ordering a meal at our favorite restaurant.

Now, I'm a realist. I know that when you get into a terrible situation, like a felony charge, or a huge estate dispute, or a monster fight over land, you are going to the land of five or six digit bills from your lawyer. You're at his mercy...you're asking him to fight as hard as he can in your version of WWII, but you want him to bill like he's just thinking about you once every two weeks. It's a nightmare. Frankly, there's no controlling these situations...they represent the metastatic cancer of the legal world.

But...c'mon. Most of our problems aren't so dramatic or expensive. We have little property line disputes, little misunderstandings with our remodeling contractor; little disputes in our family corporations, little employment problems at work. And, what do we do about these little problems? Oh, that's easy.

We wing it!!! We talk to our Uncle Fred, who used to serve papers for the Sheriff's office. Or we Google the problem and get confused and go to bed. Or we read a column in the Seniors Sunset Times and hope that Tom Brown is covering your issue this week. Or we just have another glass of wine and let the problem fester. These are all BAD IDEAS!! But we sure as heck don't want to go to the lawyer... it's too expensive!!!

Ok, smarty pants, what should we do? Great question...complicated answer. But the theme of this column this month is to use the system of lawyers "proactively" (Jeez, I hate that word) and don't shy away based on cost.

First, find a lawyer you trust (we covered this in an earlier column) and then call him (or her) up. This is the critical point in the relationship. If you have a long relationship with the lawyer, you can talk...but if you're really a stranger to the lawyer, it will be tougher. The solution? Be direct. Tell the lawyer that you have a problem that is not huge and will not produce a fee the size of Montana. Then, talk directly to the lawyer about limits. Tell him or her that you want to keep this thing on the ranch, and talk about actual dollar figures. This puts the ball in the lawyer's court. If you tell him that you don't want to spend more than $500.00, then he or she has to decide whether any reasonable work can be done within that budget.

Remember, lawyers are business people. He or she wants you as a client and maybe as a friend. The lawyer will take a beating at the outset in order to form a permanent relationship with you. The lawyer is thinking that if you are charged $500.00 for $2,000.00 worth of work, you will be his client forever. And then when you have the legendary "million dollar case" you will turn to the same friendly lawyer. It's like advertising...it's like joining the Rotary Club...it's like being in a fraternity.

One of the basic elements in this discussion is the concept that you have to be realistic. If you want the lawyer to commit to a budget of $500.00 when you have been sued for reneging on a million dollar contract, you are going to be laughed off the ranch. But, if you want the lawyer to come out to your property and look at the conflicting property lines and do a little research, and keep it under $500.00, you're barking up the right tree. Or if you want the lawyer to look over the corporate books of your family corporation that has cratered, and you want him to keep it under $750.00, you're probably making sense. Don't leave it to surprise and disagreement...get it straight ahead of time: "Tom, you're going to do "x" and not charge me more than $500.00, right?" If the lawyer waffles on that question, you don't have a deal. Much worse, you don't have an understanding.

Actually, lawyers love certainty. If you and your lawyer have agreed that that the whole banana is going to be $500.00, the lawyer is happy. He knows what he has to do and he knows what the status is. But remember, if the deal matures into something else...something you didn't agree on...the price tag is going to be a lot higher.

My suggestion to you is to take charge of the relationship. Don't go whimpering to the lawyer long after you've been sued. Don't bring him a mess that's been festering for a year. Don't wonder about how expensive this mess is going to be after it has deteriorated into a quagmire. When you have a legal problem, or something that you suspect will turn into a legal problem, confront the situation and make an appointment, supply the lawyer with a summary of the problem ahead of time (so he doesn't have to spend an hour extracting the information laboriously from you when you finally do meet), and get together and discuss it. Don't be afraid to talk money. Tell the lawyer that you can't afford to pay $5,000.00 in attorney fees, so he can tell you where you're at in this problem. He may have to tell you to file bankruptcy. He may tell you to resolve it with your opponent. But you can be sure that a lawyer who has just heard that you can't afford to pay for a long, expensive battle isn't going to sign you up for that battle, with no hope of payment.

So, here's a summary of what you should do when you hire an attorney on a smaller matter:

1. Talk openly about fees.
2. Get a commitment from the attorney on the maximum fees.
3. Be realistic...you can't sue Microsoft and fight it to the bloody end for an attorney fee of $500.00.
4. Make sure you and the attorney agreement on the scope of the project.
5. Don't expect a small fee or a fee break on a huge matter.
6. Keep abreast of the fees...demand a monthly statement if necessary.
7. On a smaller project, don't hesitate to try to get a fee "deal" from the lawyer.
8. "Package" your problem, so it's easy to understand and easy to predict how long it will take to resolve.
9. Once the lawyer has fulfilled his obligation under the arrangement, don't try to chisel additional legal service for no fee.
10. Don't pursue ridiculous lawsuits or claims...you know when it just doesn't make sense.

As always, I really appreciate it when you read my column, and I appreciate all the nice comments I get from you. Thank you for reading the column...hope you enjoyed it!!!

Tom Brown

How about an injunction against Grinches?

● ● ●

WELL, IT'S THAT TIME OF year again.

The Associated Press reports that an Ohio Christmas parade won't be held for the first time in decades amid concerns over possible lawsuits, expected protests and logistical problems. Officials in the village of Amelia, Ohio canceled their Christmas parade this year to avoid legal fees in defending the tradition from possible lawsuits by religious groups. The problem started when the **private group that for 28 years had funded the parade** in Amelia village recently announced it could no longer do so, prompting the village mayor to step in with public funds. [Good for you, Mayor!] On a lawyer's advice, the mayor decided to change the name of the event from Christmas Parade to the more neutral "Holiday Parade" to avoid lawsuits and abide by constitutional rules about the separation of church and state. "Even though it may seem silly," Mayor Leroy Ellington said, "the legal fees that the village would spend to defend 'A Christmas Parade' would be costly.... There was the likelihood that we would be sued on a first amendment issue," he added, referring to the constitutional requirements for secular government. [OK, Mr. Mayor...that's reasonable.] But then, unfortunately, in a somewhat weird twist, the name change did not sit well with local church officials, who promptly threatened to boycott the event if it was no longer called "A Christmas Parade." Faced with legal quarrels and logistical problems in organizing the parade, Mayor Ellington finally threw up his hands. "As a citizen I want a Christmas parade, as a mayor I've an obligation to prevent the village from spending unnecessary tax dollars," he said on announcing that his office was dropping out of the organization drive.

In a similar kind of story, in what looks like another one of the first goofy skirmishes for the 2009 season, a federal lawsuit has been filed by a Michigan resident challenging a county's decision to end a 63-year old tradition of his family's displaying a privately-constructed and maintained Nativity Scene on the median of a road in the city. . The county first raised an objection in 2008 after receiving a letter from the "Freedom from Religion Foundation" (Yikes!) complaining that the display on public property violates the Constitution. Plaintiff removed the display last year only because he had not applied for a permit. This year he applied, **and was denied a permit**! In addition to his speech and equal protection claims, the "Foundation" charges that the denial violates the Establishment Clause of the Constitution because it lacks a valid secular purpose and has the primary effect of inhibiting religion. The crazy part here is that the good guy is the one having to bring the lawsuit, not the whackos that want to stop the Nativity scene. For crying out loud!

Hey, I'm in favor of everyone being free to celebrate his or her own legitimate religions, or lack thereof. But Christmas is a NATIONAL HOLIDAY of the United States of America. It's not just about religion. It's about history. It's about our traditions. Christmas is all about Christmas trees, lights, angels, Nativity Scenes, snowmen, Santa, elves, reindeer, etc., etc. We love Christmas. My agnostic and atheistic friends love Christmas. Every Jewish friend I've ever had loves Christmas (but they celebrate their holidays, too!) This isn't a fight! We're having a good time because it's Christmastime.

Of course, I'm a lawyer...so I support the right of everyone to come to the Courts of our country and air their legitimate grievances. But, don't we have more important grievances than this? If we have to fight, let's fight about foreign wars or the death penalty or poverty or immigration or something that truly impacts our lives for good or evil. There's just nothing sinister or unconstitutional about a chubby little baby Jesus smiling in a manger!

Remember Dr. Seuss's "Grinch"? He wanted to ruin Christmas just for the sheer meanness of it. In my humble opinion, the naysayers who attack the expressions of joy at Christmas are just today's version of the Grinch, who are trying to ruin the joy and traditions of the Christmas season.

So, this Christmas season, let's just stick to attacking our favorite target...lawyers. Here's a funny spoof of a Lawyer's politically correct Christmas card I found on the Internet. I think you'll get a laugh out of it.

• • •

LAWYER'S CHRISTMAS CARD
In Politically Correct Legalese

From us ("the wishers") to you ("hereinafter called the wishee"):

Please accept without obligation, explicit or implicit, our best wishes for an environmentally conscious, socially responsible, politically correct, low stress, non-addictive, gender neutral, celebration of the winter solstice holiday, practiced within the most enjoyable traditions of the religious persuasion or secular practice of your choice, with respect for the religious/secular persuasions and/or traditions of others, or their choice not to practice religious or secular traditions.

Please also accept, under aforesaid waiver of obligation on your part, our best wishes for a financially successful, personally fulfilling and medically uncomplicated recognition of the onset of this calendar year of the Common Era, but with due respect for the calendars of all cultures or sects, and for the race, creed, color, age, physical ability, religious faith, choice of computer platform or dietary preference of the wishee.

By accepting this greeting you acknowledge that:

This greeting is subject to further clarification or withdrawal at the wisher's discretion.

This greeting is freely transferable provided that no alteration shall be made to the original greeting and that the proprietary rights of the wisher are acknowledged.

This greeting implies no warranty on the part of the wishers to fulfill these wishes, nor any ability of the wishers to do so, merely a beneficent hope on the part of the wishers that they in fact occur.

This greeting may not be enforceable in certain jurisdictions and/or the restrictions herein may not be binding upon certain wishees in certain jurisdictions and is revocable at the sole discretion of the wishers.

This greeting is warranted to perform as reasonably may be expected within the usual application of good tidings, for a period of one year or until the issuance of a subsequent holiday greeting, whichever comes first.

The wisher warrants this greeting only for the limited replacement of this wish or issuance of a new wish at the sole discretion of the wisher.

Any references in this greeting to "the Lord", "Father Christmas", "Our Savior", or any other festive figures, whether actual or fictitious, dead or alive, shall not imply any endorsement by or from them in respect of this greeting, and all proprietary rights in any referenced third party names and images are hereby acknowledged.

Sincerely,
Dewey, Cheetham, and Howe
Attorneys at Law

● ● ●

As always, thanks for reading my column. We'll hopefully get back to more serious stuff next month. Remember, you can drop me a comment or a suggestion at tom.brown@lawbljs.com

Tom Brown

Don't slander me!!!

• • •

OVER 2,500 YEARS AGO, THE Greek Philosopher Plato said

"Let nobody speak mischief of anybody."

A couple of hundred years later, the Roman poet Plautus joined in:

"Slander-mongers and those who listen to slander. If I had my way, would all be strung up, the talkers by the tongue, the listeners by the ears."

The concept of slander has obviously been with us for a long time, probably because it is such a nasty little part of human nature to whisper about the people around us. It happens in the schoolyard, in the lunch-room, in the office...everywhere that humans talk and write, and now everywhere they electronically send texts and e-mails.

So, what in the world does the law have to do with slander? It's just normal human conduct, isn't it?

Well, the problem is that slander can have some pretty serious effects. If somebody puts up a billboard that says that the most successful lawyer in town has been stealing from his Church that will certainly have a serious effect on the lawyer's clients. If somebody announces on the radio that the most popular restaurant in town serves food contaminate by rats, you can expect that business might drop off. If the local newspaper runs a story that the minister of the largest congregation in the city has been molesting children, there are going to be some serious consequences.

So, our legal system says that if you are damaged by slander, you can sue and recover your damages. Of course, like all things legal, it's not that simple. (You knew that was coming, didn't you?)

Let's break it down a little bit. First, our legal system has created a general category called ***defamation***, which includes written (libel) and spoken (slander) statements. In the United States, defamation is usually a tort, not a crime. This means that the defamer can be sued for damages, but not put in jail or subjected to other criminal penalties. But, if your defamation harms somebody, either by causing their customers to go somewhere else or by causing emotional pain and suffering, be prepared to get out your checkbook! (Interestingly, many nations of the world, including most of our European friends, consider defamation to be a crime! And...surprisingly...some of our states still have some rarely used criminal defamation laws.) But you are safe in saying that defamation or slander or libel is usually not a crime in the United States.

What is the essence of defamation? The statement must have these characteristics:

1. It must be false.
2. It must be communicated or transmitted to other persons.
3. It must cause damage to the person who is the subject.

Truth is an absolute defense to any claim of defamation (or libel or slander). If I say that Mayor Smith is stealing from the City treasury and he sues me for defamation; he will lose that lawsuit if I can prove that he stole $5.00 from the City's till.

The big problem with defamation in the United States is that it constantly bumps into one of our most cherished rights...free speech! We like our free press to talk about public figures, but we still want them to be fair. In a famous case 45 years ago, the U.S. Supreme Court said that a public figure could only sue for defamation if the defamer **knew** it was false or didn't even try to determine if it was false.

The chances of the average citizen getting involved with defamation or slander or libel are really slim. Nonetheless, it is one of the commonest calls I receive from the public. People are always saying that they were slandered or that they want to sue for defamation. 99 times out of 100, I discourage these people from taking any legal action. A defamation lawsuit is virtually impossible to win unless the lie is clear and the damages are huge. In my 39-year career, I've probably had less than ten cases that ever made it to a real lawsuit, and only two or three that ever made it to a courtroom. (However, one of those did result in a $1.3 Million verdict for my client...my biggest case ever!)

Here's my advice relating to defamation or slander or libel:

1. Think twice before you send that letter to the editor.
2. Think twice before you send that e-mail or text message.
3. Read all the books you can get your hands on about libel and slander cases...they are delicious and fun to read.

Finally, when thinking about defamation and slander, it is good to remember the Hebrew proverb:

"Slander slays three persons: the speaker, the spoken to, and the spoken of."

I can't tell you how wonderful you readers have been to me about this column. I enjoy this very much and I thank you for reading. See you next month!

If you have any comments or suggestions feel free to contact me at tom.brown@lawbljs.com

Tom Brown

You're FIRED!

• • •

It's NOT JUST THE CURRENT recession…employment problems are one of the most nagging group of complaints that lawyers face on an ongoing basis. I haven't kept track over the last 40 years as a lawyer, but I'll bet that at least 50% of the random calls I've received are related -- in some way -- to employment issues.

People get fired, people get "eased out", people get "promoted" to lesser jobs, people get "transferred" to another department, people get re-assigned, people get discriminated against at work, people get assigned burdensome duties that force them to quit, people can't stand the people they're working with…it goes on and on.

WHEN CAN AN EMPLOYEE BE FIRED?

Let's start our thoughtful discussion with the basic rule in Washington State…this is an "at will" employment state. That means that -- unless you have an employment contract (or unless one of the law's dozens of exceptions exist) -- your employer can fire you at any time, for any reason, without cause. You can be fired because your hair is the wrong color, or your boss doesn't like your squeaky voice, or because you're a ditzy idiot that can't figure out how to get through the front door at the office. The boss doesn't need a reason…you're fired and there's nothing you can do about it. Well…. almost nothing…

So, now, of course, we turn to the exceptions and loopholes…and believe me, they are all over the place. If there is some sort of relationship that changes the equation between the employer and the employee, then the "at will" nature of the beast changes. Examples of such relationships are:

1. Public or civil service employment. After a probationary period, it is very difficult to fire a civil servant because the law provides a complex and detailed process for challenging the firing. The employer sees nothing but lawyers and hearings and recriminations in the future and usually decides that getting rid of the employee isn't worth the trouble.
2. Union situations. Once the employee has jumped through the hoops and become a member of the union, the employee is protected by complex collective bargaining agreements that make it very difficult to fire even an incompetent employee. This is particularly true with the stronger unions, like the teachers.
3. Employment Contracts. This category can apply to employees that have influence and power or to employees that have no power and are being forced to sign a contract by a powerful employer. So it can be an advantage either to the employee or to the employer. This is the area that is the source of much of the litigation over employment issues. While most employees don't sign a contract, the courts have often agreed that a personnel manual or handbook may rise to the level of a contract. So that dusty, unread "Employee Handbook" in the bottom drawer may be a lot more important than either the employer or employee ever realized.
4. Promises. Promises by the employer can add up to something very close to a contract.

So, let's summarize the basic situation: if you're not a government employee or in a union, you can probably be fired without a good reason.

If the job is worth fighting over, have your lawyer take a look at the circumstances, including any employee manuals or handouts or promises. If you're an employer, be careful about what you put in the employee manual or handouts…it can come back to bite you. So can any promises that you make.

WHAT ABOUT UNEMPLOYMENT INSURANCE?

When someone is fired, the first thing they usually think of is unemployment insurance. That is a government program that provides limited benefits to persons who lost their jobs, while they look for work. Many factors affect eligibility for unemployment insurance. If the worker was fired "for cause" they may not be eligible. If they find other work, they're not eligible. Unfortunately for the taxpayer, the rules about having to actively look for work are often winked at, and unemployment can become an extended partially paid vacation. Most people don't realize that the employer takes a huge hit if one of their former employees goes on unemployment…meaning that their premiums go way up.

A fired worker should always consider applying for unemployment insurance unless the reason for the firing was so gross that there's no chance. Sometimes, the employer just doesn't want to go through the hassle of the appeal and doesn't contest what the employer says, and lets them have the unemployment. The employer usually regrets that decision the next year when the new premium statement arrives from the State.

Likewise, if the employer wants to keep his premiums down, the employer should contest the appeal of the fired worker who is claiming that she only quit because the environment in the office was so negative, she had to quit!

In either case, it's worth a few bucks to talk to a lawyer, who can give you an idea of what your chances are.

What about Non-Competition Agreements?

If your new employer wants you to sign something that restricts your ability to work somewhere else if you're fired or you quit, your alarm bells should be going off. This isn't just a concern for accountants and life insurance agents…it's a real concern for nurses, paralegals, office managers, salesmen, etc. A potential employee should never (that's *never*) sign anything that restricts his or her ability to work in the future, without a very careful and thorough review by a lawyer who knows what he's doing.

Our Washington courts are very critical of such agreements…and they only survive legal scrutiny if they are reasonable in terms of geography and duration. But it's too expensive to have a Court decide this kind of stuff…see the lawyer ahead of time and avoid a lawsuit.

Other stuff

Employment law is a rich and busy area of the law. Maybe in a future column, we'll talk about some of the really juicy stuff, like undisclosed criminal records; citizenship as a prerequisite for the job; whether the former employer can tell the new employer what a lousy employee you were; discrimination based on race, sex, national origin, color, familial status, age; use of false references, bad habits (smoking, drinking, chew, etc.); sexual misconduct on the job; and so on…it's just too interesting!

Thanks for reading my column, and thanks for the many nice comments! If you want to comment or suggest a topic, feel free to drop me e-mail at tom.brown@lawbljs.com

Tom Brown

You're too late! Sometimes you can't sue...even if you are in the right

• • •

OVER THE YEARS, THE LAW has evolved to serve common sense and reality. It continues to evolve as our legislatures hum away each year, creating new crimes, new laws, new time limits, and new ways to give lawyers gray hairs.

One of the problems that have always haunted the law is that people's claims do get old and stale. The witnesses forget what happened or die or simply lose interest. The evidence gets lost. The people just don't know what happened so many years ago. Let's face it...if a claim has been around for too many years, it's like last weeks' fish. It starts to stink.

In its wisdom, the law and the lawmakers have long realized that there had to be some kind of limit to how long claims against other people lasted.

So, in order to keep this thing reasonable, our predecessors created STATUTES OF LIMITATION. These are laws that say that you can't sue after a certain amount of time has passed. Some of these you won't believe!!

Let's start with personal injury cases. In Washington, if you are injured in an automobile accident, or a slip and fall, or a doctor's malpractice, you have to sue the responsible person within three years of the incident or the claim is lost forever! Unlike most things in the law that allow for our human foibles, these things are absolute! There's no second chance... there's no explaining the problem and getting a break...there's no grace period because the dog ate your paperwork. You are out of luck.

Of course, like all things legal, there are a lot of little rules surrounding this basic rule. For example, if you didn't know that somebody's negligence caused your injuries, you might have 3 years from the time you discovered the negligent act to file your lawsuit. There are other rules that modify this basic rule, but the basic rule is strong and powerful and absolute!

(Of course, one interesting point is that -- if your lawyer forgets to file the lawsuit when he should have, you are still barred from pursuing the claim. Of course, you have three years from the time your lawyer screwed up to sue him (or her) for malpractice!! In that lawsuit, you have to show the validity of the first lawsuit and then show that your lawyer screwed up.)

There are different rules for different things. Most written agreements and contracts have a six-year statute of limitations, meaning you have to get your lawsuit going within six years of the time when the contract was violated or the person should have paid or fulfilled the contract. For example, if you signed a promissory note to pay someone back for money they loaned you, and you fail to make payments when required, the person must sue you within six years or they're out of luck.

This is even true of your home loan and mortgage. If your note goes into default, your bank had better sue you within six years or they have no way to get their money back...they even lose their mortgage against your house!

There are even Statutes of Limitation for crimes! If the government within the proper time limit does not charge you, you can go scot free (believe me, it doesn't happen very often!) The statute of limitations for many crimes in Washington is three years, but the variety of different statutes is dazzling. Of course, for the most serious of crimes, like murder and rape, there is no statute and the time limit never runs out.

By the way, with all statutes of limitation -- civil or criminal -- the statute is "tolled" (or interrupted) if the person to be sued or charged hides out or leaves the state. The statute doesn't run while the person is hiding!!

The variety of statutes of limitation is absolutely astounding. There is a different statute for libel and slander, a different one for trespass, etc. etc. etc.

As you can imagine, timeliness of a lawsuit is a real headache for lawyers. If a client trusts his or her problem to a lawyer, and then the lawyer blows the statute of limitation, then the lawyer may be sued for malpractice. So lawyers and their insurance companies are very careful about the Statute of Limitations problem; and you will find that your lawyer in very concerned about the exact date that the accident happened or the contract was signed or the crime was committed...his economic health may be at stake!

As I mentioned earlier in this article, there are many, many little side rules that govern and modify the basic rules I am talking about here. You probably have already guessed the messages that I am going to preach now...if you have a legal problem, don't hesitate! It's easy for a couple of years to slide by, and a legitimate lawsuit can be lost.

Our law books are filled with cases where the Appellate Courts have struggled with the concepts of limiting the time for lawsuits in our state. The courts want to protect your right to bring a righteous lawsuit…but they also want to honor the concept that it is not good for lawsuits to last forever.

Get to your lawyer early in the game. Be accurate about ALL of the dates involved. Talk to the lawyer about the statute of limitations and what it means in your case. Double check his or her advice…if you suspect a mistake or conflict, talks to the lawyer about it. If you think the lawyer has his head in a place that has no light, feel free to talk to another lawyer.

Remember, the law is an effort to serve the best interests of our citizens…if it seems clumsy or complicated, that's because we are human beings with an almost infinite variety of distinctions and differences that the law tries its best to cope with. No matter what you think, these crazy laws stand between chaos and us.

As always, thank you for reading my column and thank you for all the nice comments I've received. If you have any comments or suggestions, feel free to drop me e-mail at tom.brown@lawbljs.com

Tom Brown

Laws, Laws Everywhere and No Relief in Sight!!!

$$\bullet \ \ \bullet \ \ \bullet$$

Every day in this country, we talk about "the law" as if it is one single, definable, thing that we can wrap our hands and minds around. But, as you might expect, it's not that simple.

Our laws basically come from two sources:

1. Our Courts on the one hand, and
2. Our legislative and administrative bodies on the other hand.

Simple, huh?

Hah! You knew it wouldn't be that easy!

THE COMMON LAW

Let's start with the Courts. For centuries, in England and in the United States, our law has been evolving in the Courts. This called "the common law" and it forms the basis of our legal system.

In a common law system like ours, the Courts decide cases based on an evolving set of rules that the Courts fashion. The Courts are supposed to follow "precedent" -- meaning that the Courts follows what other Courts have done in the past. This makes sure that people will have confidence that the law is not arbitrary, but is applied evenly and fairly to all persons...and it doesn't suddenly change for the next person.

In our system, the common law applies mostly to the areas of contracts, negligence, and property. For example, the courts have established the rule that a contract requires a meeting of the minds between parties on all the terms of the agreement. For another example, the courts have formulated the rules around how boundary disputes between landowners will be resolved. For another example, the courts have established the standards for suing doctors for medical malpractice.

The judges and lawyers involved in cases like these do legal research to find other similar cases, where our Courts have discussed and ruled on similar issues. Sometimes the earlier cases fit perfectly and control the situation; in other situations, the present case may present new issues that require the Court to expand on the earlier cases and thus create new law.

In Washington in particular, these kinds of decisions are made by our Supreme Court and by three intermediate Appellate Courts that cover three separate areas of the state. Sometimes, the intermediate appellate courts disagree on a particular point of law, and issue completely different decisions. In that situation, the Supreme Court may step in and resolve the issue.

The Courts save and publish their opinions, and they are available to the lawyers and the public, so we can see what they have done in the past and how they might act in the future.

STATUTORY LAW

While the Courts are grinding away making law the old-fashioned way...your United States Congress and your State Legislature and your State Administrative Agencies and your County Boards of Commissioners and your City Councils are spewing out new laws at a staggering rate.

These laws cover a dizzying array of subjects and are just as binding as the common law.

The statutory laws tells us what conduct is criminal, what taxes we have to pay, how our elections work, how our traffic systems work, what we can or can't put in our water, what departments our government will have, etc., etc. Just to give you a sense of how many laws there are, between 2000 and 2007, Congress created at least 452 new crimes. So the total number of Federal crimes as of the end of 2007 exceeded 4,450. That's just the crimes! That doesn't count the tens of thousands of civil laws

And...get this...the laws give the power to bureaucrats to issue "regulations" -- which are also laws that we have to follow! For example, Congress creates the Federal Aviation Administration, and then the FAA makes all the rules about aviation in this country. The airlines and the pilots and the passengers are bound by those regulations just as if they were laws.

While that's going on, your City Council is making laws about how you have to put your garbage out and how you have to control your dog.

Most of these laws make sense. But some don't. To see some bonehead laws, go to http://www.dumblaws.com/laws/united-states/washington

WHAT CAN WE DO?

How do we know what all these thousands of laws are? Isn't it true that "…ignorance of the law is no excuse"?

Well, no one person could ever learn what is in all of our laws from Courts and legislative bodies and administrative agencies. One of our great Supreme Court Justices, Charles Evans Hughes, once said that "The United States is the greatest law factory the world has ever known." That's probably true, and we don't have to tear our hair out about knowing all these laws.

Under our system, we are expected to make a reasonable inquiry into laws that relate to what we are doing. If I am hiring myself out as a plumbing contractor, I'm expected to know about registration as a contractor and about the plumbing codes. If I am going to build a huge fence between my house and my neighbor, I'm expected to learn a little bit about property codes and boundary disputes (I might have to see a lawyer!) If I'm going to practice law, I'm expected to find out what the requirements are before I can hang out my shingle. If I'm going to drive, I'm expected to know the rules of the road.

When will these stops? When will they quit making laws? When will the Courts stop changing and expanding the law? Hah! You know the answer.

A famous philosopher, Azarias, put it simply: "Laws are not invented. They grow out of circumstances."

I couldn't have put it better myself!

Thanks for reading my column…see you next month!!!

Tom Brown

Who cares about the Supreme Court?

• • •

PROBABLY, WHEN YOU ARE READING this column, the furor over the next appointment to the United States Supreme Court will be at high tide.

You know what we're talking about...will President Obama choose a woman, an Hispanic, a liberal, an activist, a Black, a gay person, or what? And how big of a fight will there be in the Senate, which has to confirm any potential appointee?

Well, let's start with the obvious. The next member of the Supreme Court is likely to be a person who has sat as a judge in the Federal Appeals Court system. There are 94 Federal District Courts with about 2700 judges. There are 12 "Circuits" with about 700 judges. Every single member of the present Supreme Court has sat as a Federal Circuit Appeals Judge. Every single one! What kind of diversity is that?

The 700 Federal Circuit Judges do one thing and one thing only. They hear appeals from lower courts, mostly from the 2700 judges in the Federal District Courts. Most of these 700 Circuit Judges have a blue ribbon background. They have gone to the finest law schools, they have served as clerks for prior judges, and they have held important jobs as government lawyers.

To be appointed as a Federal Judge at either one of these levels, you have to have some very serious political "pull." An appointment as a Federal Judge is the cream appointment of a lifetime. Did I say lifetime? That's how long the appointment is for...for the rest of your life!!!

If you're getting the impression that this is an elite club of wealthy and politically connected lawyers, who now steer the Federal Judicial system, you're right.

But back to our point...why are all the Supremes taken from this pool of candidates? Aren't there other people who are equally qualified -- or better qualified -- to be Supreme Court Justices? Absolutely, and that is the point of this month's diatribe. Is it good for us to have all of our eggheads in one basket? I say absolutely not. The business of the Supreme Court of our country is too important, too critical for us not to do what we usually do in this great country...trust our high-level decision making to a mixed group of quality people, who will disagree and argue and compromise and -- hopefully -- come up with a decision that reflects our National will.

A perfect example of the validity of this theory was the first woman on the U.S. Supreme Court, Sandra Day O'Connor. Justice O'Connor was never in the Federal Judiciary. She was a practicing lawyer in Arizona, who later served in the Arizona legislature, and who later served on a lower appellate court in the Arizona judicial system, and who later served with distinction on the Arizona Supreme Court. What a fabulous range of practical and professional experience she brought to the Supreme Court...the classic "breath of fresh air." She was a centrist with good judgment who made the Court better.

Back in the "good old days" when Justices came from every corner of America's legal system, the Supreme Court had character and personality.

One of the greatest, most quoted Justices of all time -- Oliver Wendell Holmes, Jr. -- fought in the Civil War, went to law school, and ended up as a Judge on the Massachusetts Supreme Court...where President Teddy Roosevelt found him and appointed him.

...Or how about Earl Warren, one of the greatest Justices the Court has ever known? Whether you agree with his judicial philosophy or not, he was a *force*. And where did he come from? Not from the Federal Judiciary. He was a practicing lawyer in California, who got interested in politics, became a district attorney, then was elected Governor of California, and then ran for Vice-president of the United States with Thomas Dewey (beaten by Harry Truman) and then almost ran for President! What a history, and what a rich palette of experience and knowledge.

Since we know it so well, we could argue persuasively to President Obama that Washington State has many, many strong and brilliant individuals who could bring balance and light and justice to the Supreme Court.

Look at our Supreme Court...it has strong and articulate members of both sexes who have toiled in the trenches and now lift our Supreme Court to its position of greatness among the States. Look at our Attorney General. Look at our Governor.

I'm not saying it's likely that Barack Obama is going Justice-shopping in Washington State, but he does need to turn his gaze outward. It is time to return the Supreme Court of the United States to its roots...a diverse, brilliant, eclectic body of men and women of all stripes that reflects who we are as a country.

Is any of this important? Well, think back over recent history. Our Supreme Court has decided a Presidential election; forced the disclosure of critical evidence from the grip of a President; forced the government to let us see the Pentagon Papers; decided the most controversial issue in America with Roe v Wade; refused to toss out the death penalty; protected free speech; ended segregation in schools, ...and the list winds through the history of this great land.

The United States Supreme Court is truly one of our great institutions, and it deserves the richness and diversity of all of our citizens of all races, of all states, of all levels of service. It's too valuable of a pillar of our society to let it wither under the weight of Federal Appeals Court Justices.

Look to the West, Mr. President...there are a lot of great Judges and lawyers out here.

As always, I thank you for reading my little column each month, and thank you for your generous comments and compliments.

Tom Brown

Just Don't Bring Your Lawyer
to the Clubhouse!

• • •

WHEN I WAS GROWING UP, I knew I wanted to be a lawyer, but I never thought that the law had anything to do with one of my other loves... which was sports. I grew up in the era of Mickey Mantle and the Yankees; Johnny Unitas and the Colts; Bob Cousy and the Celtics; Rod Laver in tennis...well, you get the idea.

These guys were genuine heroes who "...didn't need no fancy slick lawyers..." to make things right with the ownership of the team in question. They supposedly came in and laid their cards on the table and took whatever was fair. Hah!

Well, whatever happened then, we know now that sport is up to its eyes in lawyers (and probably was back then, too -- we just didn't know it). Anyway, this is all an opening to our discussion this month: What is the role of lawyers and the law in sports today? As you probably guessed, it's huge.

Probably the most interesting aspect of the relationship between the law and sports is the fact that sports is a business...and -- like all businesses -- the owners don't like lawyers or lawsuits or judges or juries. It's just not efficient and economical. That's why we hear so much about

Arbitration by players these days. Many or most of the major league professional contracts provide that -- if there is a salary disagreement -- there will be no strikes, no lawsuits, no holdouts, no picketing, no judges, no juries. No, there will be an arbitration...short, sweet, run by somebody who knows the sport, and not subject to appeal.

This is nothing new to American business. If American businesses could eliminate lawsuits and replace them with Arbitration, they'd do it in a heartbeat.

But player contracts aren't the only part of sports where lawyers have become entrenched in the last few decades. No, sirree! Sports are such big business that antitrust considerations come into play. But, as far back as 1922, the lawyers all went to the Supreme Court of the United States, where the Justices upheld Professional Baseball's exemption from anti-trust legislation. Behind the scenes, at all levels of sport, amateur and professional, lawyers are at work to keep the players on the field.

The sports lawyer finds himself dealing with a huge variety of legal issues, including sports betting, drug use and testing, league structures, game rules, franchise relocation, violence on the field and in the stands, facilities (all the way from Yankee Stadium down to the local little-league park), fan misbehavior, injuries to fans, food poisoning by the hot dogs, excessive drinking, etc. When you think about it, sports is just like the rest of our lives...there's almost an unlimited number of ways to get into legal hot water.

But, as you've come to expect from me in this monthly column, I like to look at how the law has improved our lives, which it constantly does. In sports, one of the most important lawsuits in modern history was the famed 1972 lawsuit that forced colleges and universities to allow equal opportunity for female athletes as males. This caused a boom in women's college athletics in the 1980s and '90s, leading to such events as the Women's World Cup and leagues like the WNBA. That case, and the series of lawsuits that followed, shook professional and amateur sports to its roots.

And how about discrimination, drug testing, immigration? All problems that simmered below the surface until our legal system was willing to shine the light of day on them in the legal system and help us emerge from "...the good old days."

So, as you're enjoying your favorite ball game at the stadium or on the TV, just remember to thank your friendly lawyers for keeping the system oiled and running smoothly. Hey, we lawyers are just like you... we love our Mariners and our Seahawks and our Sonics...oops! That's one where the lawyers got there too late. Oh, well!

Tom Brown

July 4th, 2010

• • •

ONE OF THE BENEFITS OF writing a little column like this is that you get to take the stage and say what you think. Mostly, over the last 27 months, I've had the honor to try to tell you how our legal system works and how it sometimes stumbles.

My goal has been to make the system more understandable, more accessible, and even more fun.

But, once in a while, particularly when we are calling each other traitors and liars and un-American and everything else we can throw in each other's faces, it's good to put on the brakes and take a fresh look at our system of laws and government and ask ourselves how we got here and whether we have come to a good place.

When we complain that there are too many laws, too many lawyers, too many judges, too many trials, etc., we are right. It would be so much easier if we all just agreed and didn't fight so much about every issue that popped up. But, let's face it...that's not human nature. We believe strongly in what we say and preach and we want everyone else to agree with us and act the way we want.

Of course, that was the beauty of what our forefathers did over two hundred years ago when they created this framework that we are going to celebrate on July 4th. Those were some pretty smart guys. They recognized that there were tough decisions and tough arguments ahead.

That's why they fought with each other over every word of the Constitution...so it would last as a framework for many different ideas and many different changes in the future.

Some people...good-hearted people...argue that the Constitution was a rigid structure that should be followed religiously to preserve basic principles. They don't think we should "interpret" the Constitution, we should just follow it. Other good-hearted people insist that the Constitution that was written 240 years ago can't possibly meet the changes and challenges of modern society, without being followed in a way that honors those principles, but doesn't cling to them religiously and blindly.

We lawyers, especially small town lawyers in places like Port Angeles, Port Townsend, Ocean Shores, Aberdeen, Montesano, Westport, Raymond, South Bend, have the burden and the joy of telling our neighbors every day that this system of laws and principles actually works.

Because of this beautiful system of laws and justice set up before we were even born, we don't kill each other over a property dispute, we don't burn down each others' buildings because they're too big, we don't throw troubled children into pits like they did in the middle ages in Europe. No, we trust our judges and juries to look backward to a set of principles that will never die, and to look forward to a set of goals that will continue to keep us growing in wisdom and fairness and justice.

So, as we stand at the threshold of another July 4th...another celebration of who we are, let's remember that one of the most powerful building blocks of our "system" is the collection of laws and judges and lawyers and courts that keeps us true to our goal of being a free society that works out its problems in an honorable way, and trusts both the past and the future.

Many of you will never have a "legal" problem. Many of you will. But both groups should keep their eye on the ball. This is a country of laws, of compromise, of growth, of change, of goodwill toward our neighbors and enemies, of fairness, of justice. Let's stop hating our judges and political representatives and elected officials. They want the right thing just like you do...we're just trying to work out the correct path.

Justice Scalia of the Supreme Court is not a bad man...he's a wonderful, brilliant man who loves his children and his country. Nancy Pelosi is not an evil presence...she's a powerful woman who loves her country and loves the Congress of the United States. Sarah Palin is not an idiot...she's a smart woman who thinks that she can change things for the better. Barack Obama is not a socialist spendthrift...he's a guy that wants this country to be great just like you do.

The law is not an obstacle...it's a vehicle to continued greatness of this country, just as it has been for over two centuries. Let's continue to talk about the law for another few years, while we smile at what it has done for us and will continue to do as America becomes greater and stronger.

Tom Brown

Remember, It's Your Government

• • •

DESPITE ALL THE WHINING BY the tea party, and all the shouting and finger-pointing by the Right and by the Left, one essential fact remains: the government of your city and your county and your state and your country all belong to you. You are the boss!

I know how intimidating it seems to deal with the government, but in recent years we have been given extraordinary weapons as citizens. The State of Washington in particular has taken very seriously the concept that we regular citizens are entitled to see everything (almost) that our government does.

In our state, it began with an initiative – The Public Records Act – written by Washington public interest groups that was voted into law by the citizens of this state in 1972. Since that time, the law has been expanded and strengthened by amendments and by Court decisions, and is now part of the fabric of our government in Washington State.

This law is so incredible that you have to listen to and enjoy what it says:

"...Free and open examination of public records is in the public interest, even though such examination may cause inconvenience or embarrassment to public officials or others."

WOW! That's some pretty powerful stuff!! Here's some more:

1. "The people of this state do not yield their sovereignty to the agencies that serve them."
2. "The people, in delegating authority, do not give their public servants the right to decide what is good for the people to know and what is not good for them to know."
3. "The people insist on remaining informed so that they may maintain control over the instruments that they have created."

This isn't some fancy-pants, off-the-wall theory by some ACLU lawyer arguing with the government. THIS IS THE LAW!

You have the right to march right in to your PUD or School District or Police Department or County Assessor or Fire Department and request their records about the things you are concerned with. No one can question why you want the records or what you are going to do with them.

This is your government and you have the right to see what's going on.

If you think you have been wronged in some way by the government and you plan to file a lawsuit, you can do all your preparation in advance by making a public records request and finding out what the government did or did not do.

The agency involved cannot hide or change the records. If the Agency violates the law and doesn't supply the records, you can sue them to comply and they will have to pay your attorney fees and court costs.

Our Courts...and particularly our State Supreme Court...have been particularly strong in support of this law. Incidentally, the Supreme

Court of the United States – the big boys – within the last month, ruled that our Public Records Act even trumped a claimed right of privacy by people who signed an initiative petition to put a law on the ballot.

Of course, like all situations, there are limits. The Public Records Act does not allow us to see certain things and there is a substantial list of exceptions… but under this law they are mostly things you would assume, like personal information about employees, social security numbers, child molestation information, job applications, open criminal investigation files, real estate appraisals, health care information, etc.,

The really good news is that – if you want to exercise your rights– you are not "on your own."

There is plenty of help out there for you. The first place to go is to the State Attorney General's office. They have a special department to assist citizens who want to make a records request. If you have Internet access, go to http://www.atg.wa.gov/obtaining-records and click on "A guide to obtaining public records." You should also look at "The Open Government Internet Desk book," which you can click on at that website.

Believe it or not, there's even a Fully Automated, Fill-in-the-Blanks State Open Records Law Request Letter Generator, located at http://www.splc.org/page/lettergenerator …you just fill in the blanks and it spits out a letter to use in requesting information!!! Amazing!

OK, what about fees? Well, you cannot be charged for just "inspecting" the documents. If you want copies, you can be charged a reasonable fee for the copying, but not more than the agency's actual copying cost, and generally not more than 15 cents per page.

Everything I've been saying here is about the State of Washington's situation, but the Federal Government has a similar law, called the

"Freedom of Information Act" commonly referred to as FOIA. If you're interested in pursuing that angle, go to http://washingtoncog.org/freedom-of-information-act/

Or go to: http://www.justice.gov/oip/doj-guide-freedom-information-act
Or go to: http://www.rcfp.org/federal-open-government-guide

By the way, it's a little off subject, but if you want to look at the salary of every public official, every teacher, every state government employee, etc., just go prowl around this website for a while. You'll probably end up angry, but at least you'll be informed! http://lbloom.net/

OK, that's it! Don't just sit around griping about your government.

Get involved!

Order up those documents!

Go to the next City Council meeting!

Write a letter!

You're an important person – YOU'RE A CITIZEN!

Tom Brown

Your Government Can Do No Wrong!!! REALLY?

• • •

FOR MANY CENTURIES, OUR GOVERNMENTS could just do as they pleased, and the people just had to shut up and take it. They could steal our crops; burn our houses, slaughter our children...and we all just understood that was the way it was. It was terrible, but that was what government and royalty and privilege was all about.

In the middle ages, when we were "growing up" as a race, we began to examine basic questions about our relationship to our various governments around the world.

The basic rule was still something called "sovereign immunity" which meant that "the king could do no wrong" and so the government was immune from the legal system and immune from lawsuits for the wrongs that government had done. But, about the time of the Magna Carta and other huge advances in government, we began to question whether government or kings could just do whatever they pleased, and we all just had to shut up about it.

Sovereign immunity survived into the United States of America and still exists in some forms around this great country of ours. Believe it or not, it is still a big deal to sue the government...your city, your county, your state, or your federal government.

Some of us might say that's a good Idea, government shouldn't be sued…it's not American!

Well, let's think about that for a minute. If the FedEx driver is speeding and reckless and kills a child, we would all probably agree that FedEx could be sued for the terrible damages the family suffered. Well, isn't that equally true if the negligent driver is driving a United States Postal Service delivery vehicle? Or a city worker driving a garbage truck?

What if the Air Traffic Controller is drunk and his supervisor ignores it, and a planeload of people crashes and dies as a result?

What if a school district knows about a very dangerous condition on a school playground and does nothing about it and a child dies? Shouldn't the School District be responsible for not being alert to the dangerous situation?

What if the parole people allow a crazed killer out of jail, and he kills nice families in suburbia?

Shouldn't the State be liable for the terrible loss suffered?

What if the city puts up a barricade to keep cars from running off the road, but the barricade actually kills people who just lose control because it's a bad corner? Shouldn't the city be held to a duty to make the right decision?

Think back to some of our earlier columns about why there is a "tort" system at all -- we believe that if people are held financially responsible for being stupid or negligent or irresponsible, then the financial consequences will force them to be more careful and to take precautions to be sure that people aren't hurt.

It's a good system!

The question we are talking about today is whether or not it's a good idea that our various governments should be bound by the same rules.

In Washington, the concept of "sovereign immunity" has been almost completely abolished. We can sue our State, our counties, our cities, our Port Districts, our school districts if they do something negligent or stupid or fraudulent and it causes harm. Most of us would agree that our cities and counties and state should be held to the same standards as our businesses or our citizens.

However, it's definitely different than making a claim against a private individual or company. The vestiges of "sovereign immunity " still exist and create a lot of roadblock to a suit against "the King." The law requires a special kind of notice to the public body that a potential claim might be made. If you don't file the special claim...you're screwed -- no claim.

The claims against the government in Washington are big business. The Attorney General's office in Olympia has a whole section of high-powered attorneys defending claims against the state for dozens and dozens of different mistakes claimed against the state, from poor highway design to letting killers out of jail to failing to protect children on welfare to medical malpractice at the UW hospital.

The cities and counties each have their own agencies that collect premiums (your tax dollars) from its members and then deal with claims like an insurance company. They are defending claims every day. The claims range from the mundane (auto accidents) to the esoteric (employment issues).

The transit authorities around the state have their own group that defends claims for bus accidents and discrimination complaints and similar stuff.

On a national level, our Federal government still holds strongly to the notion of sovereign immunity, but has passed two important laws, the Federal Tort Claims Act (which allows the Federal government to be sued for the negligence of its employees) and the Tucker Act (which allows the Federal government to be sued for breach of its contracts). Like the state laws, these laws are very technical and require strict adherence to the procedural requirements of the laws.

So there it is...where we used to say "The King can do no wrong!" we now look at the situation and say: "Hey, our government can make mistakes and harm people and violate its contracts just like the rest of us, and they ought to be held accountable just like we would."

Interestingly enough, in most countries where there is still a King or Queen (like Denmark, Malaysia, Norway, Spain, Sweden, etc.), the King or Queen is still immune from legal proceedings, but the governments (or the King's ministers) are not immune. The City-State of the Vatican strongly insists on the immunity of the Pope, but has international agreements with other countries that allow normal business transactions to be protected.

The concept of "sovereign immunity" is an historical oddity that will continue to develop and merge into our present-day concepts of what is right and wrong and what is necessary for the orderly running of a government.

As always, thanks for reading my column and thanks for the wonderful comments you have sent me.

Tom Brown

Security? What's THAT?

• • •

SECURITY IS A WORD THAT carries so many meanings. In the day-to-day world we live in, security means a sense of comfort about our financial situation. "Mary and I have a lot of security in our retirement." In the world of military and business protection, it means a quality of protection that we can rely on. "The security at the base was very strong." OR "The security at the plant was well-planned and thorough." In the financial world, it's a product...like stock. "He bought and sold securities in the market." Whatever it means, it has a nice, comforting sound about it. It sounds...well, secure!

To lawyers, there's a special meaning to security. Security to us usually means the way of guaranteeing that you will live up to your bargain. For example, if you borrow $1,000.00 from me and sign a promissory note to pay me back in one year, I have an enforceable claim against you for repayment. But it is not secured. You may not pay me and I have to chase you and sue you.

Even if I get a judgment against you, I still haven't gotten my money back and I'd have to garnish your paycheck or attach your bank account – obviously a very expensive headache, just to get my rightful money back from you. However, if I get a mortgage on your house, or a lien against your car, or an assignment of your bank account, then that obligation is secured. That means -- even if you don't pay me back -- I can get the money back from your house or your car or your bank account, with a lot less trouble and expense.

Smart lenders (like banks) usually get security. They won't loan you money unless you give them security in your house, or your business inventory, or your bank accounts. That means they can get their money back, even if you are not able to pay. They will just tap your bank account or foreclose on your house or pick up your car and get back most of what you borrowed. They know very well that your bare promise to pay the money back may be well intentioned, but it's not going to mean anything when you are hurting for money.

How does all this impact us on a day-to-day basis? We see it all the time. Most of us don't have enough money in cash to buy a house...so we borrow the money from a bank or other lender, buy the house, and pay back the money at the monthly rate that makes sense. In the meantime, the bank has a mortgage or deed of trust (just two of the many forms of a security interest) in our house. If you can't pay the bank back, they foreclose on your house and sell it to get their money. The same is often true of a car or other major purchase.

So, you're never going to get a substantial amount of money from a bank or credit union or smart lender without putting up security...like your house or your car or your bank accounts.

Remember, it's not just the promissory note that you're signing. That's not enough. It's the security interest.

Now, let's get to meat of this month's column: In the non-bank situation, when should you demand security and when should someone demand security from you?

Here's my rule of thumb: If you loan money to a friend or a family member or business associate, and the amount is $1,000.00 or more, ALWAYS, ALWAYS have security. Tell the person that you have limited money and your lawyer advised you to have security for this loan. I know it's difficult and sensitive, but tell them that your lawyer and your wife or husband insisted on security. The security should be in their best asset -- usually their house or some other real estate. Next would be a car or other valuable property. You could even agree to hold something of value that they own, like a piece of equipment.

If you are going to have security, don't try to do it yourself. I know it's tempting to go on the Internet and try to figure it out or get a form from the stationery store. Don't. Security interests are very complicated and need to be "perfected" in a manner that will make it last and cover your loan. It's a complicated process that sometimes even challenges lawyers.

Make it clear to your brother-in-law or uncle or whoever wants to borrow your money that this is standard stuff in the making of a loan. Keep it friendly and make it seem like "business as usual."

If the person doesn't have a house or a business, then you've got to get creative. What else do they have to protect you? Do they have a cabin on a lake? So they have a retirement account?

So they have a collector car? Don't be ashamed...they have come to you for money...you have a right to protect yourself in case the stuff hits the fan and they simply cannot pay you back.

Now, here comes the most important part. Don't do this on an informal basis. If they just hand you the deed to their house to hold, or hand you the title to the car or truck to hold, THAT DOES NOT DO ANY GOOD!! IT DOESN'T WORK! You have to go through a very formal procedure to get one of these security interests. Do not try to do it yourself...see a lawyer! It's not really that expensive. Holding the title to the car or a deed to the house does not cut it. A separate document called a security agreement or mortgage has to be signed and THEN there has to be another procedure to file it in the right place with the county or the state. I'm not kidding here!!!

Don't try to do this without a lawyer.

Now, what is the situation if the shoe is on the other foot? What if you need the money? What if you're borrowing from your Dad or brother or cousin or best friend or business partner? Well, it would be wonderful if they just forked over the money, and there were no formalities about it. But if your brother has a brain in his head, he will want you to sign a note and a security agreement, and he will "perfect" it in the way that makes it effective.

Especially if you are borrowing a substantial amount of money, you will want to reduce this down to some documents that set the rules. Go see a lawyer...it won't cost that much to figure out what the documents should be and how complicated it has to be.

Remember the mantra from both sides: if someone is asking for your money, you want to make sure that when the friend or relative melts down, you are going to have something to show for the hard-earned money you handed over. On the other hand, when you are the one borrowing money, try to give the least security possible...if you can't pay it back on time, every piece of security you gave will be tied up and possibly lost.

Over my 40 years of lawyering, I've heard many, many sad tales about people who handed over cash to their best friends or family members or church members or neighbors, fully expecting that they would get their money right back after the immediate crisis passes. The problem is that if there is a crisis to begin with, there is an underlying problem that is probably going to get worse. When it does get worse, you are seen as just another part of that problem because you want your money back, and the dear friend or neighbor begins to resent you for being so insensitive! And you thought you were being a Good Samaritan.

By the way, none of this affects the situation where you are helping someone out of the goodness of your heart and you don't expect the money back. If it's a gift, you don't need to do anything about protecting yourself. (But if it's a really big gift, talk to your accountant about the tax consequences!)

There's always a big temptation to go on the Internet or go to the stationery store and do all this yourself. If you've read my earlier columns, you know I'm all in favor of avoiding legal bills if you can. But this is not the place to save on attorney fees. If you're loaning over $1,000.00 or if you're being asked to put up security, talk to a lawyer...as they say: you'll be glad you did.

As always, I am very grateful for you readers who take the time to read my column and the many positive comments I get about it.

Tom Brown

I went to Court this morning

● ● ●

IT WAS A RAINY, SLOPPY morning and I had to drive to South Bend to argue about a case that has been going on for nearly two and one-half years. The case was frustrating in many ways, and I knew that going to Pacific County would involve not only a 45 minute drive in the rain... but would also probably involve a lot of delays and wasted time, sharing the "motion docket" with a bunch of other lawyers.

In the world of lawyering, we lawyers are very familiar with the concept of a "motion docket."

That is a day set aside every week for motions for the Judge to hear and decide. In small counties like Grays Harbor and Pacific, it is the day that many of the lawyers show up at the courthouse to argue motions and other matters that have been set for that day. The Judge has a list of all the cases scheduled for arguments (the "docket"), and he or she goes through them one at a time, and the lawyers are called up to argue their points and the Judge makes a decision. There are many varieties of things that are before the Judge on Motion day, and the Courts have come to realize that it just makes sense to combine all the motions and other stuff in to one big cluster, once a week, and get it out of the way. Actual trials and hearings take place during the rest of the week, one at a time.

The motions that are before the Court run the entire gamut...from motions that the Judge order the other party to reply to requests for information about a case to a motion that an upcoming trial be postponed for various reasons to a motion that the Court impose sanctions (a fine) against the other party for misconduct...and on and on. The variety is almost unlimited. Sometimes Judges are cranky on Motion Day, sometimes they're overworked, sometimes they're amused by the squabbling of lawyers, sometimes it's just a job, and sometimes it's magical...you never know what to expect.

Today, I wasn't late, but it was raining and I trotted across the parking lot and up the steps to the doors of the Pacific County Courthouse. I wasn't in a very good mood, because the case was turning out to be more of problem than it should have been. The other attorney was refusing to see everything my way...an irritant that we keep bumping into. Anyway, my mood changed the minute I walked in the doors. The Pacific County Courthouse is a wondrous place. I know I raved about it in an earlier column...but you just have to see it. I walked through the rotunda to the twin steel circular steps that wind up to the second floor, where the railing overlooks the rotunda and the beautiful, unbelievable stained glass ceiling dominates. Then it's through a ridiculously incongruous metal detector into the Courtroom. The effect is always stunning; no matter how many times you enter this Courtroom...the room is dominated by dark rich wood everywhere. The windows, the moldings, the Judge's bench, the impossibly heavy tables and chairs from another era...all in heavy wood that says weight and gravity and important things transpiring. All of that is balanced by the recurrence of the stained glass. The huge ceiling panel of stained glass and the cupola over the Judge's chair remind you of the rotunda ceiling you just left. And then, as if to remind you that you are deep in the natural heart of the Northwest, huge windows frame the trees and leaden sky. Ornate sconces with hanging ball lamps surround the room, punctuating the effect.

Precisely at nine, the Judge enters in his black robe that the law requires him to wear, and the 12 people in the Courtroom rise...a solemn ritual that repeats our pledge that we honor the law by showing our continuing respect for the institution and the person that represents it.

I can see that I am going to have to wait. There are obviously a number of matters that the Judge will have to hear. I see and greet my opposing counterpart...he looks ready to go. Right away the Judge plunges into a nasty domestic matter about people who can't co-exist, and they have actual Court orders dictating how close they can be to one another (100 yards), and where they can sit if they're both at a football game or track meet. Some sparks have flown and the Judge calmly reviews the problem, asks them questions, and rules on their dispute. It seems like common sense should have prevailed earlier, but there are clenched jaws and the Judge tries to impose reason. When he sends them on their way, he has them leave 5 minutes apart so they don't clash in the Rotunda.

Next, two feisty lawyers who seem not to like each other very much wrangle over the wording of the final papers in a divorce. They argue about car titles, air conditioners and other minutia.

They told the Judge their matter would take ten minutes...it lasted nearly an hour. As my eyes glazed over, I wondered how the Judge could remain an island of calm in these turbulent waters.

My eyes roam the Courtroom...to the ancient American flag in a frame with 13 stars in a circle, to the pictures of all 14 of the previous Judges that ruled this Courtroom (beginning with Nathaniel Bloomfield in 1889). The room is a kaleidoscope of contrasts: here is an ancient steel ballot box that the jurors' names were once drawn from...there is a flat screen plasma TV with video camera...here are the refurbished church pews for the gallery...there are the computers for the court reporter and clerk...here is a selection of ancient typewriters on display...there is the headphone for the Spanish language translator.

Finally, our case is called, but disappointment reigns when we realize that the judge hasn't seen one of the things we're arguing about, and I haven't seen another one of the things for some reason...so we're delayed while the Judge and I catch up.

But, by the time we're ready to go, other matters have squeezed to the top. The Judge hears a case where parents can't control their child and they have turned, out of desperation, to the State to help them... the facts are terrible and you can see that the Judge wishes supernatural powers for himself so he could solve these unsolvable problems. Then another family's wreckage plays out in front of him. He can't put a mother and a daughter back together again.

Crushing.

OK, we're up again. It's getting late in the morning, but the juices are flowing and my opponent and I hurl arguments at each other while the Judge serenely tries to get to the bottom of the arguments and claims and accusations. He takes the prudent route of giving himself some time to reflect on what has been argued and takes our papers with a promise to review and decide.

We leave somewhat unfulfilled, but grateful that a human being can withstand the battering of unsolvable problems all morning, and still calmly deal with our contentious issue. Finality will have to wait a little bit, so that correctness and justice will rule the day. Not a bad deal, really.

So, it's time to leave the Pacific County Courthouse. She is truly a grand piece of Washington history, having celebrated her 100th birthday this month. Something about what happened here this morning lifts my spirits. The miracle is that among the historic relics, and inside the 1910 architecture, and despite the doubts some of us harbor about our system, a very personal, very thoughtful brand of justice still reverberates inside that storied courtroom as people, lawyers, Judges, jurors, witnesses and observers struggle to do the right thing. Beautiful.

I went to Court this morning.

Tom Brown

'Twas The Night Before Christmas (Legal Version)

• • •

WHILE TRYING TO COME UP with something fun and light for the Holiday season, I ran across this "legal" version of a Christmas card and the infamous story of Santa. Credit goes to the author, Ralph Ostermueller and to the SBS Diva Blog and to the "Law is Cool" Blog out of Canada. Hope you enjoy it as much as I did, and I hope you have a very Merry (you know what) and a Happy New Year.

Please accept without obligation, express or implied, these best wishes for an environmentally safe, socially responsible, low stress, non-addictive, and gender-neutral celebration of the winter solstice holiday as practiced within the most enjoyable traditions of the religious persuasion of your choice (but with respect for the religious or secular persuasions and/or traditions of others, or for their choice not to practice religious or secular traditions at all) and further for a fiscally successful, personally fulfilling, and medically uncomplicated onset of the generally accepted calendar year (including, but not limited to, the Christian calendar, but not without due respect for the calendars of choice of other cultures). The preceding wishes are extended without regard to the race, creed, age, physical ability, religious faith or lack thereof, choice of computer platform, or sexual preference of the wishee(s).

THE NIGHT BEFORE CHRISTMAS:

Whereas, on or about the night prior to Christmas, there did occur at a certain improved piece of real property (hereinafter "the House") a general lack of stirring by all creatures therein, including, but not limited to a mouse.

A variety of foot apparel, e.g., stocking, socks, etc., had been affixed by and around the chimney in said House in the hope and/or belief that St. Nick a/k/a/ St. Nicholas a/k/a/ Santa Claus (hereinafter "Claus") would arrive at sometime thereafter. The minor residents, i.e. the children, of the aforementioned House were located in their individual beds and were engaged in nocturnal hallucinations, i.e. dreams, wherein vision of confectionery treats, including, but not limited to, candies, nuts and/or sugar plums, did dance, cavort and otherwise appear in said dreams.

Whereupon the party of the first part (sometimes hereinafter referred to as ("I"), being the joint-owner in fee simple of the House with the party of the second part (hereinafter "Mamma"), and said Mamma had retired for a sustained period of sleep. At such time, the parties were clad in various forms of headgear, e.g., kerchief and cap.

Suddenly, and without prior notice or warning, there did occur upon the unimproved real property adjacent and appurtenant to said House, i.e., the lawn, a certain disruption of unknown nature, cause and/or circumstance. The party of the first part did immediately rush to a window in the House to investigate the cause of such disturbance.

At that time, the party of the first part did observe, with some degree of wonder and/or disbelief, a miniature sleigh (hereinafter "the Vehicle") being pulled and/or drawn very rapidly through the air by approximately eight (8) reindeer. The driver of the Vehicle appeared to be and in fact was, the previously referenced Claus.

Said Claus was providing specific direction, instruction and guidance to the approximately eight (8) reindeer and specifically identified the animal co-conspirators by name: Dasher, Dancer, Prancer, Vixen, Comet, Cupid, Donner and Blitzen (hereinafter "the Deer"). (Upon information and belief, it is further asserted that an additional co- conspirator named "Rudolph" may have been involved.)

The party of the first part witnessed Claus, the Vehicle and the Deer intentionally and willfully trespass upon the roofs of several residences located adjacent to and in the vicinity of the House, and noted that the Vehicle was heavily laden with packages, toys and other items of unknown origin or nature. Suddenly, without prior invitation or permission, either express or implied, the Vehicle arrived at the House, and Claus entered said House via the chimney.

Said Claus was clad in a red fur suit, which was partially covered with residue from the chimney, and he carried a large sack containing a portion of the aforementioned packages, toys, and other unknown items.

He was smoking what appeared to be tobacco in a small pipe in blatant violation of local ordinances and health regulations.

Claus did not speak, but immediately began to fill the stocking of the minor children, which hung adjacent to the chimney, with toys and other small gifts. (Said items did not, however, constitute "gifts" to said minor pursuant to the applicable provisions of the U.S. Tax Code.)

Upon completion of such task, Claus touched the side of his nose and flew, rose and/or ascended up the chimney of the House to the roof where the Vehicle and Deer waited and/or served as "lookouts." Claus immediately departed for an unknown destination.

However, prior to the departure of the Vehicle, Deer and Claus from said House, the party of the first part did hear Claus state and/or exclaim: "Merry Christmas to all and to all a good night!" Or words to that effect.

Tom Brown

What about our criminal justice system?

● ● ●

Since the last two columns have been pretty light-hearted, I thought we might start the new year on a more serious note; and I'll share with you something that's been on my mind this last week or so.

You've probably heard about the trial in Salt Lake City of the scary lunatic who kidnapped and molested Elizabeth Smart. The defendant sang hymns during the trial, as if he were some sort of religious being that was above it all. Of course, the jury saw right through his shenanigans and found him guilty of molesting that poor, beautiful child. I really felt sorry for her and her family that they had to endure the trial, but they did it with grace and dignity.

The thing that bothered me was what Elizabeth Smart said after the defendant was found guilty. She was widely quoted as saying: "I hope that ... This is an example that justice can be served in America..." as if to say that usually outrageous creeps like him get away with terrible crimes in America. And it's not just her...people in general in the good ol' USA like to poor-mouth the criminal justice system, as if it's some sort of quirky, unreliable jalopy that allows all manner of terrible criminals to escape justice. Brian Mitchell got convicted just like everyone thought he should.

I'd be willing to bet that you -- my loyal and thoughtful readers -- suspect that it's true. That the criminal justice system just doesn't work reliably. Well, here's the news flash of the day that I want you to take to your next bridge game, or house party or wherever...the American criminal justice system is one of the most successful, reliable systems on the planet. Nearly every criminal that gets delivered to the American criminal justice system ends up convicted of what he or she was charged with, to one degree or another.

Let's break it down. The "system" of dealing with our society's criminals is really three systems. As you've heard for years on "Law and Order" -- the first part of the system is law enforcement -- the cops. They investigate, build a case, and arrest the bad guys. Then they present the case to the second system, the criminal justice system, which consists of the prosecuting attorney, the defense attorney, and the Court. That part of the system decides if the person is guilty of a crime and exactly what that crime is.

Once the criminal justice system has dealt with the criminal, the case moves on to the third part of the system that punishes or incarcerates or rehabilitates the criminal. This is the penal system (jails), the fixing system (counselors, probation officers, etc.) and the monitoring system (parole officers) and parole boards. (Think about it...Charles Manson doesn't go back to the judge that sentenced him to life in prison to ask for parole...he goes before a parole board, probably appointed by the governor.)

Most of us don't realize this, but the second part of the system is working at an almost unbelievable level of efficiency. People that are charged with crimes are usually convicted of those crimes (or a lesser version of those crimes) by a system of prosecutors and defense lawyers and judges and juries with a remarkable record for changing criminal charges into criminal convictions. Sure, "deals" are worked out to get a conviction and avoid a risky and expensive trial...but the primary goal of this part of the system -- to convict of a crime if guilty -- works pretty darned well. And on the rare occasion that a jury of your neighbors finds someone innocent, you can be that there was a lot more than just "reasonable doubt."

The place where our society has problems is usually with the third part of the system. What do we do with people who have been convicted or pled guilty to a crime? Put them all in jail? Ha! We don't have half of the jails and halfway houses and minimum-security facilities necessary to take care of all the criminals that the criminal justice system is pumping out. Why? It's simple. It's about money. We simply don't have enough money to build and staff the necessary facilities. We don't have enough money to hire, train and retain the guards, counselors, cooks, janitorial staff, gardeners, etc., etc. To man the prisons and jails that we so desperately want to fill up. Judges send them to jail, parole boards let them out.

It's simply a fact of life that we are not willing to commit the kind of resources necessary to incarcerate and isolate the criminals that our society produces. So, they end up on the street and quit reporting to their parole or probation officer, and end up committing another crime -- maybe a terrible one. What do we do? We get mad...and we say, what's wrong with the judges and lawyers that allowed this to happen. Hey, the guy was convicted and sent to jail. The Judge can't control if he's paroled or given work release out of the state penitentiary.

My goal here is not to cover for the Judges or the prosecuting attorneys. My goal is to have us all understand that the decision to make our streets and alleys safe is our decision to make. Are we willing to commit the funding necessary to house dangerous criminals, to provide intensive supervision if they're out of custody, and to protect our citizens from the ones who are just too dangerous to be free? The criminal justice system will continue to convict criminals at an unbelievably efficient rate...what are we going to do with them after that?

Getting back to Elizabeth Smart, I would say to her that the easy part is over. Our justice system has no trouble identifying and convicting creeps like Brian Mitchell and sending them to jail. The tough part is keeping them there.

Tom Brown

...neither a renter nor a landlord be?

• • •

WITH ALL OF THE FORECLOSURES the last couple of years and with all the economic problems, the rental market has absolutely gone crazy.

I don't know about other lawyers, but one of the commonest calls I get these days is about rental situations. People want to know if they need a lease. People want to know if they can get out of a lease. People want to know what to do about insurance. Landlords want to know how to deal with troublesome tenants. Tenants want some help with outrageous landlords. It's crazy!

Let's start with the basics: why rent at all? It's not always an economic issue. The mobility of our society has created a class of people who don't want to be wedded to a house. They want to be mobile. Or they want to test out a certain style of living before they commit. Lots of houses are for rent, ranging from dumps to multi-million dollar ocean-view mansions. The wild housing market has created all kinds of "situations" out there that give us a lot of options.

If you are thinking about buying or renting a house, you owe it to yourself to explore all the financial options...that's not a question for your lawyer...it's more for your banker or real estate professional. But, if you do decide to rent rather than buy, spend a little time with your lawyer on how that rental will be handled. A month-to-month arrangement is the simplest, cleanest, most fragile arrangement. If you hate the place, you can get out with a month's notice. You can also put pressure on your landlord to do a better job with maintenance, upkeep, security, or whatever. If your landlord thinks you might bolt next month, he's more likely to try to keep you happy. On the other hand, if you're stuck with a lease, you have no leverage with your landlord until it's time to renew the lease. But, on the other end of the stick, a month-to-month lease has the least security for the tenant. The landlord can kick you our on 30 days' notice...no exceptions, you're outta' there!

Leases are amazing documents. A lease can govern everything about your relationship with your building and with your landlord. The cost, the rules, the parking, pets, children, noise, garbage, television, use of the "common areas", etc., etc. What most people don't know is that a lease usually sets up the parties for the next rental period. Sometimes it renews automatically if you do or don't do something. Sometimes it sets the rental rate for the next term, to start automatically. We lawyers look for clauses in leases that say: "...if you don't do something by such and such a date, then you automatically have agreed to another year's tenancy at an increased rate!" WOW! How do you deal with that...set up a good reminder system!!!

Anyway, the point is clear...NEVER, NEVER sign a lease without having a lawyer look it over...and that applies to you landlords, too. I've had landlords come to see me about leases they made their renter sign... AND THEY DIDN'T EVEN KNOW WHAT WAS IN IT!!!! Now, that's nuts! On a more serious note, it is very important to know and understand what is in your lease, no matter which side of the table you are on. They typically last for a year and that's a long time if you're dealing with a destructive tenant or if you're dealing with a harsh, intolerant landlord.

Let's talk about some specifics.

INSURANCE

This is directed mostly at tenants. Remember that your landlord's insurance will probably not protect you in any way. The landlord's insurance typically protects him against fire or other casualties, but does nothing for the tenant. You need to protect yourself against fire, theft, windstorm and all the other mayhem that the world can inflict. Your stuff is valuable! Imagine if it was all gone tomorrow. Most insurance companies have evolved to a nice, comprehensive package that merits your attention. It can also provide liability insurance so that you aren't sued for something that happens in your apartment where someone got hurt.

Sit down with the insurance person and talk about the insurance. What does it do? Why do I need it? How much does it cost? Do I have to take it all or can I pick and choose my coverages?

EVICTION (FOR TENANTS)

It is not easy to evict someone from an apartment or a house. If there is a lease, the person has to be in clear violation of the lease. The clearest is non-payment, but the complicated ones are usually related to a long-standing problem between the landlord and the tenant. If there is no lease, the landlord can give 30 days' notice and the person has to leave.

What most people don't understand is that when someone has been given notice to leave the premises, THEY USUALLY DON'T! What happens then? Well, it's a lawyer's nightmare and a landlord's nightmare. Because of the abuses over the decades, the laws are very protective of people that are in the premises. In order to evict them, the landlord has to serve some very specific and very detailed papers on them. They either have to be served by handing it to them or it has to be nailed to the door. If they don't leave, the landlord has to start a lawsuit and serve some more papers, telling the tenants that they have to show up in Court and "show cause" (which means tell the Judge) why they shouldn't be thrown out of the house or apartment. If they have a real issue, it is set for a trial within a very few days, and each side can come in and tell the judge what happened and why. Most of the time, it's about paying the rent, and the eviction is fairly routine.

If you are a tenant, *never, never, never* ignore papers that are served on someone at your house or papers that are nailed or taped to your house. You have to respond or bad things will happen.

One positive note for tenants is that the landscape has changed dramatically over the last couple of decades. Tenants now have a whole basketful of rights that protect people from arbitrary and capricious actions by unscrupulous landlords. There are many protections built into these newer laws that give expansive rights to tenants in apartments, houses, mobile home parks and other situations.

EVICTION (FOR LANDLORDS)

If you're going to be in the rental business...even if it's only your downstairs unit...be prepared to do it right. Don't *ever, ever, ever* do a do-it-yourself eviction without the advice of a lawyer.

While there are circumstances where you can pack out someone's apartment and put it in a storage unit, those instances are few and far between.

Most tenant crises require a calm approach, with a strong dose of diplomacy. Try to get your tenant to comply peacefully with whatever the issue is. Allow payments to be made weekly, rather than monthly. Buy them a garbage can, so they won't throw their garbage in the hall. Talk to them at a sober moment about the decibel level of their stereo or TV. If all else fails, and you need to evict them, it is time to go see the lawyer. Yes, it's going to be expensive to get them out if they resist; but it's better than the alternative, which will end up being 10 times as expensive.

Look for compromise. Let them temporarily leave their furniture in the shed or garage. Give them a tip on a cheaper, more manageable location.

Never lose your head and just move all their stuff into the yard and change the locks...you'll probably end up regretting it.

HIGH END RENTALS

If you're in the market for a nice house on a rental basis, you should not sign a form lease without seeing a lawyer first. The form lease is probably going to be from a stationery store or off the Internet, and it is not going to be designed for the exact situation you are facing. In other words, it isn't going to fit your situation or the house you want to rent or the relationship with your new landlord. Just to show you how crazy it can be, I know of a situation where a really nice two-story house is being rented as two units -- the upstairs as one unit and the downstairs as another. Well, the upstairs has nice wood floors, but the people downstairs don't like the people upstairs walking heavily on the wood floors...the noise and vibration annoys them!

Without a little research or inquiry first, this has the ability to blossom into a first-class nightmare. All parties -- tenants and landlord -- need to be tuned in to the problem, and make sure it is covered in the two leases and in the handshake.

Also, people who are paying more than rock bottom for rental space expect amenities...parking, outdoor recreation space, landscaping, dining space, etc. The creative landlord will snag the tenant and the smart tenant will maximize the available space. Just make sure that it all doesn't end up in the lap of a lawyer!

As always, thanks again for reading my column and thanks for all the nice comments. See you next month.

Tom Brown

In loco parentis

• • •

ARE YOU A PARENT? ARE you loco? What is *in loco parentis*?

One of the toughest areas of the law for lawyers and judges and educators and law enforcement is dealing with children...you know, those little people under 18.

As a society, we long ago made a decision that our children would be treated in a special manner. The goal -- of course-- is to steer the kids in the right direction and to protect them until they can fend for themselves in the "adult" world.

In particular, the Washington State legislature has long ago passed comprehensive legislation to protect children that need help and to deal with children that have fallen into a pattern of self-destructive behavior. Our state law provides for personnel and facilities to protect our youngest, most vulnerable citizens

Most larger communities have a juvenile facility with a courtroom and with secure and non-secure holding areas for the kids. Every county or community has to have a facility separate from the "adult" facilities.

Part of every Superior Court in every County is something called Juvenile Court -- the regular Superior Court Judges in most counties take turns serving as judges and being presented with impossible situations every day.

Our society trusts the parents as qualified custodians of children until they manage to prove otherwise and start to screw up their own kids. Fortunately many institutions and agencies exist to serve "in loco parentis" (or, "in the place of parents")

Some of these stand-in parents get their job naturally and some get it by Court order. The most obvious of these agencies are our schools, which stand in the place of parents every day, in a world where school is mandatory. At the other end of the spectrum is the juvenile court system, which will take control of the children by Court Order.

As you might expect, our juvenile court system is presented with a bewildering array of situations that confront our society's children: serious crimes, petty crimes, failure to attend school, terrible home situations where the natural parents have utterly failed, insufficient or nonexistent medical care, the need for psychiatric care, and on and on and on.

To cope with this huge range of problems, our juvenile facilities accommodate situations that range from the need for VERY SECURE housing of a belligerent, angry, destructive child to a residential-type situation for a scared child that needs a safe place to sleep and a square meal to eat. Whatever the situation, we -- as a society -- have to ready to stand "in loco parentis."

Our juvenile system and our juvenile facilities have a broad array of weapons and tools to meet the difficult situations presented every day. There are detention officers, juvenile probation officers, juvenile counselors (these three are often wrapped into one very talented package), also representatives from the medical community when the problem is physical, representatives from the psychiatric and psychological communities when the problem is other than physical, and -- of course -- those long-suffering judges who have to make the hard calls on what society should do to fulfill its duty to stand *in loco parentis*.

Obviously, as you are learning from this analysis, it doesn't make any difference whether we are real parents or not.... we all stand together in *loco parentis* to save, protect, educate and inspire the kids in our society, who have not had the opportunities that some of their peers have had.

Those who work in this system (the juvenile probation officers, the prosecutors, the defense lawyers, the judges, the doctors, the psychiatrists) will tell you that it is grueling, sad and scary work. There are so many kids that have jumped the tracks and are too far-gone to get them back to normal. But the real news -- the real story-- is the successes:

* A kid who came back to school and then graduates.
* A kid who kicked a bad habit of alcohol or drugs and then lived clean.
* A kid who got out of an abusive home situation and into the care of someone who cared.
* A dangerous kid who is off the streets and away from other kids

If this has piqued your interest at all, you can ask the Superior Court Clerk when and if you can attend a session of Juvenile Court...it will open your eyes. (Sometimes proceedings are closed to protect the kids). If you are able to do this, you'll be amazed and you'll have a new view of your society, and you will have a new appreciation of the people who pick up the battered, neglected, troubled children of our world and carry them to a safe place to see if they can be put back together.

I hope that you will be proud and I hope you will believe that your society has a right and a duty to stand "in loco parentis."

Tom Brown

Aren't all lawyers perfect?

• • •

THERE'S NOTHING FUNNIER THAN A good lawyer joke...we all enjoy taking a jab at lawyers. Maybe it's because they seem so powerful, so immune...they can get away with anything! Right? Weeeeelllll, not quite.

Lawyers are one of the most closely policed professions in America. Every state has a "Bar Association" that does a lot of things involving how lawyers act...The most visible thing to most of us is that the Bar Associations receive and process claims against lawyers ... not necessarily claims for money, but claims that the lawyer acted dishonestly, or unfairly, or in violation of the many rules (mostly invisible to the world) that we lawyers live by.

To understand the whole business about lawyer misconduct, we need to first go to the basics. All lawyers in America are bound by a strict code of ethics. It varies a little bit from State to State, but it's pretty much the same across America. It's a set of rules about how a lawyer must act in order to stay within the bounds of ETHICS. This code has a whole bunch of provisions, but it can be summarized by saying that lawyers have to be honest and truthful with their clients and with judges and with other lawyers. Lawyers can't make false statements to Courts. Lawyers can't steal from their clients. Lawyers must communicate openly and regularly with their clients. Lawyers can't commit serious crimes even if it has nothing to do with their practice.

Lawyers have to be careful not to have a conflict of interest, by having a relationship with both sides of an issue. Lawyers have to keep their client's money separate and accounted for. These rules (and many more) are in the Rules of Professional Conduct, which you can read by going to the Bar Association website at: www.wsba.org/

Most State Bar Associations have a very active and professional discipline function that investigates complaints and prosecutes cases against lawyers. Ultimately, the authority to discipline a lawyer in Washington rests with the Supreme Court, which ends up handling the most serious and most hotly contested discipline cases. Most are resolved one way or the other before they get to the Supreme Court.

The Bar Association in Washington is known to be very active and very diligent in pursuing and dealing with lawyers who have jumped the tracks. When a complaint is received against a lawyer, the Bar Association investigates, collects information, and then either resolves it or sends it to a review committee for further handling. In a serious case, a lawyer's license can be suspended for a period of time or taken away altogether. Some kinds of conduct are almost certain to result in disbarment or suspension, such as stealing from a client, being convicted of a serious crime, or defrauding a Court.

The Bar Association has to deal with all kinds of complaints about lawyers . . . many of them don't really have anything to do with ethical problems. For example, the Bar Association's Disciplinary folks don't handle fee disputes or simple mistakes in judgment by a lawyer. (There are other ways to deal with those things – to be dealt with in a future column.) While they take every complaint seriously, there are a lot of frivolous and unfounded complaints filed every year that have to be weeded out.

The American Bar Association, the organization that supposedly speaks for all of the lawyers in America, has developed a set of guidelines for the State Bars, telling them what the punishment should be for certain kinds of violations. For example the suggested punishment for stealing a client's money is disbarment; whereas the suggested punishment for something much less dramatic might be a reprimand to the lawyer that goes on his/her record. The ABA also lists common aggravating and mitigating factors in lawyer discipline. For example, a clean record and a first offense might lessen the punishment; but a history of similar problems and a bad attitude might get the lawyer a stiffer punishment.

Some lawyers make the mistake of treating the Bar Association like the Prosecuting Attorney and not cooperating with the investigation. Bad idea. Bar discipline isn't like criminal law . . . the accused is required to cooperate with the Bar Association . . . or it could make the penalty worse!!

The most serious penalties are disbarment and suspension . . . meaning a lawyer loses his license to practice permanently or for a period of stated time. In the year 2010, there were 21 disbarments and 24 suspensions and 5 lawyers who chose to resign rather than fight it out. In the less serious category, there were 32 reprimands and 11 admonitions. Most of the complaints related to lawyers who were practicing criminal law (30% of all complaints) or family law (17% of all complaints.)

The Bar Association doesn't just punish lawyers . . . it also helps people who have been hurt by the dishonest acts of lawyers. In 2010, the Bar Association voluntarily paid $554,270 (YES! half a million dollars!!!) to people who have been harmed by dishonest lawyers. This money came from the pockets of the lawyers who – in the vast majority – are honest and hard working and believe that victims should be taken care of. Over the last three years, those payments have totaled $1,893,759 . . . WOW, almost 2 Million dollars!

So what does all this mean to Joe or Josephine Citizen, who needs a lawyer once or twice in their life? Well, the good news is that the huge, overwhelming majority of the 27,000+ lawyers in Washington State are honest, fair, hard-working citizens, who are governed by a strict code of ethics that is aggressively enforced. Your chances of ending up with a good, honest lawyer are very good. The better news is that the tiny percentage of bad-news violators are reported and dealt with by a professional and aggressive group of people who want to keep the legal profession squeaky clean.

As always, thanks for reading my column! Also, many thanks for all the nice comments!

See you next month.

Tom Brown

Where There's A Will, There's A Lawyer

● ● ●

DID YOU EVER WONDER WHY wills have to be such a big deal?

Why not just leave your intentions scribbled on the back of an old envelope?

Or, why not just whisper to your loved ones on your deathbed how you want your property divvied up?

Why does everything have to be so formal, so complicated, so . . . legal?

Well, the answer to those questions is all about human nature. The law never makes its own path . . . it response to the needs and actions of the people it serves. In the case of wills, the formal nature of these tools is a response to how humans act. Unfortunately, we humans have a history of lying, cheating, forging, altering, destroying, or doing almost anything to make sure that one person's wealth makes it to their pockets rather than go where the deceased wanted it to go.

The law's response to this has been to do everything in its power to make sure that wills are legitimate and truly reflect what the deceased wanted. If you comb through the hundreds of thousands of court cases and written laws in American and English legal history, you will find a common theme: the lawmakers and judges want to make sure that what the deceased wanted is actually done, while preserving a forum for legitimate disputes and questions.

The result is a very rigid set of rules for wills and how they are handled.

It's really not that often that we have to deal with wills (fortunately!); but it is good to review some of the basics, just in case. Let's see if we can identify to things that will make us a little more savvy about wills. (This is in partial fulfillment of the promise I made to you in May 2008, to answer some more questions about wills and probates.)

What in the world is probate? It's simple . . . probate is the court-supervised enforcement of the will. The Court makes sure that notice is given to all persons entitled; makes sure the Executor follows all the rules; make sure that all the bills and creditors are paid; and makes sure the deceased's property goes to the correct persons. Probate has a bad reputation for being expensive and long lasting, but it's usually very inexpensive and orderly. It's only when there's a dispute that things get gnarly.

What if someone I know dies and I know there is a will and where it is?

Well, congratulations! Now you're in a situation where the law is very specific. If you are the custodian of that will (meaning . . . if it's in your possession or control), you have a legal duty to make sure that the will gets safely into the hands of the Superior Court. You can discharge this duty by taking it to the Clerk of the Superior Court in your County and filing it with the Clerk. (There's a small fee.) If you already have a lawyer or you know the lawyer who prepared the will, you can discharge this duty by delivering the will to that lawyer.

What if a husband or wife dies and they have wills and a Community Property Agreement?

This is the most common situation that is encountered. Most lawyers advise people of moderate means to have a Community Property Agreement, which has the effect of transferring all of the assets of the family to the surviving spouse, without reference to the will. No probate is necessary, and the will of the deceased is not even referred to. Technically, the will should be filed with the Clerk, but that requirement is often ignored in this situation, because the will has no effect.

What about the Power of Attorney that Uncle Joe gave me before he died?

Forget it. When Uncle Joe died, his Power of Attorney died too. But you will have to account for everything you did under the Power of Attorney while he was alive.

What are the formal requirements of a will in Washington?

The person making the will must be competent.

The will must be in writing.

The will must be signed by the person making the will (or signed by someone at his direction if he can't sign).

Two independent and competent witnesses must confirm by signing that the "testator" actually signed the will and that he appeared to be competent and that the "testator" asked them or directed them to sign the will.

If either of the witnesses is a beneficiary under the will, that witness is disqualified, and the will is probably invalid.

My cousin told me you could do a will in your own handwriting with no witnesses and it was legal. He said it was called a "holographic' will . . . is this true?

Nope. The problem is not that it's handwritten . . . the problem is that it is not witnessed as required by Washington law. Not a valid will. However, holographic wills are legal in some states.

What about contesting a will, because the "testator" was incompetent or because he/she was under the influence of someone? My cousin Vinny says this happens all the time.

The law and courts of the State of Washington fiercely protect the right of a person to direct the way his or her assets are distributed. If a will is challenged, the burden of proof is very, very high in order to upset the will. It can happen, but it is rare.

Where should I keep my will? Safe Deposit Box?

Remember that you want somebody to see the will if you're gone. Don't hide it where it will never be seen. Safe deposit boxes are OK for the original . . . but keep copies where your family or friends will see it: in your desk, with your lawyer, give copies to your children . . . you get the idea. Don't hide it. Some lawyers keep the original wills for no charge and give you enough copies to make sure you let your family know where it is.

What happens if I don't have a will . . . the state gets everything, right?

Absolutely not. The State of Washington (like most states) has an "intestate succession" law, which spells out who gets your property, if you don't have a will or community property agreement or other arrangement. The law is simple and commonsense. The law says that your property will go to your family members, in order of their relationship to you.

First to your spouse (or "domestic partner"), then children, then parents, then siblings, then grandchildren, then grandparents . . . well, you get the idea. Only in the most extreme cases does the property ever go to the state.

Who should I appoint as my executor?

Someone you trust without reservation. Someone who is organized, smart, efficient. Someone who is smart enough to hire a good, honest lawyer. Someone who cares about you and your family.

Beware of the relatively new law that says that if you get divorced or your spouse dies and you later re-marry, your new spouse is automatically entitled to part of your estate if you die, whether you want that result or not. If you get remarried, go see a lawyer about bringing your wills up to date.

If you had your will made while you lived in another state, and your will was legal under the laws of that state, the state of Washington will honor that will, even if it conflicts with Washington law.

Well that should hold you for another month!

Remember, our probate laws and systems are designed to protect you . . . not to harm you.

Thanks for reading my little column . . . and thank you for all the wonderful comments and suggestions I've heard from you!

Tom Brown

I Can't Believe It! I've Been Sued!

• • •

It's a beautiful late spring day. It's warm, sunny and the world is full of promise. The buzz of distant lawnmowers tells you what the neighbors are up to. Your husband just breezed in early from work and decided to take a shower. You're making his favorite dinner.

You're mildly irritated at the sound of the doorbell, hoping you don't have to fend off some religious zealots or pay the paperboy right now. But when you answer the door, it's somebody in uniform. A policeman? ...no, more like a deputy sheriff. He smiles, introduces himself, and tells you that he is here to serve some legal papers on you. You're still waaaay behind the comprehension curve, but you obediently put out your hand and take the papers he hands you. As you just start to come up to speed, questions erupt from your dazed mouth. What is this? Who sent you? What does this mean? The deputy politely deflects your questions, repeating a stock disclaimer and telling you that he is only a messenger. He leaves.

The buzzing of the lawnmowers is now a roaring in your head. Wait a minute, that's not the lawnmowers...it is a roaring in your head! What is this? What just happened here?

You've been "served."

One of the most basic rules of our American legal system is the concept that anyone who is being sued has to be personally "served" with a copy of the lawsuit and also with a piece of paper -- usually called a "summons" -- that tells them what is going on. Lawsuits come in all sizes and descriptions, and they cover a wide range of human conflicts. Automobile accidents, collection of debts, property line disputes, mortgage foreclosures, domestic violence complaints, slips and falls on someone's property, etc., etc., -- they almost always start with someone handing someone papers, telling them that a lawsuit has been started against them.

Fortunately, most of us never have to experience the trauma of being sued. Statistics tell us that only one in ten of us will ever be served with these papers in our lifetime. But, still, that's over 25 million of us here in the United States, and that number may be going up if we believe that this is truly a litigious society.

How do you respond? What do you do? Are there any terrible mistakes you can make at this early stage? Who do you call? Should you talk to anybody about it? What do you do with the papers? How do you find a lawyer? Do you need to find a lawyer? Is your life over?

Let's examine what a person who's just been sued should do in the early stages.

TAKE A DEEP BREATH

This is America. The world hasn't ended. You have the right to dispute whatever you are being sued about. No matter what you've heard, we have a smart, fair, open legal system that bends over backwards to protect the people that are involved in the system. Nobody is going to suddenly grab your home, or empty your bank accounts, or decide the case against you without you having a chance to fairly present your side of the story. Of course, it seems like everything is a red blur right now, but it will settle down. You're probably going to end up with a lawyer who is going to explain this to you and comfort you and protect you. Take a deep breath.

Be Smart

Take a moment to write down the facts of what's happening. What date were you served? What day of the week? (Could be important in some jurisdictions if it was a Sunday or a holiday.) What time were you served? What's the name of the person who served you? (Didn't ask? That's Ok, what did he look like? How was he dressed? Street clothes or uniform? What agency? Police? Sheriff? Federal Marshal?) What papers were given to you? How many sets? One or more? Was he just serving you or someone else also, like your husband? Did he ask you to sign anything?

Don't Panic.

The most important thing to remember at the beginning is that you probably have some time to deal with this on a rational basis and you probably don't need to do anything TODAY. Most state and federal courts allow a reasonable amount of time for people to respond in some way to a new lawsuit. This amount of time usually ranges from 20 days to 45 days, and it will be clearly spelled out in the papers that were just handed to you. Look at the papers and see how long you have to respond. Then sit down with your spouse or partner and have a martini or a latte or a nice dinner. Although your head will be filled with lawsuit thoughts, try to take a deep breath and talk about something else. Nothing bad is going to happen to you today, and you have lots of time to get your game together. (If the papers include an injunction or a restraining order, you will need to obey what it says from the moment you are served, so be careful not to violate a direct court order, like an order to stay away from someone or an order not to dispose of property or an order not to go on someone else's property.)

WHO DO YOU NEED TO TELL?

The automatic response is to think that a lawyer is the most important person in the world right now. While a lawyer is certainly a good idea at this time, there may be other choices. For example, if this lawsuit is about a car accident or about a slip & fall on your property, the most important person in your life right now may be your insurance agent. The chances are that your insurance will "cover" this lawsuit, and your insurance company will hire a lawyer to defend you. Make a quick call to your insurance agent, and it's possible – emphasis on the word *possible* – that you may not need to see a lawyer at all. Your insurance agent deals with this all the time. He or she will let you know if you need to see a lawyer or if they will take care of everything.

If you are being sued because you are the employee of a company or business, it's entirely possible that the company's lawyers will be protecting you as well. Let your boss know that you were served, and see what the company does. If their lawyer moves in and assures you that you are protected, it's likely that you are OK without hiring your own lawyer (at least for right now.)

If you see on the papers that there are other defendants besides you, it's possible that one of those other defendants may be required to provide you with a defense, and they may do it immediately and without question – it happens all the time.

But, if you have any doubt at all...or, if you're not absolutely sure that someone has stepped up to the plate to protect you, call a lawyer. Make it clear to the receptionist or the lawyer that you have been served with papers and that there is a time limit that you are concerned about. Don't be put off on the timing. Insist on an appointment right away so that the arrangements can be made for the lawyer to "appear" in the lawsuit with time to spare.

Don't talk about the merits of the case.

Watch out for yourself.

Save your papers and evidence.

Make a chronology for the lawyer.

Write things down for the lawyer.

Trust the system.

Tom Brown

Your Required Summer Legal Reading (and movie watching)

• • •

Hey! A guest columnist! For only the second time in three and one-half years, I'm going to bring an outsider to our chummy monthly discussion. Bob Sigler, a high school friend of mine, is a deputy United States Attorney for Nebraska and a voracious reader and a really good writer.

I just found out that Bob writes a monthly column mostly for lawyers, and I got a chance to enjoy this month's column, which is Bob's light look at summer reading and movie watching on legal issues. Some of his recommendations may be a little on the heavy side, but – hey – this isn't Disneyland.

So here he is...enjoy!

• • •

Summer is here -- the time to downshift a gear or two. As you head off to the beach or the mountain streams or just the back yard, it's time to read a book. Now, since this monthly essay is supposed to have some relation to the law; I will confine my recommendations to books, which have some relation to that discipline even if the link is a bit tenuous. I am also going to indulge in some movie suggestions since I think that some films are as good as, or better than, the book. Be advised there is no John Grisham. Sig strives for higher ground. All of the titles discussed can be found on Amazon - many at a very low cost.

Did you ever wonder how the Supreme Court is able to turn everyday disputes into great principles of constitutional law? John Garraty provides an excellent start to the answer in ***Quarrels That Have Shaped the Constitution***, a collection of essays which detail the historical context of some of the Court's most important constitutional cases. You will learn about the stories behind *Marbury v. Madison*, *Dred Scott* and many more. If you are an "originalist" (as is our friend Justice Scalia), this entertaining walk through history will challenge.

A bit more academic, but still centered on the person, is John T. Noonan Jr.'s ***Persons and Masks of the Law: Cardozo, Holmes, Jefferson, and Wythe as Makers of the Masks.***

Noonan is a Senior Circuit Judge on the 9th Circuit and has written a number of books on legal and moral subjects. He makes you think.

And if you really want to stretch your mind, try Judge Richard Posner's ***How Judges Think*** or Ronald Dworkin's ***Justice in Robes***. Posner is beloved by the right. Dworkin is to the left. Pick your opposite and set out to understand the other side. If these guys make your head hurt, remember that Bacon also counseled "Some books are to be tasted, others to be swallowed, and some few to be chewed and digested."

There has been many a social change in America whose catalyst is law since the baby boom stork arrived with me in 1946. Richard Klugler's ***Simple Justice: The History of Brown v. Board of Education and Black***

America's Struggle for Equality tells the story of how the most important of those changes got to the Supreme Court and why the Court decided as it did.

I don't know any films that tell that story but I highly recommend *Amistad*, an historical drama film with Anthony Hopkins and Matthew McConaughey based on the true story of a slave mutiny that took place aboard a ship of the same name in 1839, and the legal battle that followed. It shows how, even though the case was won at the federal district court level, it was appealed by President Marin Van Buren to the Supreme Court, and how former President John Quincy Adams took part in the proceedings.

In the area of criminal law most of you dimly recall *Gideon v. Wainwright*. For the historical story read *Gideon's Trumpet* by Anthony Lewis. The 1980 movie starring Henry Fonda is worth two hours. And if you live in Nebraska and have never seen Spencer Tracy and Frederic March in *Inherit the Wind* or read *Summer for the Gods: The Scopes Trial and America's Continuing Debate Over Science and Religion* by Edward J. Larson, then I'm a monkey's uncle and you didn't go to Bryan High.

And to be involved in criminal law in Nebraska you must know the name of Charles Starkweather. Several books have been written. My recommendation is *Caril* by Omaha reporter Ninette Beaver. The movie *Badlands* with Martin Sheen and Sissy Spacek is a fictionalized version of the 1958 murder spree that terrified people all across Nebraska - me included.

In the realm of fiction, for one of the best ever TV studies of the America that keeps criminal law in business, try season one of the HBO series *The Wire*. If you are involved in criminal law somehow and you are not hooked for the remaining four seasons, then I can only lament with Gray: "where ignorance is bliss, 'tis folly to be wise."

Finally, and for fun, meet John Mortimer's Old Bailey hack, Horace Rumpole. A good introduction is *The First Rumpole Omnibus*. Or enjoy the inimitable Leo McKern's portrayal of She-Who-Must-Be-Obeyed's spouse in the DVD of the TV series *Rumpole of the Bailey*. You will learn that "Even judges are human. Not many people know that." (Horace Rumpole).

I could go on. Films such as *12 Angry Men* and *Anatomy of a Murder* are in the introductory course for criminal lawyers. Another film about true crime in Nebraska is *Boys Don't Cry* for which Hillary Swank won an Academy Award for Best Actress. The Penguin Books *Famous Trials* series is endlessly interesting. Fred W. Friendly's *The Constitution: That Delicate Balance* is yet another work about the people and the drama behind landmark Supreme Court cases.

But I am out of space. (And I have to finish *Bleak House* to see how *Jarndyce and Jarndyce* is resolved.)

So become a full man or woman this summer. Read - and watch. At summer's end you will be refreshed, renewed, and full. Full? "Reading maketh a full man, conference a ready man. And writing, an exact man." Francis Bacon.

• • •

Thanks, Bob. And thank you again faithful SST "de minimis" readers.

I hope Bob's observations motivate some of us to jump into some thoughtful legal reading or legal movie watching this summer. And, I have to add...there's one fantastic book that is not really about the law, but it's about one of the greatest American lawyers who ever lived: Abraham Lincoln. I'm reading Doris Kearns Goodwin's magical book about Lincoln, *A Team of Rivals*. It's just flat awesome. Read it.

See you next month.

Tom Brown

Are Lawyers Neanderthals?

● ● ●

Obviously, we are all living in the world of technology unleashed.

Every day brings a new device, new software, a new way of communicating, a rejection of the "old ways" of doing business.

What is going on with lawyers during this revolution?

Are lawyers still closeted in their dusty libraries; dictating to stenographers who record their every nuance in shorthand; are they checking legal precedent in dusty, crumbling books that haven't been opened since King John signed the Magna Carta in 1215; are they calling their clients and colleagues on rotary dial phones? That's what we expect, isn't it? That lawyers and their whole antiquated system are hopelessly behind the times, as the nation and the world rocket forward?

As my kids would have said 20+ years ago: "Not so fast, Judgment-Face!"

We lawyers have been dragged kicking and screaming into the 21st century...there's simply no escaping the tsunami of technological advances that have engulfed the rest of the business world. By God...we are connected!

First, the books. What was in those rows and rows of moldy looking books, anyway? Well, those books fell into four basic categories:

(1) collections of every single case decided by state and federal appeal courts; (2) Summaries of the law divided into categories based on the kind of issue (landlord & tenant; crimes; divorces; wills, etc.); (3) Books written to exhaustively cover certain areas of the law; (4) the laws and regulations passed by Congress and state legislatures and administrative agencies. That's what we poor lawyers used to plow through to figure out what "the law" was. Now, of course, you know where we go...yes, we go to the keyboard. All of those court decisions and laws and treatises are now online and we lawyers can access them through sophisticated (and expensive) programs that let us search the issues or areas we are concerned with and get the printout or summary of all those sources... it's magical!

How about the way we communicate? Just to give you an idea, I've been practicing law for 41 years. During the first 35 years or so, I spent my days at the office with a Dictaphone in my hand, dictating letters, pleadings, briefs, notes, etc. to a secretary that transcribed all of that into typed hard copies. Now, I don't even own a dictating machine. Nearly 90% of my communications with other lawyers and clients and courts is by e-mail. I prepare my own e-mails on my computer and send them from my computer. The responses are almost instantaneous. Scheduling issues in a complex case that may have taken weeks to work out are now solved in days, maybe hours. Even more important, documents are rarely mailed...usually we copy them in a format that can be e-mailed (like PDF) and send them by e-mail. Lengthy telephone conversations are rare, because the participants usually agree to send the materials by e-mail and digest them and talk later. Lengthy disputes over the wording of an important document are reduced to hours or minutes, as the revised versions of the documents fly back and forth.

Recent years have also marked the use of video in very innovative ways. It used to be very difficult to schedule witnesses for a trial, because trials could get postponed or we couldn't predict when the witness would testify. That's not too big of a problem, unless your witness is a neurosurgeon charging $750.00 per hour for sitting around twiddling his thumbs waiting to testify or unless your witness lives in London, and it would cost $20K to get him to a courtroom in Montesano. Now, we go to the witness at a time certain, videotape the testimony with the lawyers present just as if it was in the courtroom...and show the video to the jury at trial. Voila!

At trial, we used to write and draw diagrams and timelines on white "butcher paper" on big easels for the judge or jury. Now, it's very different. Now, lawyers create materials before the trial starts (like timelines, graphs, charts, etc.) and these are shown to the jury in an electronic form (computer or projector) and everyone is spared the tedium and anxiety of the lawyer trying to draw the correct diagram 3 or 4 times while the jury giggles over the ineptitude of the lawyers.

The Courts themselves are up to their eyes in the technology revolution. The Federal Courts require that all filings be by computer, and the whole court file is electronic. The state courts of Washington haven't gone that far yet, but you can still get a printout of every filing in every Washington State Superior Court Lawsuit by going to http://dw.courts.wa.gov/

Just to show how flexible and user-friendly the system has gotten, I had a case last week where all of the lawyers agreed to totally suspend the rules of service of documents by mail, and agreed to e-mail service, thereby cutting at least 3 days off every exchange of documents.

And how about timekeeping and billing? This is how lawyers bill you...have things changed in that department? Well...yes and no. The system depends on the attorney recording his or her time at the time the service was performed. I can tell you that in a lawyer's day, it's very difficult to catch every activity, every phone call, and every e-mail. But, with the hard record of e-mails and the hard record of faxes and with the hard record of long distance phone calls...it just gets more and more likely that the time the attorney spent will be captured and will show up on your bill.

Now, of course, every time slip and every charge and every fax and every e-mail exists in electronic form...so it's more likely that it will find its way to your bill...lucky you!

So...I suggest that we smooth, charming lawyers are not Neanderthals. We are modern, hip, connected, savvy, and cool. Wired, "with it" professionals who are making our way in this screaming technological world.

But, if I send you a note on a torn-out telephone directory page, or if I push the wrong button on the telephone and disconnect you; or if I send you an e-mail with an attachment and forget to attach the attachment...don't think I've fallen off the technology cliff...I just faded back to the good ol' days for a minute.

As always, I really appreciate the opportunity to talk to you about the law; and I absolutely cherish the comments you make about the column...you make it all worthwhile. And speaking of technology, you can e-mail me at **tom.brown@lawbljs.com**

Tom Brown

What about Court Reporters

• • •

LAST MONTH WE TALKED ABOUT how technology had impacted lawyers, and what a nerdy bunch of techno-whizzes we were now with our e-mails and scanners and search engines, etc.

Well, a good friend of mine who owns a Court Reporting service told me she was disappointed that the column didn't talk about the effects of technology on the business of Court Reporting.

Of course, she was right...but -- more importantly -- it got me to thinking about the whole business of Court Reporting and how invisible it is to the public. So, let's take the time to examine what Court Reporting is and how essential it is to the everyday business of the law.

There are many reasons and many situations where it is critically important that every word spoken is accurately recorded. We usually think of the courtroom and the recording of testimony and arguments in trials. Of course, that is the obvious situation and perhaps the most well known. But there are literally dozens of other venues and situations where the Court Reporter may turn out to be the most important person in the room.

When I started practicing law in 1970, there were still many, many Court Reporters who took their notes with a notepad and pen or pencil in shorthand. They often backed up their work with a tape recorder so they could check the accuracy of what they had written down, or fill in the blanks where they missed something.

But that era was dying, and most Court Reporters were beginning to use the Stenotype, a machine that looks like a tiny little typewriter on a stand, between the knees of the court Reporter. The keys on the stenotype are oddly shaped and placed and have no letters on them. The Court Reporter is trained to strike certain keys to represent certain sounds and the machine created a strip of paper with images on it that would be "read" by the Court Reporter or an assistant. Then came the laborious task of typing the information with a regular typewriter so it was in a format that the lawyers and judges could use and understand.

That system was state of the art for many years, until along came...guess what? Of course, the computer. Pretty soon, the little machines were hooked up to computers and many of the intervening steps were eliminated. As the Court Reporter keyed the information into the Stenotype, it appeared magically on the computer screen as text. Welcome to the new world! Now, instead of re-typing every word from the Stenotype notes, the Court Reporter would check the output to the computer and clean it up in perhaps 10% of the time it took before. And, of course, the computer would take care of many of the formatting and spelling problems that used to plague the Court Reporters.

Court Reporters are a crucial part of the legal system. Their role is so important, that certain levels of education are required and they are licensed and regulated by the state. It takes from 2 to 4 years to acquire the skills necessary to be a stenotype reporter. Then, the reporters have to have ongoing education every year to keep their licenses. They are closely regulated by the state, and are subject to many of the whims of the courts where they work.

Many Court Reporters don't work for Courts or Public agencies. They are "free-lance" and take whatever work needs to be done. The scope of free-lance Court Reporting is huge...but it mostly is attending depositions (taking of testimony outside court) and arbitrations (mini-trials without a judge or jury) and special kinds of "hearings" (like little trials) of State agencies.

Of course, the technology tsunami has swept the Court Reporters along as well as the lawyers and judges. Now lawyers take a deposition of a critical witness and want to see the transcript of the deposition the same day. Shockingly, it often happens. And the Court Reporter makes it clear that the transcript has not been vetted or checked or proofread and attaches it to an e-mail and off it goes. The harried lawyer is marking up the printout even before the printer is done!!

Free-lance Court Reporting has become big business. The ability of a lawyer to call a known entity and rely on the fact that a competent reporter will be waiting at 5:30 o'clock AM in a doctor's parking lot in Shelton, Washington is just magical. Hours later, that deposition transcript may be in a Courtroom, taking center stage in an important dispute.

Virtually every trial in Washington State will involve testimony by video. In this situation, the Court Reporter takes down all the testimony for the official record; the lawyers act as if they are in the Courtroom; the video expert records everything on high-definition video, and the Doctor testifies from his office in Longview for a later trial in South Bend. Months later, at the Courthouse, the jury watches him on video, hears the questions of the lawyers, and watches the doctor demonstrate how the bones work and show the x-rays on screen. It's a magical world!

If the witness is in New York State, the deposition can be taken there, with the lawyers in Washington State at separate offices and the Court Reporter at her office. Everything gets recorded!

But, it's not perfect. I had a case years ago where the driver on the other side had testified in his deposition: "I was going 35 miles an hour." That was great because it was over the speed limit. In front of the jury, I asked him how fast he was going at the time of the accident. He said 20 miles per hour. I attacked him...I said "...didn't you testify that you were going 35 miles and hour?" He said: "No, I didn't say that." I showed him the deposition. He stubbornly refused to admit that he had said that. In the middle of the trial, on a break, I called the Court Reporter and told her to get ready to come to court and testify to what the guy said. I told her to double check and listen to the audiotape just to be sure. She called me back in shock and told me she had mis-heard and mis-typed the answer. She said when she listened to the tape, the witness didn't say, "**I** was going 35 miles an hour." He said: "**The guy** was going 35 miles an hour." Oops! We settled the case.

Court Reporters are witnesses to the most outrageous, funniest, scariest, incredible things that humans say. Here are a few samples to keep you laughing until nest month. These are supposedly actual testimony in actual trials and hearings:

Q: What is your brother-in-law's name?
A: Borofkin

Q: What is his first name?
A: I can't remember.

Q: He's been your brother-in-law for 45 years, and you can't remember his first name?

A: No. I tell you I'm too excited. (Rising from the witness chair and pointing to Mr. Borofkin). Nathan, for God's sake, tell them your first name!

Q: James stood back and shot Tommy Lee?

A: Yes.

Q: And then Tommy Lee pulled out his gun and shot James in the fracas?

A: (After a hesitation) No sir, just above it.

Q: Doctor, did you say he was shot in the woods?

A: No, I said he was shot in the lumber region.

Q: What is your name?

A: Ernestine McDowell.

Q: What is your marital status?

A: Fair.

Q: Do you know how far pregnant you are right now?

A: I will be three months November 8th.

Q: Apparently then, the date of conception was August 8th?

A: Yes.

Q: What were you and your husband doing at that time?

Q: Doctor, how many autopsies have you performed on dead people?

A: All my autopsies have been on dead people.

Q: Mrs. Jones, is your appearance this morning pursuant to a deposition notice that I sent to your attorney?
A: No. This is how I dress when I go to work.

Q: When he went, had you gone and had she, if she wanted to and were able, for the time being excluding all the restraints on her not to go also, would he have brought you, meaning you and she, with him to the station?
A: MR. BROOKS. Objection. That question should be taken out and shot.

Q: Please state the location of your right foot immediately prior to impact.
A: Immediately before the impact, my right foot was located at the immediate end of my right leg.

Q: And lastly, Gary, all your responses must be oral, O.K.?
A: Oral.

Q: How old are you?
A: Oral.

Thanks for reading my little column and thanks for all the nice comments. See you next month!

Tom Brown

Can you sue God?...Canada?...
an Indian Tribe?

● ● ●

WE AMERICANS HAVE A REPUTATION for being lawsuit-happy...filing a lawsuit for every slight, every injury, and every problem that confronts us.

Of course, the truth is far from that silly reputation, but we do tend to rely on our courts to iron out the knotty differences that we can't resolve ourselves. I would argue that the volume of lawsuits is not anywhere near what our reputation is; but that discussion is for another day...another column.

Today, the question is this: Whom can you sue?

Seems like an easy question...but, hey, we're lawyers! We can complicate anything.

Basically, the law says that – if you have a legitimate claim – you can sue anybody or anything that is within the reach of the court...we call it jurisdiction. So, if you are in the State of Washington, you can sue people who live in Washington, people who own property in Washington, corporations created under Washington law, corporations from other states that do business in Washington; people who drive their cars in

Washington, people who negligently harmed you while they were visiting Washington, and almost anybody or any corporation that has "significant contacts" with the state of Washington.

But there are certain people or entities that you cannot sue, even if they are doing their business or living their life in our state. The most obvious of these situations are foreign countries or foreign citizens. Those entities -- like the country of Canada or its citizens -- are immune from suit in our courts, unless they have *consented* or agreed to be sued in our courts. While this may seem kind of abstract, think about how many Canadian drivers are operating motor vehicles in our state every day and how many accidents there are...it would be chaos if we didn't work out a way to establish responsibility for stupid or negligent driving. So we have agreed by treaties and other international agreements to allow us to sue them in our courts if they drive here and vice-versa. It only makes sense.

But, if you rent a car in Canada and it blows up and injures you seriously, where are you going to sue? Not in the good ol' USA...nope, welcome to the Canadian legal system. Maybe your favorite lawyer can cooperate with our friends in Canada, but their system is the place where your issues will be decided and you will have a Canadian lawyer.

Foreign countries have something called "sovereign immunity." That means they are immune from suit in certain courts. It's the death knell for a lawsuit unless there's a treaty or other situation that covers the issue.

Does all of this seem too abstract? Too improbable? It could never involve you? Well, think about your last trip to your friendly neighborhood Indian casino. What if your slot machine had been installed or maintained improperly and short-circuited and electrocuted you? What if the fancy chandelier was not checked regularly and had fallen on your head and killed you at the blackjack table? What if the casino's fire suppression system failed due to negligence or inattention and a fire killed all the gamblers? All of those injured people or their survivors would just file a lawsuit against the Indian Tribe for their damages, right? Not so fast, American citizen.

That Indian Tribe is an independent nation, just like Canada or Mexico, and has SOVEREIGN IMMUNITY. What Court are you going to sue in? Washington's Superior Courts in every county? Sorry... sovereign immunity. Federal Court in Seattle or Tacoma? Sorry...sovereign immunity.

Where? Can't you sue the Tribe anywhere? Sure you can. You can sue in the Tribal Court...it has jurisdiction over this sort of thing...and it also has a set of rules written by the Indian Tribe and it also has a Judge who is probably a member of the Tribe. I'm a proud member of the bar of the Quinault Tribal Court and I would never impugn the integrity of the Court or its Judge by suggesting that it wouldn't be fair. But I'm also a realist, and I would not suggest to my injured client or his surviving relatives that the ideal or perfect venue for his multi-million dollar claim against the Tribe was in that Tribe's Tribal Court.

Fortunately, we have a system where the Indian Tribes can *waive* their sovereign immunity and allow our courts to decide issues. For example, when the Tribes construct casinos, they agree to *waive* their sovereign immunity when it comes to building codes and fire codes and health codes, so that our state and counties and cities can regulate these things for the health and safety of the public just like any other business. So, if the casino doesn't comply with the local building code, the county can come in and enforce it -- even with a lawsuit, if necessary.

In some other states, the Indian Tribes who want to operate casinos waive their sovereign immunity as to tort liability (tort liability is what we are talking about here – the responsibility for hurting or killing somebody by their negligence -- like the chandelier or the electrocution)...but not in Washington. In Washington, the tribes so far have not waived this immunity and people are left to whatever they can work out with the Tribe's insurance company (Hah!) or end up in Tribal Court.

In my humble opinion, the various tribes could agree that they are subject to the jurisdiction of the State Courts in this crucial area. This would be part of their licensing agreement with the State. Certainly the State has the power to do this...California does it. Other States do it. Why not Washington?

Most important, when we think about someone that was horribly injured in a casino by a negligent or stupid oversight, shouldn't that person be able to ask a Washington State jury of his peers to decide whose fault it was and who should be responsible, rather than asking those same questions of a Tribal Judge? Just sayin'...

And then, referring back to the title of this particular column, what about suing God? As weird as it sounds, some people have actually tried this...obviously with no success. If nothing else, it's a little tough to figure out how to serve the papers!

As always, thanks for your terrific comments about my columns and thanks for reading this great little newspaper!!!

Tom Brown

McDonald's 'hot coffee' case still burns people

• • •

WSAJ EAGLE MEMBER ANDREW BERGH has written a monthly column for the *Daily Journal of Commerce* for 19 years – upwards of 400 articles. His hope was that his columns would help shape and improve opinions of lawyers and the law. His commitment to our mission is worthy of our gratitude and admiration. As his final article, he chose to discuss the movie "Hot Coffee" and the ongoing impacts of Stella Liebeck's case against McDonalds. With our thanks, we reprint his column here. Originally published in the *Daily Journal of Commerce*, July 2011.

By Andrew Bergh

Can you name the plaintiff in the infamous McDonald's coffee case?

Didn't think so.

For the record, the plaintiff was 79-year-old Stella Liebeck, the drive-through customer who spilled hot coffee between her legs. But despite her relative anonymity, the McDonald's coffee case – once touted as "the poster child of excessive lawsuits" – continues to be a cause célèbre since it achieved notoriety 12 years ago.

First of all, let's discuss a case recently decided by the Utah Supreme Court.

While walking in a crosswalk in a grocery store parking lot, John Boyle was hit by a truck. As a result, the Salt Lake City resident suffered a serious back injury that led to surgery, and also lost his job because he couldn't work for months.

Unfortunately, Boyle still suffers from chronic pain that prevents him from sleeping through the night or in a bed, driving for extended periods, or working an eight-hour day. Although he now works for a golf shop, he can't lift two buckets of golf balls at the same time or perform other job-related tasks. And once a professional golfer, his golf game has gone downhill.

Boyle later sued the truck driver, Kerry Christensen, for damages in Salt Lake District Court. After Christensen admitted liability, the case went to trial on damages only.

During closing argument, defense counsel referred to the McDonald's coffee case for the very first time, incorrectly representing that plaintiff's counsel in both cases had used a so-called "per diem" analysis for determining damages. (Under this perfectly acceptable approach, the jury is urged to calculate damages for pain and suffering by using a daily dollar amount and then multiplying it by the number of days that the plaintiff was hurt and/or disabled.)

Although Boyle's attorney immediately objected on the ground that the McDonald's coffee case wasn't in evidence and was prejudicial, the trial court overruled his objection. In the short time allowed for his response, Boyle's lawyer couldn't say much to mitigate the impact of opposing counsel's remark.

The jury later returned a verdict for $62,500, which included less than $28,000 for Boyle's pain and suffering. (The balance was for his economic losses.) This paled in comparison to the amount requested by his attorney - $458,724, to be exact – which included $370,000 for his pain and suffering.

In his appeal, Boyle argued, among other things, that the reference to the McDonald's coffee case was irrelevant and improper, and that he deserved a new trial. Although a Utah appeals court disagreed, Boyle convinced the Utah Supreme Court to hear his case.

In a unanimous decision, the justices recently reversed the lower courts and awarded Boyle a new trial.

At the outset, the high court discussed the "cultural context" of the McDonald's coffee case.

What made the headlines and what most people remember, said the court, are the size of the verdict and the source of the injury. With "$2.9 million for spilled coffee" etched in their minds, the McDonald's coffee case has come to symbolize "greedy plaintiffs and lawyers who file frivolous lawsuits and win hugely excessive sums in a broken legal system," said the court.

When limited to a "superficial view of the facts," the justices acknowledged that this negative perception is "understandable." But when the "details and issues" of the McDonald's coffee case are examined more closely, the court continued, one's perspective can be "dramatically alter(ed)."

First of all, the high court observed how the temperature of the spilled coffee was so hot – 180 to 190 degrees – that within seconds

Liebeck suffered third-degree burns on her thighs, buttocks, and groin. As a consequence, the elderly plaintiff underwent skin grafts during an eight-day hospital stay, was disabled for two years, and left with permanent scarring over 16 percent of her body.

The justices next pointed out how McDonald's had received approximately 700 prior complaints about coffee-burn injuries, including some that were settled for six-digit sums. The fast-food chain never lowered the temperature of its coffee, however, because the number of prior injuries was deemed "statistically insignificant."

Third, the court emphasized how Liebeck's verdict included $2.7 million in punitive damages. (This amount had "nothing to do with a per diem analysis," the court explained, which is why the reference to the McDonald's coffee case by Christensen's attorney had been misleading.)

The jury awarded this sum, said the court, because it believed the "extreme temperature" of the coffee was too dangerous, and that McDonald's had "callously disregarded" this danger in light of the prior injuries. Moreover, the $2.7 million figure matched McDonald's revenue from just two days of coffee sales.

Given the "uniquely iconic nature" of the McDonald's coffee case, the ensuing media frenzy, and the "general misunderstanding of the totality of its facts and reasoning among the public," the Utah high court said it would be "hard to imagine a scenario" where defense counsel could properly mention the case to a jury. It instead seems, said the court that the "sole purpose" of such reference would be to appeal improperly to the jury's passions.

So were the jury's passions wrongly inflamed in Boyle's case by the improper reference to the McDonald's coffee case?

Hard to say. But after considering various factors, including the small amount of pain and suffering damages awarded by the jury, the justices ultimately said there was a "reasonable likelihood" that Boyle would've fared better if the infamous coffee case had never been mentioned – and that he was therefore entitled to a new trial.

So are you more of a movie buff than a legal beagle?

If so, perhaps you've already seen "Hot Coffee," which is a 78-minute documentary released last month (so far only on HBO) that reveals "what really happened" in the McDonald's coffee case. For example, did you know Liebeck offered to settle her claim for $20,000 toward her substantial medical expenses but that McDonald's offered only $800? While I don't know if "Hot Coffee" will get two thumbs up from Roger Ebert, it's definitely a must view if you're at all curious about how and why the McDonald's coffee case attracted so much media attention and who funded the effort.

In short, it looks like the McDonald's coffee case will have an even longer shelf life. Ironically, at the end of the day, it might be best known as the "poster child of corporate greed."

Andrew Bergh, WSAJ EAGLE member, former prosecutor and insurance defense attorney, now limits his practice to plaintiff's personal injury cases, including medical malpractice and insurance bad faith.

Tom Brown

Could you go to jail for honking your car horn?

• • •

Most of us – including lawyers – don't really understand how much access we have to the business of our government. In this new computer world, we can sit in on committee hearings when people testify about their favorite bills; we can watch the legislature debate and vote; we can watch administrative agencies make rulings that dramatically affect our lives.

Among all these other things, we can also watch lawyers argue to the Washington State Supreme Court on the various issues it confronts every day. Wow...how boring, huh? Well, not as boring as you might think. Some of these cases are really, really interesting and touch our lives in ways that would surprise you.

First of all...here are the basics: You can watch lawyers argue to the Washington State Supreme Court within a day or two of the actual arguments. The whole thing is recorded and played back on TVW, one of the most outstanding public access, a governmental access institution that's ever hit the airwaves. It's fun to see them joust with the nine justices...and sometimes it's funny and downright entertaining. This stuff is not edited or trimmed or rehearsed or choreographed...it's real. I'll grant that some of it is boring as hell...but all of it is important.

Here's are a few important things for you to know about the Washington State Supreme Court:

i.   It is like the United States Supreme Court in one very important way: they get to pick and choose their cases. This means that they don't have to accept every mundane, routine appeal that comes through the pipeline...no, they get to decide what cases they will hear. This means that they will pick the juiciest, most important, gnarliest, coolest cases with the most impact on our citizens.

ii. Our State's system of elected Supreme Court judges, with gubernatorial appointments, insures that we don't end up with a bunch of old drones; sitting in cobwebbed, padded chairs; snoring while their law clerks write the opinions. To the contrary, our state's system has consistently generated "cream of the crop" judges who are smart, active and involved. The current Court has a mix of appointed and elected Judges that is the envy of Court watchers across the country.

iii. Our State Supreme Court is not a chummy club where the Judges try to come up with some ridiculous consensus, just to be able to say that they all agreed. To the contrary, our State Supreme Court is nothing short of lively...with a lot of dissenting and concurring opinions...meaning that great minds differ and state why they differ, with emphasis and vigor. Far from being a problem, this process enlivens the law, keeping it a growing, tangible evolutionary process that reflects the norms (and abnorms) of our society.

So, you might ask: What does all of this have to do with honking your horn?

Well, before I launch into that part of this month's column, let me tell you that you have the ability to receive and read every single decision written by the Appellate courts and the Supreme Court in this State. (There are three Appellate Courts – Seattle, Tacoma and Spokane) that takes all the appeals. They don't have the discretion to simply deny, "review" – no; they have to address every single case that is appealed.

You can set your computer to deliver to you every single case from the three Courts of Appeal and from the Supreme Court or just some... like the Supreme Court only. In order to do this, you go to http://www. courts.wa.gov/notifications/ and you can set it up so that you receive JUST Supreme Court opinions or JUST Court of Appeals decisions or whatever mix you choose.

Remember, the Courts of Appeals HAVE to review every case, so they are not going to have the same caliber of "sexy" cases that the Supreme Court has, but every case is an interesting story that bears reading.

So, once again, what does all of this have to do with honking your car horn?

Well, believe it or not, a woman in Monroe got charged with a crime for honking her horn at her neighbor who had complained about the chickens in the woman's yard. Her case made it all the way to out State Supreme Court...remember what I said about being able to choose your cases? You gotta love your Supreme Court judges who picked this one out of the basket.

Anyway, Helen Imelda lived on a cul-de-sac in a neighborhood that was controlled by a neighborhood owners' association. Her neighbor complained about the noisy chickens in her yard and the neighborhood association sent a letter to Helen telling her she couldn't have chickens.

Welllllll, Helen didn't cotton to that and retaliated by honking her horn in front of her neighbor's house for 5 to 10 minutes before 6:00

o'clock AM on the next Saturday morning. The neighbor called the sheriff's office and a Sergeant showed up.

Just to make sure there was no doubt about the facts, Helen drove by while the Sergeant was there at 7:00 o'clock AM and delivered three more long horn blasts. Predictably, the Sergeant was not amused and arrested Helen. She was charged, convicted and sentenced to 10 days in jail. (Author's note: TEN DAYS IN JAIL??? Is the glue used on the Dreamliner wafting around the County?)

Anyway, as this debacle ground its way through the Courts, our Supreme Court was waiting quietly in Olympia for the package to arrive at its doorstep. When it did, the Supreme Court did not disappoint. In generating three separate opinions, the Court covered the entire gamut of First Amendment thought and held that the law in Snohomish county was simply too broad to be consistent with the dictates of the First Amendment. The first Amendment???? What does honking your horn have to do with the First Amendment? Well, as Justice Debra Stephens pointed out, we honk our horns for a lot of reasons, some of which are very expressive, like..."a driver of a carpool vehicle who toots a horn to let a coworker know it is time to go, a driver who enthusiastically responds to a sign that says 'honk if you support our troops,' wedding guests who celebrate nuptials by sounding their horns, and a motorist who honks a horn in support of an individual picketing on a street corner" all legitimate expressions of our right to free speech.

Well, as we all know...when you mess with free speech in this country, you are on the heavy, smelly side of the dung ball. Anyway, notwithstanding the objections of the dissenting Justices, the decision by Justice Stephens won the day; and the Supreme Court declared that certain conduct was free speech, and when you are dealing with free speech, the rules are very strict and very powerful.

If you elect to receive all of the appellate court opinions by e-mail, you will probably end up with too much to read and too much to absorb. So pick and choose. See if anything interests you. But try it...you'll be amazed at how readable and interesting these Appellate Court opinions are.

But, the message I hope to get across this month is that there is a world of incredible, amazing judicial thought out there for the reading. It will change your view of the law forever if you stop to enjoy and savor what is in these opinions. Remember, these opinions are not the invention of some academic...this is real world stuff...unedited...unrestricted...full of the human experience.

So, thanks again for letting me come into your lives. Thanks again for all the wonderful comments I've received about this column. If you have any suggestions or comments, please feel free to send them to Lora.

Tom Brown

New Year Meanderings

● ● ●

I'M A LITTLE BEHIND THIS month, because we took a long trip in late November and early December to visit our children and grandchildren (including a brand new one!) in California and then visited my mother-in-law in Minnesota to celebrate her 95th birthday. She is a faithful reader of Seniors Sunset Times and especially my column...Hi, Betty!

Anyway, while pulling my greying hair out -- trying to come up with an entertaining idea for this month's column, I realized that the answer was right in front of me...what does everybody do in January? We make lists or "resolutions" of the things we need to do this year. Unfortunately, most of us don't think about the legal issues that are facing us each year, but we really should take stock at least once a year and make sure our legal house is in order.

So, here's my checklist for the New Year. If an item applies to you... fabulous! Otherwise, just cross it off and have another eggnog. I'm also going to make a few non-legal suggestions here that might simplify your lives.

1. Let's get that estate planning in order. If you saw your lawyer 30 years ago and had your wills done, they are probably factually and legally obsolete now, and it's time to go back to your lawyer and get things spiffed up. Some of the documents we have

discussed in this column over the last few years (It will be four years in April!!! ...eek!) are Community Property Agreements, Durable Powers of Attorney, Powers of Attorney for Health Care, Wills, Trusts, "Living Wills", etc. Some or all of these may have application to your lives and your attorney can guide you through the maze. Simple estate planning is usually surprisingly inexpensive and there are always changes in the law and changes in your life that need to be addressed. Don't put this off another year.

2. Check your insurance package. If you use an insurance agent, it's a good idea to sit down with her/him periodically and make sure that you are properly insured. There are some particularly critical areas. In your auto insurance, make sure your liability limits are high enough...the minimum of $25K is simply not enough in this day and age. (I just had a case where the people had $50K coverage and got in an accident with a bicyclist, whose hospital bills alone were over $100K...they had to pay money out of their own pocket to settle the case!!) You should have at least $100K liability coverage...or more if you have a lot to lose. (This is also true of your homeowner's policy.) Also make sure that you have substantial "Uninsured/Underinsured Motorist Coverage" Some people elect to not include this coverage with their auto insurance...Don't do it!! This coverage is critical these days with so many people wandering the highways with little or no insurance. There are other insurance issues too numerous to list here. Have a serious and critical session with your insurance agent to make sure that you have the right coverages, and then have you lawyer review it again, just in case.

3. Protect your critical documents. If you put things in a safe deposit box, remember that they are sealed off from your family members...not to mention that you will ultimately forget what's in there. Make a list of everything in the safe deposit box and give a copy to your kids, or your brother, or whomever you

trust. You can also put copies of the critical documents and the list in the "cloud" by signing up for DropBox.com (https://www.dropbox.com/) on your computer (it's free!) and your documents and information are safe from any calamity and you can retrieve them from any computer. Many lawyers provide Safety Deposit Box protection -- free of charge -- to their clients to keep wills and other important documents, so you can keep copies in a conspicuous location where your family will see them.

4. While we're mentioning computers, I'll share a couple of my secret gems that you can and should take advantage of as part of your New Year regimen. I already mentioned Drop Box, which is sensational and is free. (You can buy more space than the minimum, and store all your pictures and videos.) Another free program that I use every day is Memo tome. (http://www.memotome.com/) This is a fabulous program that reminds you of birthdays, anniversaries, appointments, meetings, when your passport expires, when your insurance is due, etc. etc. You can set it to remind you a day or a few days in advance (or a week or a month) and it will send you an e-mail AND/OR send you a text to your cell phone! It can handle daily, weekly, monthly, and periodic events. It's free! For keeping my business and family calendar, I have been using "Calendar Creator" by Broderbund (http://www.broderbund.com/) for well over 20 years. It is simply the best...I print it out every two or three weeks and write new entries all over the hard copy and then update it on the computer and print it out again...the display is awesome and the program is easy to use. This one is not free...I think it's about $30.00. For the New Year, you should double-check your computer security and maybe consider getting a backup rescue program like Carbonite. If your computer bites the dust, you'll wish you had it. (Within the last year, I had three computers go down...very annoying!)

5. Don't rely on yourself for big purchases. Within the last 6 months, I've had discussions with two older folks who each tried to buy a car on their own. It was a disaster both times. We Medicare-card-carriers are considered easy targets for some auto dealers (both new and used) and for sellers of "big-ticket" items. If you're going to buy something that costs more than $2,000.00, a warning light should go off in your head. Talk to your children or your other younger relatives or your lawyer about getting help in making this purchase. You want to avoid unplanned and unnecessary charges that somehow find their way into the deal. If you have someone with you who is asking the hard questions, it helps avoid any embarrassment or reluctance you might have to challenge the salesperson that is trying to "help" you. My son-in-law went along on our last big purchase and it made all the difference in the world on product selection, what "extras" were needed, and price.

6. Let your spouse (and children) know what happens if the worst happens. This advice isn't necessarily for us MCC's (Medicare Card Carriers) only. When someone -- regardless of age or situation -- has a disabling incident or dies unexpectedly, confusion reigns afterward. One of the best things you can do for your spouse or your survivor is to make a memo of all the stuff that's hidden away in your head. I did this for many years for my wife, and called it the "Crosswalk Document" because it was for the day when I got hit by a bus in the crosswalk. Anyway, it listed all the bank accounts, all the insurance, where the safe deposit box was and what was in it, how much money we owed (mortgage, cars, etc.), where the deed to the house was, what the arrangements were for succession at my workplace, what stuff I had at the office that was personal, what estate planning documents there were (wills, community property agreement, etc.). In 42 years of practicing law, I've had a front-row seat to the terrible uncertainty and confusion that prevails when someone dies or

becomes incapacitated unexpectedly. Make it easy on your survivors...and, if you do live another 40 years after you make the Crosswalk Document, you will have had the satisfaction of organizing your life and taken care of business!

7. Use the power of the written or electronic word. When we are dealing with the various people we encounter in life, we have to remember that they are human beings with the same frailties we have. For example, my doctor is flat out the best, smartest doc in the world and I trust him totally. But I also know he's human, and he has a zillion patients. Do him a favor...put it in writing! Put what in writing? How? Well, if you had an odd reaction to that drug... send a note or e-mail. It will end up in the chart. Bring a list of issues or problems to your next appointment and a copy for the doctor...it will end up in your chart. A phone call to the receptionist might not. If the information is in the chart, the chances are much greater that the Doc will make the correct call. If that tooth hurts in a certain situation, bring your dentist a note for your chart. If you call your lawyer and tell him that he misspelled your name or the last page was left off the will, follow up with e-mail or a note. We lawyers take as many as 50 calls every day, and we simply forget some or fail to make a note of some. If it's important enough for a phone call...it's important enough to confirm in writing. I can't tell you how crucial this is when real-life disputes get into the hands of the lawyers. If you wrote down every contact with your lousy contractor, it's like a bonanza for your lawyer later.

So...that's all the advice I have right now for 2012. I hope you have a wonderful and well-organized year; and I hope you keep reading Seniors Sunset Times. Once again, thank you for all the wonderful comments and suggestions I've received.

Tom Brown

Let's get rid of the bad lawyers!

• • •

Happy New Year!!! We made it to 2012...can you believe it? I was born in 1946, and I'm pretty sure that I'm now in my late 30's or early 40's. (I can hear my children chuckling at this self-delusion.) Anyway, I feel young...and that's the most important thing!

Those of you that have been reading this little column for the last four years know that I am pretty upbeat about things, including aging and including the law. I love the law and I think it does a pretty good job of keeping us grounded in common sense and goodwill...it has its problems, but it's better than the alternative.

Anyway, this month I want to talk about the darker side of lawyers and lawyering. I don't necessarily like the subject, but I think we all need to know about what happens when lawyers go bad or when they simply fall off the turnip truck. You also need to know what to do when your lawyer is no longer serving you, but is serving himself or herself.

First of all, the good news. We lawyers get it pounded into our thick skulls, over and over again, that the client comes first. We are never far from the mantra that we have to be totally honest with our clients. That we have to tell our clients everything -- good or bad -- about their case. That we have to confess to our clients when we screw up. That we owe a sleighful of duties to our clients that we are obligated to keep. And so forth. And so forth. From the first day in law school, in every seminar we attend, in every article in our monthly journal, from the mouths of every Judge...we hear it and learn it over and over: the client comes first.

Most of the lawyers I know understand this truth and live by the message. When things go to you-know-where-in-a-hand basket, when we make a terrible mistake, when we forget a deadline...we can't cover it up or lie about it or conveniently forget it. No, we owe a duty to our client to let them know every significant fact about their case and every problem we've encountered. It's hard...but it's what we signed up for. If we are going to hold peoples' business or fate in our hands, we have to keep those hands above the table.

Now comes the tricky part. What about the lawyers who don't come clean about their mistakes? What about the lawyers who are just plain dishonest and steal from their clients? What about the lawyers who become raving alcoholics or abuse drugs to the extent that it hurts the business of their clients? What about the lawyers who lie to judges? Sadly, it happens. Not very often...but it happens.

Happily for the citizens of the State of Washington, we have the Washington State Bar Association, which has many duties...but one of its most important is to monitor and enforce the rules of conduct that have been set up for lawyers. Some people would scoff at this concept, making a joke about the wolves guarding the henhouse. Hah! Nothing could be further from the truth, particularly in our State. Our Bar Association, which is overseen by the Washington Supreme Court, is one of the toughest, most aggressive, most professional discipline organizations in the United States.

First of all, Joe or Mary Citizen can go to the WSBA website and see what's going on. You can read the rules of conduct. You can read the decisions in other cases. You can get step-by-step instructions on how to register a complaint against your lawyer. You can call them and shoot the breeze about how the system works. In the area of discipline, the WSBA definitely does not see itself as an organization whose job it is to protect the lawyers. On the contrary, they are dedicated to making sure that justice is done and the public is protected...even if it costs a lawyer his or her career. They work for you.

Even more importantly, the whole process is overseen by the Washington State Supreme Court, which reviews (or can review...depending on the situation) every case of lawyer misconduct. Believe me, those nine people -- who face the voters ever few years -- have no qualms about using the sword of justice.

Many times, when a lawyer jumps the tracks, it can be traced back to a terrible life event that changed everything. The Washington State Bar Association and the system it serves recognize that the quality of mercy is not strained. The people who run the system and the Supreme Court do everything they can to save careers, while protecting the injured clients. The ultimate ruling often includes counseling, treatment, and ongoing supervision.

From the point of view of the lawyers, the disciplinary process of the WSBA is certainly not a joke or a simple irritant. Lawyers respect the power and efficacy of the system that oversees them. Who am I kidding? Those people scare us to death!!! Hopefully, we lawyers toe the line because we are ethical, honest lawyers...on the other hand, it doesn't hurt that there is a tough, aggressive agency making sure we follow the rules.

If you're interested in how this system works, take a virtual trip to the Washington State Bar Association discipline section at http://www.wsba.org/Licensing-and-Lawyer-Conduct/Discipline Take some time to look around. Look at some of the decisions. See how careful, but how aggressive the Bar Association is. Put in the name of your favorite lawyer and see if they've ever had a discipline problem. You can even make sure that your favorite lawyer has license to practice law! (If I'm not there, call me fast!)

You will see that the Bar Association and the Supreme Court sometimes take away the lawyers license...sometimes they put him/her on probation under very strict supervision...sometimes they simply warn him/her...sometimes they find out that the client was crazy and the lawyer did everything he/she could, but it didn't satisfy the complainant. It's really just a microcosm of how human beings act...surprise!!! Anyway... the important thing is that it's a credible, responsive system that protects you from unscrupulous or runaway lawyers.

Here's what I'd like to leave you with this month: You are the clients of the Washington State Bar Association because you are citizens of the State of Washington. Most of my brother/sister lawyers are hard-working, conscientious professionals who want to do the right thing. If you have the unfortunate circumstance to run into a lawyer that doesn't hew to that creed, be comforted that you can go to the WSBA for help. But... first...call up your lawyer and say: "What the hell is going on?" Maybe you can work it out...who knows?

As always, I thank you for reading my little column and for reading this fantastic monthly...the Seniors Sunset Times. Thanks for all the wonderful comments about this column and I hope to see you next month!

Tom Brown

A fresh look at government money

● ● ●

WE LAWYERS SOMETIMES HAVE THE privilege of enjoying an "inside" look at the system. We are lucky enough to learn from our clients about little "ins and outs" of society and government that the rest of us may not always be exposed to. It's not always pretty...but it's always interesting.

This month, I felt possessed by the conflict between "public" and "private" money in our state and country, particularly in these desperate times when money is really, really tight.

This came to my mind as a possible topic for the "de minimis" column during a lunch discussion with my wife this week. She was telling me about some of the people she had heard about second-hand that were enjoying the government largesse of the "Employment Security" system...OK, OK, I know. Its real name is simply "Unemployment." Anyway, she was ranting and raving because she believed that the system was funded from the general tax base of our states and federal government and is abused by a lot of people at the expense of the taxpayers.

I don't think any of us would disagree that there are abuses of this system, just like there are abuses of a lot of our systems. But, along with the abuses, are the thousands and thousands of cases that are consistent with the original idea...to protect people whose jobs disappear because of the economy. So...what's the truth?

The truth, as we business owners know so well, is that this "Unemployment" system (like others I'll talk about later in this column) are funded (at least in part) by very specific taxes on the employers!! It's not the government alone that is handing out this mountain of benefits...it's the employers in partnership with the government. That's why it's called "unemployment insurance"...the employers are creating an insurance pool, run by the state, that is funded by a tax on those employers for the privilege of doing business in the state. We employers all pay "premiums" each month to create a pool of money to provide unemployment checks to people who lost their jobs because of the economy. A noble purpose, right?

Yes, but there are problems. Let's face it; a lot of people abuse this system. They aren't fired because of economic conditions, they're fired because they are not making it as quality employees and the employer is willing to take the hit on the premiums, just to get rid of them. "Take the hit?" what do you mean?...we already paid the premiums! Not so fast, employment-man! If you have an employee who gets unemployment benefits, your premiums go way up!! It's just like insurance, you get in an accident, and your premiums rise, right? A lot of employers are surprised --even shocked -- to find out that when they let that marginal employee go, their unemployment premiums shot up. Surprise!

Anyway, the point I want to make this month is that there are a lot of government programs where our lawmakers have done a pretty darn good job of trying to keep the public money out of the "game" and keep it funded by the people who benefit from the system.

Perhaps the most obvious and well-known agency in Washington that does not depend on the general taxation system is the Department of Labor and Industries. In theory, that system is funded by the contributions of the employers. Maybe it's true that we taxpayers don't fund that monster system, but I'm not totally convinced. I was surprised to learn, in the course of representing, a couple of clients, that there is a separate judicial agency to hear all of the L & I appeals. This agency (The Board of Industrial Insurance Appeals) has approximately 70 judges, making anywhere from $75K to $105K per year, just to hear the appeals from what the Department does wrong. (By comparison, the Courts of Appeals -- that hear all appeals in the state -- criminal, civil, divorces, accidents, guardianships, etc., etc., has only 22 judges!) It makes you wonder.

Anyway, our government has been attentive to the problems that our economy presents, and our lawmakers are pretty inventive in responding to those problems.

A good example in in the "tort" system, where people sue each other for car accidents, slips and falls, medical malpractice, and all manner of things. When people recover money from the responsible party, it usually includes the medical bills and lost wages and other "out of pocket" expenses that these injured people had. The catch was that somebody (an insurance company, Medicare, Medicaid, Labor & industries, etc.) had paid that money and ought to get it back, when the injured person got paid for his or her injuries. Of course, the insurance companies had this figured out for years, but the government was a little slower to arrive at the dance. Now, there are elaborate rules and regulations about making sure that Medicare and Medicaid and the State and L&I (and whoever) get paid back out of the settlement money. It's a constant battle, because the lawyers want to keep more for their clients, and the government wants its money back. The result: CHAOS!

What does all of this mean to us, the regular Joes and Marys on the street? Here's the message: If you receive a government benefit, our legislators have made it so that the government will try to get that benefit back from you, or your employer, or your insurance company, or from the proceeds of your lawsuit. Money is so tight these days that legislators are constantly exploring every possible way to return these precious dollars to the government coffers. So don't be surprised, after you are done celebrating your victory in scoring government dollars, that a government employee (whose salary you are paying) shows up to suggest that the money you scored was really the government's money and you should send it back.

So...is all of this good or bad or indifferent? And what does it have to do with the law? Well, we lawyers are the ones that will be working these complicated issues out for you...our clients.

The judgment as to whether it's good or bad for society is a political one that only time can resolve for us.

Meanwhile, we lawyers will keep plugging along for you, trying to maximize the benefits you hired us to protect.

As always, thanks for reading my little column. I feel like this month's column was a little too heavy, but I was motivated by a lot of recent events. I very much appreciate the nice comments you have made about this column, and I hope to continue to entertain you, provoke you and make the law seem more accessible to you.

Tom Brown

No courts. No justice. No freedom.

• • •

THAT CATCHY LITTLE PHRASE - **NO COURTS NO JUSTICE NO FREEDOM** - is the official theme of Law Day 2012.

Probably, when you are reading this, it will be early or mid April, so you'll have a good start on Law Day, which is celebrated on May 1 of each year.

It was back in 1958 that then-President Dwight D. Eisenhower first proclaimed May 1st to be Law Day.

But long before that, the first day of May had always been known as May Day and celebrated as a time to remember workers who suffered or died in their fight for decent wages and safe working conditions. Particularly in other countries, the first day of May was observed as International Workers Day or Labor Day. To a lot of people this had communist or socialist overtones that were perceived as being inconsistent with American values.

The actual idea came from a lawyer (surprise!). Charles Rhyne was President Eisenhower's legal counsel and he was also serving as the President of the American Bar Association. He encouraged president Eisenhower to declare a special holiday devoted to celebrating the rule of law in our country. So the President declared May 1 as

Law Day and Congress -- three years later-- passed a law that made the observance permanent.

Although it is very important that our country formally recognizes and celebrates the rule of law over rule by force, the existence of Law Day is pretty low-key and is not really honored with enough gusto to satisfy a lot of us...including me.   I submit that Law Day should be a National holiday, with the same kind of weight and pomp as President's Day or MLK's Birthday or Veteran's Day, to underscore our belief in the rule of law. (Write a letter to your Senator!) ...and how about another day off?

Anyway, this year the theme of Law Day is "No Courts, No Justice, No Freedom" to remind us that open and accessible courts are the cornerstone of a free society.

This isn't a new or radical idea. The framers of the Constitution recognized the importance of the rule of law when they made the Judiciary one of the three co-equal branches of our government. Also remember that Justice is blind (most of the statues of Lady Justice depict her as blindfolded, holding the scales of justice. The blindfold represents objectivity, in that justice is or should be meted out objectively, without fear or favor, regardless of identity, money, power, or weakness; blind justice and impartiality are two of the strongest symbols of our Justice system.)

Read the opening lines of our U.S. Constitution to see what place Justice has in forming a more perfect union...it's the very first component!!!!

Now, our Lady Justice and we face a crisis. Recent budget cuts at all levels have seriously compromised the ability of the courts to function effectively and keep the wheels of justice turning. That's why Law Day this year has a theme to remind of a simple basic truth: **NO COURTS NO JUSTICE NO FREEDOM**

No matter who you are, or what you do, or how much money you have...you depend every day on the Courts of our land to stand guard over your rights.

Last year, the American Bar Association recognized the fact that cutbacks in Court funding were forcing courts -- at every level -- to freeze hiring, to make critical staff layoff, to increase fees to the public, and even -- in some instances -- to close! Criminal cases, Civil cases, Will Probates,

Divorces, Injury Claims, Important patent disputes, contract disputes, small claims hearings, child custody matters, child protection matters, juvenile justice proceedings...all of these and many more are impaired or frozen. Perhaps the scariest point is that society's most disadvantaged people: the poor, the disabled, the homeless, the victims, the jobless now have no place to turn.

The American Bar Association Report had these chilling words for us:

Given their historic role as the protectors of the least advantaged in our nation, the courts have rightly been called, "Society's Emergency Room." And never is that title so warranted as in times of economic distress. The same recession that has led legislatures to reduce access to our justice system has obviously increased the number of people who need it.

Strong, effective and independent justice systems are a core element of our democracy. Even the most eloquent constitution is worthless with no one to enforce it.

So, what should we do?

I've always believed that, as citizens, our first responsibility is to our closest, most immediate corridors of government. When we decide to "get involved" we doesn't necessarily look to Washington, D.C. or to our State Capitol first. Rather, we need to look around us...at our cities, counties, PUD districts, Port districts, school boards, etc. In other words, places where our statements and positions can have a real impact.

In the case of our Courts, we just suffered through a dramatic example of what reduced funding can do to one of our most cherished institutions. In Grays Harbor County, the Judges have been begging, arguing, pleading, cajoling, threatening, and politicking with the County Commissioners to get necessary funding to run the Courts and to install even minimal security to protect the Courts from harm from outside. (Grays Harbor County has the least secure Courthouse in the state...no security personnel, no metal detectors, no minimal package searches, etc.) Those efforts fell on such deaf ears that the Courts **were forced to sue** the County Commissioners to require them to fulfill their responsibilities. While the suit was pending, and while the County Commissioners were posturing and foot-shuffling, a troubled and dangerous man strolled into the Courthouse...the home of our county's justice system...and assaulted a Judge and shot a law enforcement officer and escaped after firing shots.

Residents of Counties in Washington State can impact the functions of government. It's relatively easy to figure out who your County Commissioners are, what their addresses and/or e-mails are, when they meet, and how to get on their agenda. *Your* agenda, as a citizen, should include a category that tells your County Commissioners that you want your Judges and Courthouses to be safe, so that the business of justice and law can be conducted without threat or interruption.

On the State level, your legislators in Olympia will also listen to you. Tell them how important the protection of Justice is to you and your families. Tell them how important it is that each and every citizen of this great country -- no matter how poor or downtrodden -- ought to be able to access our Courts to protect their rights, their homes, their children, their lives.

Sometimes we smile or wince at the outspoken people who make a pest of themselves to our lawmakers and our Courts. Sure, some of those people are crackpots...but most of them are good, law-abiding, tax-paying citizens who believe strongly that our country can do better. Speak up. Get involved. Make our world better.

How to begin? Maybe Law Day this year is your starting point. The American Bar Association has put together a beautiful website, devoted to Law Day 2012. The website is full of information, motivation, talking points, events you can organize, how to reach out to the community, planning for a winning Law Day, Web Resources, a Catalog of resources, and even stuff you can buy to promote Law Day.

That website is at www.lawday.org

If this is too organized or complicated for you, consider just plain getting involved as a citizen. You can start with a simple, no-brainer issue, like protecting and funding your courts. Find out how to get heard before your County Commissioners at their next meeting...just call them and ask...they work for you...they have to respond...they have to listen to you.

Follow your State Legislature. They are messing around with cutting education and cutting the Courts and cutting programs that help people get access to the Courts...what's more basic and important than that? It's time for you to be heard about things you believe in!!! Don't let another day go by where you just grumble about how crappy government is. It's only going to get better if people like you get REALLY involved.

Remember.........NO COURTS NO JUSTICE NO FREEDOM. It's true!

As always, I really appreciate you folks who read my column and let me know how you feel. I really appreciate the nice comments and suggestions I get! This month's column marks four years of monthly columns. I thank you and I thank Lora...the brilliant and gifted soul of this publication...for the opportunity to say what I think.

Tom Brown

What in the world is a grand jury?

• • •

ONE OF MY FAITHFUL READERS got in touch with me and wanted to know what in the world a "Grand Jury" was...what it did, what was it for, and why do Grand Juries even exist? (The beauty of a small newspaper is that your readers have direct input into the content, so we writers get to be responsive to what you want...I love it!) Anyway, what a great bunch of questions. We hear about Grand Juries all the time on television, but nobody tells us what they are or why they exist. Most of us (even we lawyers) have never come into contact with a living, breathing Grand Jury, so we don't even know what it's for or how it works. So...these are excellent questions.

What does a Grand Jury do? What's it for? Do we even use them? OK, let's start with the basics. There are two kinds of juries: Grand Juries and Petit Juries. We talked a lot about petit juries in an earlier column. "Petit" means "little" or "small." A Petit jury is the kind we know the most about. It's the 6 or 12 person jury that sits in judgment in criminal and civil cases and decides what the truth is. If you've ever been called for jury duty and selected, you sat on a Petit Jury. Even though the name suggests otherwise, the Petit Jury is a thousand times more important than a Grand Jury. Petit juries are the workhorses of the judicial system. They sit in civil and criminal cases in thousands of courthouses around the country every day. They decide. In contrast, a Grand Jury doesn't really decide anything...rather it investigates and recommends, usually about whether a crime has been committed and whether there is enough evidence to convict somebody. In this context, the word "Grand" doesn't refer to anything spectacular that the Grand Jury is doing...it is only a reference to its size. A Grand Jury usually has many more jurors than a Petit (small) Jury. The job of the Grand Jury has always been the same: to determine whether a crime was probably committed and to issue a finding (sometimes called an "indictment" or "true bill" or something else, depending on the jurisdiction) that the prosecutor should go ahead and charge the person (s) with a crime and proceed to trial. In the early days of the United States, Grand Juries were all over the place, issuing indictments of all sorts of mischief...crimes, misconduct of public officials, corrupt government, etc., etc. As the roles of public prosecutors (or "district attorneys" or "prosecuting attorneys" or "county attorneys") expanded, the decision-making shifted from the Grand Juries to elected or appointed prosecutors. Every single State in the United States has a provision for Grand Juries; only 22 states require their use and only about half the states ever use them. By contrast, the Constitution of the United States requires the use of a Grand Jury to charge someone with a Federal crime, so a Federal Grand Jury is almost constantly in session in every Federal District in every state. A Grand Jury does not decide what it will investigate. In practice, it only hears cases brought to it by the Prosecutor and only hears evidence that the Prosecutor produces.

So, as a practical matter, the only Grand Juries that affect the smaller counties of Washington's Olympic Peninsula and Coast are Federal Grand Juries investigating Federal crimes, usually drug related, but sometimes dealing with violation of Federal criminal statutes relating to ecological issues or species protection. In contrast, most of the "local" crimes are investigated by local law enforcement agencies, which turn their investigations over to County Prosecuting Attorneys, who then make the decision who to charge and what to charge them with -- without convening a Grand Jury. An interesting side note here is the Trayvon Martin case in Florida.

Lots of people were screaming for a Grand Jury investigation, but the local prosecutors put their heads together and made the decision to charge Mr. Zimmerman without the formality of a Grand Jury investigation or indictment. However, the Prosecutor had to present to the Court an affidavit setting forth the basis for the charge and why the specific charge was being brought. This is very similar to what would happen in a Washington county...the decision to charge with a crime would be made by an elected prosecutor, not a Grand Jury. (BUT REMEMBER...EVERY PERSON CHARGED WITH A CRIME HAS THE ABSOLUTE RIGHT TO HAVE A PETIT JURY HEAR ALL THE FACTS AT A TRIAL, AND DECIDE IF THE PERSON IS GUILTY OR NOT.)

Many people who understand the system scoff at the Grand Jury system, because it is so controlled by the Prosecutors. There's an old saying that a Prosecutor could get a Grand Jury to indict "a ham sandwich" – meaning that a Prosecutor is so in control of the Grand Jury Process, that getting an indictment (or "true bill" or "charge") is ridiculously easy. The need to protect the citizenry from unchecked prosecutors is probably served by the electoral process...prosecuting attorneys in most states have to run for office and face the electorate every few years. Here's an interesting sidelight: Under Washington law, a County coroner has the right (and duty, I guess) to convene a Coroner's inquest, with jurors drawn from the county, to look into suspicious deaths and then to issue arrest warrants. This happened recently in Lewis County, when a female State Trooper died under somewhat suspicious circumstances. When there was no criminal prosecution, the County Coroner acted on his own and invoked this procedure, and the inquest jury found that the Trooper's death was a homicide. Many people, including some journalists that should have known better, referred to this proceeding as a "Grand Jury." It was not a Grand Jury, but it had some of the same features. It's my understanding that the Prosecuting Attorney in Lewis County is still trying to figure out what to do with a Coroner's Inquest finding that there was a criminal homicide...it should be interesting! In the Federal system, and in most state systems, Grand Jury proceedings are secret, and the panel works behind closed doors. No judge is present. A prosecutor pretty much controls the proceedings.

When witnesses testify, prosecutors typically control the questioning, although grand jurors can -- and sometimes do -- ask questions of their own. Although they appear alone, witnesses can ask for permission to leave the grand jury room and consult with their lawyers. A witness who asserts a Fifth Amendment right against self-incrimination and refuses to answer can be taken before a judge of the court, who can grant the witness immunity from prosecution. Those who still refuse to answer -- even with immunity -- can be jailed for contempt. So, in summary, unlike trial (or petit) juries, Grand Juries don't decide if someone is guilty of criminal charges that have been brought against them. Grand Juries listen to evidence and decide if someone SHOULD BE CHARGED with a crime. A famous example of what can happen in a Grand Jury "system" is the O.J. Simpson case. In that wild case, the prosecutors were going to ask a grand jury to charge Simpson with murdering Nicole Brown Simpson and Ronald Goldman; but the defense attorneys persuaded the Court that the grand jurors (that is, the people who lived in that County) had heard too much about the case to be able to make an impartial decision. They did this by filing a motion saying the grand jurors were too prejudiced by what they had seen on television and read in the papers to be able to review the evidence against Mr. Simpson impartially. The judge agreed with the defense attorneys, which is very unusual. Normally, defense attorneys fail when they try to claim that a grand jury is biased. Courts reject these claims on the theory that all the grand jury does is bring charges, so even if a grand jury is biased; the person they charge can still prove their innocence at trial. But the judge bought the defense's argument in the case of O.J. Simpson (perhaps because of the extraordinary publicity surrounding Mr. Simpson) and, instead of trying to start all over with a new grand jury; the prosecutors used another method to charge Simpson with the murders. Then, as we all know, the trial jury -- the "petit jury" -- heard all the evidence and decided Mr. Simpson was innocent. In my County -- Grays Harbor -- there has not been a Grand Jury convened in well over 40 years. Like most of America (except the Federal System) and like most of Washington State, we rely completely on the professionalism and expertise of the elected Prosecuting Attorney to make the charging decisions arising out of a criminal investigation. In turn, that Prosecutor relies on the competence and aggressiveness of multiple law enforcement agencies to supply the Prosecutor with evidence to support the charging decision. Well, I hope this is clearer than mud. The chances are that you will never encounter or be involved in a Grand Jury proceeding. But -- WOW! -- would it ever be interesting!

As always, I thank you for reading my little column and I thank Lora for the opportunity to be in this great little newspaper. SST is growing every issue...and just seems to be getting better and better. Thanks to all of you for the wonderful comments and suggestions!

Tom Brown

I've got a will...so what's a testament?

• • •

My Great-Great-Grandfather is buried in a little Church cemetery in western New York State. I've never visited his gravesite, but I have pictures of it. There's not much information on his tombstone...mainly his date of birth and his date of death. But he did tell us on his gravestone where he came from -- a little area called Thomond Gate in County Clare, Ireland, just across the River Shannon from St. Johns Castle in Limerick. Without that brief testament on John Brown's grave about his birthplace, my uncle (the family historian) might never have been able to trace the family history.

The word "testament" is bandied about in our language to mean many things. It's very closely allied with testimony...like the giving of the truth in Court. It's also about history...as in the New and Old Testaments. But, oddly enough, it almost always shows up on the front page of a person's will...as in your "LAST WILL AND TESTAMENT" (drum roll). What in the world does your last will have to do with the concept of your last "testament"?...and what is your last testament?

Well, my great-great-grandfather's testament was a permanent shout to the world that said: "This is where I came from and this is how long I lived." Really, when you think about it, that's a pretty important slice of life, and John managed to make sure it lasted for a long, long time

(140 years, so far!). And, glory be, it turned out to be important, so we could trace the family genealogy. His last testament came on a gravestone rather than in a will.

As a lawyer, I've been writing wills for people for almost 42 years. The process is wonderful...you get to explore peoples' lives with them and learn what they want to leave behind, when they go to the big nursing home/party in the sky. Although I love the process, the ultimate product is pretty boring and unimaginative. Wills tend to follow a recipe, because lawyers love safety and they want to be sure that the will is safe...meaning: it will work. It won't get thrown out by a judge or successfully challenged by a secret mistress or a forgotten child or a disgruntled heir. We lawyers like our wills to be safe. Unfortunately, that usually means that they are boring and unimaginative. We follow tried and true tracks and everybody's happy, right?

Well, all of my will-writing habits were shattered recently by one of my clients. I had done this person's will earlier, to straighten out some unfortunate stuff that had been imposed on the family by lawyers who were less interested in simplicity than in fees. I thought we had the situation nicely in hand, with a simple, easy to understand will that had eliminated all the previous garbage. Things were fine. But then my client came back to me and told me that he wanted to change his will again because he had changed his mind about the distribution of his assets.

This was a little unusual, but not alarming, particularly since he was definitely in the final quarter of his life. He wanted to take charge of the arrangements and I totally respect that in a person. So, I thought we would sit down in my office and put the standard language into the standard paragraphs and come up with a standard will.

Boy, was I wrong!

My client sat down and said: I have some things I want to say in my will. I said "Sure"...we can talk about specific language. He said: "No, I want to read it to you." ...and he did. It was beautiful. He expressed his love for the individual members of his family. He explained why he left certain things to certain people. He mapped out the simple ceremony he wanted instead of a funeral. He specifically described the beautiful and heart-wrenching disposition of his ashes. He asked his children and grandchildren to remember his beloved wife. He discussed his favorite charities and beneficiaries and made sure that they received something from his largesse. And, most important, he left a TESTAMENT for his family that will probably live on for many years. His descendants will be reading and cherishing that will for generations and his TESTAMENT will have survived.

So, I put the will together, preserving as much of his language as I could legally get away with (that's most of it...you can say whatever you want in a will!!). The final product was a joy. I told him that he had re-energized me with regard to the writing of wills and that I was going to change my *modus operandi* and make wills more of a "testament" and make them a family document that will live for generations in a family, reaching out to future genealogists and historians.

I told him that I was going to offer every future client of mine the opportunity and option to make their will also a true "testament" with family history, special intentions, special instructions, words of love, memories, instructions, and history.

Of course, none of this is a news flash. People have been writing imaginative wills for centuries.

Janis Joplin -- a rock and blues singer, ("Me and Bobby McGee.") in-famous for her heavy drinking and drug use, purportedly made changes to her will just two days before her death, setting aside $2,500 to pay for a posthumous all-night party for 200 guests at her favorite pub in San Anselmo, California, "so my friends can get blasted after I'm gone." [Actually, some 25 or 30 years ago, one of my clients persuaded me to provide in his will that the executor throw a "big (expletive omitted... although it wasn't omitted in the will) party" to celebrate his life.]

When S. Sanborn died in 1871, he left his body to science. The will stipulated that two drums were to be made out of Sanborn's skin and given to a friend on the condition that every June 17 at dawn he would pound out the tune "Yankee Doodle" at Bunker Hill to commemorate the anniversary of the famous Revolutionary War battle.

The last wish of Charles Dickens was that people "who attend my funeral wear no scarf, cloak, black bow, long hatband, or other such revolting absurdity."

Jack Benny provided that his wife, Mary Livingstone, would receive a rose everyday for the rest of her life...she lived for nine years after he died...that's over three thousand roses.

Anyway...you get the point. A will can be a dry and lawyer-like legal document...or it can be your "TESTAMENT" -- a statement of your wishes, of your observations, of the things you want to say to the world, of whatever is on your mind. You can even recite your family history! List all of your relatives and heirs. Work with your lawyer, he or she knows best about what will screw up a will and make it useless. Even if you are withholding or re-directing assets, you want your will to survive scrutiny and be accepted as a legitimate will.

And...don't forget your tombstone. Why not leave a message to the world?

As always, I want to thank you for the nice comments and observations about this little column every month. If there are issues you think should be discussed here, or if you have a great idea for a "...de minimis..." column, just let us know.

Tom Brown

When is a law not really a law?

● ● ●

As I WAS STRUGGLING TO come up with a thoughtful and entertaining topic for this month's column, my wife was on a different page. She was wondering out loud why laws that have been passed by the legislature and signed by the governor are still "up in the air" and subject to all kinds of chess moves by various groups.

Isn't it final when the Governor signs a law passed by the Legislature?

Hah! Not even close, my friends!

Your most recent memories of this phenomenon would be with the so-called "Gay Marriage" bill and the liquor initiative.

The Legislature debated and politicked and voted, approving the concept of gay marriage, and the Governor took all kinds of flak (even from her own religion) and finally decided to sign the bill into law.

In the liquor department, the people rose up and adopted their own law (...to hell with the legislature!!!) approving the privatization of liquor distribution and sale.

In both cases, after millions of dollars were spent, and after thousands of hours of politicking were expended, you'd think the game was over, right? Hah! ...we know better, don't we?

Our forefathers were a suspicious lot. They had watched the British legal system work its "magic" for many years. The legislature would ignore the true needs of the people or would pass laws that served special interests and hurt the interests of the people on the street.

So the architects of the American system of laws and justice decided that the people would have a way to say "No!" to a bad law, or say "Yes!" to a law that needed to be passed.

In addition, our justice system recognized – early in the game – that if a law was in violation of our beloved Constitution, it could not be allowed to continue unchallenged.

Let's talk about these one at a time.

JUDICIAL REVIEW
In 1800, the Supreme Court of the United States faced a real nasty problem in our young country.

A law had been passed that was in conflict with the rights of our citizens. The question was whether the Congress could fiddle around with the laws and do whatever they wanted, even in violation of the newly minted Constitution of the United States. This spawned a heated discussion of the doctrine of "judicial review"…in other words, whether a Court has the power to say that the act of the legislative branch of the government is illegal or unconstitutional and – therefore – has no right to exist.

WOW! What a concept …the Judicial Branch of government at war with the legislative branch!

Who wins? Well, in the case of *Marbury v Madison,* and in the case of every similar concept since then, we have accepted (sometimes grudgingly!) that our Courts have the right – and duty – to examine laws passed by the Congress (or legislature, or city council, or County commission} and determine whether they are in accordance with our Constitution. If they are not...then the Courts may and will strike them down. So, if our State Legislature passes a law that says – for example -- that citizens of Hispanic or Irish origin don't have the right to vote – that law will be struck down by the Courts, even if the legislators and the public thought it was a great idea. (Most situations aren't that clear, of course!)

So, to bring us back to the present, every single law passed by our Legislature (or by our National Congress or by our city council) is subject to scrutiny by the Courts to make sure that the law is not in violation of our state or federal constitution. This scrutiny doesn't happen automatically...no, somebody must file a lawsuit asking the Courts to strike down the law. The bar is a very high one...Courts don't like to take on the legislature or Congress and don't like to second-guess the will of the people. But, when the Constitution of the Unites States is under attack by a certain law, the Courts will not hesitate to say "NO!"

Initiatives

What if our legislature just plain won't do something that the voters want? We can write letters to our legislators, we can lobby like crazy, we can write letters to the editors...still no results. Well, in most states, the citizens can say: "OK, Legislature... If you won't do it, we'll gather signatures of voters and put it on the ballot ourselves!"

Yes, our forefathers recognized that the legislature cannot always be the guardian of what is wanted or needed by our citizens, so they gave the citizens the right to ORIGINATE laws and place them before the voters. This is the concept of "initiative" – which is very robust and topical in the State of Washington.

In recent history, the activist Tim Eyman has been one of the most visible users of this political tool, but the real story lately has been the battle to privatize the distribution and sale of liquor in the State of Washington. As we all recall, there were millions and millions of dollars poured (get it?..."poured") into taking this responsibility away from the State and putting it in the hands of private business. But my wife asked the legitimate question: If it was such a fancy-schmancy political coup, why did it end up in the courts...and then before the Supreme Court? Well, that's a good question...does everything have to be reviewed by the Courts? Answer: No.

The forces that wanted to keep the liquor business in the hands of the State, scoured the liquor initiative and found two things that they said made it invalid:

1. The language of the initiative that the voters approved created new taxes;
2. Initiatives can only have one subject at a time.

The Supreme Court accepted the case on an expedited basis and ruled against the challengers, leaving the Initiative totally intact; and – as you all know – it took effect as scheduled. (So...here's to the State Supreme Court!)

When you think about it, we should feel comforted by the process here...the initiative was written by professionals...we had the chance to argue and dissect the issues during the election process...and the Supreme Court took a close and scholarly look...what more could we ask for?

REFERENDUM

Perhaps the most interesting issue, from the point of view of the political fanatic, is the situation with the so-called "Gay Marriage" Act, which was passed by the Washington State Legislature and signed by the Governor.

Where do the opponents of this law go? To the courts? To the people? Which of the political tools do they choose?

Well, they chose the route of Referendum...the power that our forefathers gave to the people to review and challenge laws passed by the legislature.

The enemies of this law have now collected 240,000 signatures (they only needed 120,577 signatures) and that means the law will be on the ballot for the voters to decide. Once that occurs, the losing side will examine everything that has happened with a microscope to see if there are any loopholes or mistakes, and take it to the courts for review.

That would **not** be the Courts deciding the issue on the merits. The Courts would not decide if gay marriage is good or bad or indifferent... they would decide if all of the maneuvering was done according to law and done precisely as the laws dictate.

So, at the conclusion of that round of political wheeling and dealing, what will we have?

Well, I almost hate to bring it up...but if the law is upheld, someone is going to challenge it in the Courts as unconstitutional.

That's judicial review...right back where we started! EEK!

The moral here is that we do have a complicated, intricate system for creating our laws.

Fortunately, thanks to the wisdom and forethought of our founding fathers, there are safety valves and quality controls that prevent the system from impairing our rights as citizens and/or our rights as human beings.

We trust our institutions...our legislatures, our city councils, our county commissions, our lower courts, our appellate Courts, our elected officials. But we know that they are not perfect.

Sometimes politics creeps in. Sometimes, rigid beliefs interfere with our common sense.

Sometimes public outrage turns our heads. Sometimes, we are reminded that our institutions are created and peopled by human beings and we need to turn to the safeguards that reside in our systems to keep us free and keep us human.

As always...thank you for reading my little column. I welcome and enjoy your comments and suggestions. I hope I've added a little something to your understanding of the law.

Tom Brown

Should lawyers advertise?

• • •

WHEN I WAS A YOUNG lawyer...a year or two ago...lawyers did not advertise.

We were told that it was not in line with our image as defenders and advocates, and that it was cheap, and tawdry and just plain grotesque. But the most important thing that kept us from advertising was the power of the state bar associations and the American Bar Association and all the other bar associations that it was simply prohibited. That was it. If you advertised, you would be subject to discipline...you could be censured, you could be punished, ...in theory, you could lose your license.

What happened? Why the big change? Well, basically, America happened. The good old American system kicked in like it always does and said "Hey, this is America...if people want to advertise then – by God – they can advertise. This is America. Land of the brave, home of the free.

Believe it or not, lawyers started suing their own Bar Associations, pointing out that this is America, where people are free to say and do what they want (within limitation, of course). Slowly but surely, the advertisements of lawyers started to creep onto the yellow pages of your local telephone book, and then onto the sides of buses, then onto the backs of your church bulletins, then onto television...well, you know the rest.

Now, lawyer advertising is part of the landscape. Our yellow pages are packed with all kinds of ads, both gross and dignified. Television ads try to lure in victims of drugs or asbestos. Lawyers sponsor athletic teams, fight for space on church bulletins, show their smiling faces on bus stop benches, sponsor golf holes, do mailings to targeted audiences, etc., etc. And it's not just for criminal cases and car crashes.

You can find lawyers advertising to handle estates and wills, to help you with the patent for your sure-fire method for walking on water, to get you a divorce from that terrible spouse, etc., etc. Advertising now crosses all boundaries for lawyers. It's in newspapers, phone books, on television, on the radio, etc. etc.

So, let's talk turkey...is it a good or bad thing? Well, like all controversial issues, you can find a lot of competing ideas and thoughts. Basically, from my perspective as an "old-timer" that has been around as a lawyer both in the days when advertising was forbidden and now when anything goes, it's a good thing.

I'm a strong believer in the concept that openness is good. I think people should be exposed to all the various levels and types of advertising, to help them judge what is acceptable and what is off the chart. Let's face it: the American consumer is savvy and very, very curious.

They want to know what a lawyer does, how to make contact, how much it will cost, and what the outcome will be. They want to know if the lawyer has a history...if the lawyer is any good...and what other lawyers think of this particular lawyer.

This new world of openness has spawned all kinds of services to "help" the consumer find out that the right lawyer is for this particular person or job. In the old days, everybody had to rely on a dusty collection of books called "Martindale – Hubbel" to determine if a lawyer was respected by his or her peers and clients. Now, of course, that concept has expanded also. There's a new services in town (based in Seattle, as a matter of fact) called AVVO, which collects all kinds of information and rates the lawyers accordingly.

Judging lawyers is a tricky business – very subjective – so it is hard to be too critical of the results. But AVVO does a pretty good job of reporting on various lawyers' achievements, but it is still in its infancy and seems to be growing very slowly.

In short, it's hard to know who is the right lawyer for a particular job. If you know a lawyer who you trust, ask her or him for advice on who is the right person to handle a particular job. If he or she says: "I'm the right person for the job" – proceed with care.

Maybe the best advice I can give here is to trust your instincts... if the person you are dealing with is honest and respectful and is obviously trying to do his or her best for you...maybe you've found the right lawyer.

Tom Brown

What about the children?

• • •

"In the little world in which children have their existence, whosoever brings them up, there is nothing so finely perceived and so finely felt as injustice." Charles Dickens, Great Expectations

Through the centuries, societies and legal systems have been judged by how well they protected children...their rights, their lives, their health, and their dreams. What justice have the children enjoyed?

Once in a while, it's good for us to look at our own legal system here in America, and ask ourselves if we do a good job of taking care of the legal rights of children.

This came to my mind this week because I am involved in doing something that will amaze you, will make you glad that you live in America, and will give you a new feeling about our legal system. I am acting as a "Settlement Guardian *ad litem*." Wow! That's a mouthful... what does it mean?

Well...here's the story. A little girl, about 7 years old, was hit by a car in a crosswalk.

Fortunately, she wasn't critically injured; but she did have a fracture of one of her leg bones.

Her parents hired an attorney to recover damages from the driver of the car and his insurance company. There was only so much insurance available, so the attorney worked out a settlement where the medical providers agreed to take less money, and the balance (after attorney fees and costs) was to be placed in a locked bank account for the child, that couldn't be touched by the child or the parents until the child was an adult or only by Court order after a hearing.

Well, fortunately, we have a legal system that is suspicious of chummy little settlements that might end up benefitting the parents (HEY! ...a new flat screen TV!!) or the lawyer (HEY!...I'll take half as my fee!), so our Court rules say that any settlement for a minor child must be reviewed by a totally independent lawyer, appointed by the Court, who has experience in cases like this, to make sure that the child is not getting sold down the river. (If you're thinking that this is a sign of greed in an earlier era...you're right!)

So, the Settlement Guardian *ad litem* takes all the information and puts it under a microscope...the amount of the settlement, the amount of the medical bills, the amount that the attorney is charging for reaching the settlement, the nature of the injuries, etc., etc. And the SGAL writes a report to the Court, telling the Court if the whole thing is OK or if it stinks. If it stinks, the Court has the power and duty to disallow the whole deal and send everybody back to the starting gate.

So, what's the point?

Well, the point for this month is that our Court System in America is highly evolved to take care of our weakest and most helpless citizens... the children.

An actress that you may have heard of -- Jessica Lange -- once said that:

"There can be no better measure of our governance than the way we treat our children, and no greater failing on our part than to allow them to be subjected to violence, abuse or exploitation."

What an incredible sentiment!! We are defined as a society by how we treat our children and how we protect them from the negative aspects of the seamier side of our lives. If that could be the final testament of our society...it might be enough.

Fortunately for all of us, our legal system takes this duty seriously, and goes out of its way to protect our children.

Think of all the ways our legal system stands as a protector of our children:

We have created a system of Courts...totally separate from our other Courts...to deal with the problems, issues, concerns and rehabilitation of our juvenile citizens. We recognized long ago that the practice of throwing 12 year olds in prison with hard core criminals was pathetic... so now we treat them by having trained professionals deal with counseling, protective incarceration, education, and even Court Appearances... in front of judges trained in dealing with young offenders or young children who have lost their way.

We have special rules for the testimony of children, if they are witnesses to a crime or to an incident that is the subject of a civil lawsuit. The child witness is provided with counseling and expert assistant to make sure that his/her testimony is not tainted by someone else's ideas or suggestions. The Courts make the setting for the child witness as non-threatening as possible, and the Judge assists the child in delivering the evidence with due regard for the rights of the parties and the fragile psyche of the child.

In domestic legal matters (divorce, custody, visitation), the Courts have special tools in the form of rules and procedures to make sure that the children are not traumatized any more than they already have been by the terrible events of the domestic discord. Again, the judges have the ability to provide rules, settings, limitations, procedures, and even counseling to make sure that the children are not being brutalized under the guise of "giving evidence."

As I've mentioned in earlier columns, we do a lot of complaining about our legal system and its shortcomings. But the system is evolutionary...it sees its own problems and tries to correct them or at least to implement systems or controls that will minimize those problems.

In a country that has withstood the ferocity of racial discord; the anguish of civil disobedience; the anger of international wars fought with the blood of our children; the horror of unrestrained terror; we repeatedly look to our legal system for strength and direction. Simply put, it's nice to re-discover that this legal system not only does its job efficiently, it has the ability to bend down and take its children into protective hands.

Tom Brown

Are Class Actions Evil?

• • •

THE PEOPLE THAT CRITICIZE OUR legal system often point to "class actions" as a symptom of everything that is wrong with the law and as a symptom of lawyers out of control. Nowadays, we often hear about "class actions" as some sort of evil, destructive force that is ruining the American justice system. Before I begin defending the whole concept of "class actions"...let me say that I understand the negative publicity that this particular legal device has received.

Class actions are complicated, expensive, difficult to manage, and full of pitfalls for the average consumer, like you and me. In addition, they are now the subject of intensive media advertising, which tends to be a little less than uplifting and responsible. In fact, a lot of the ads are downright crass. The basic concept of a class action is that one big lawsuit against a company that has done something that hurts thousands, or even millions, of people is better than a million lawsuits. Why? Lots of reasons.

If a million different lawsuits are brought, the cost of defending all of those lawsuits alone will probably bring down the Company involved, even if that Company didn't do anything wrong. Even worse, if there are a million different lawsuits, there may be a million different results in different courts in different states. I think we can all agree that if 500,000 courts rule that the company was not at fault, and 500,000 courts rule that the company was at fault, we've got a difficult...but certainly unfair...situation on our hands. Some good current examples of the "class action" phenomenon are the lawsuits about hip replacement hardware, the lawsuits about vaginal mesh implants, and the lawsuits about exposure to asbestos in the workplace. I'm sure you have all seen the television commercials by national law firms, trying to convince patients to call them about these cases. Obviously, those firms are anxious to sign up people who have had trouble with these medical procedures, and they want to add folks to their stable of cases.

Is this a good thing or a bad thing?

Well, it's difficult to tell without examining, or "vetting" each of the law firms involved. It is important to understand that there are excellent, skilled law firms right here in Washington that handle these cases very well...it's just a matter of getting pointed in the right direction. For example, I had a client who had me handle a couple of different matters. It turned out that she also had a potential claim for damages because of a defective vaginal mesh implant. I recognized my limitations, and told her that I couldn't handle the case...but I would find her someone who would. After a little research, and after weeding out the national advertisers, I was able to connect her with a fine, competent firm in the Seattle area that handles these cases on a very reasonable basis. Frankly, I shudder to think what would have happened if I had just told her to respond to one of the television advertisements for lawyers that claim to do this kind of work...you just don't know what you're getting...without a lot of homework.

But, it's important to understand that there is nothing inherently wrong with the concept of class actions...in fact, most legal scholars, and most people that have faced the situation, would agree that class actions are an economical, organized, and intelligent way to deal with the situation where zillions of people have claims against the same manufacturer or distributor of a product that may or may not be dangerous or defective. The concept of class actions dates back in time to around the year 1200 in England, when "group litigation" became popular as a way to enforce the King's will or a way to control the people, so the King would institute a lawsuit to enforce his will against groups of people. This fell out of favor after about 1400 and English class (or "group") actions pretty much disappeared until around 1700. In America, the movement to use class actions was fueled by two different things: the rise in Civil Rights/consumer/civil rights litigation and the realization by government that its regulation efforts would be helped immeasurably by consumer litigation. Accordingly, class action activity increased dramatically until 1966, when the Federal Rules of Civil Procedure, which governed Federal Courts, was amended to grant easier access to this legal tool. After 1966, the use of class actions was greatly streamlined and many more class actions emerged. So, here we are in 2012, with television ads blasting in our ears, telling us to call this or that 800 number if we have hip implant problems or mesh implant problems or asbestosis or any number of legal/medical problems that haunt us.

What should we do?

Number one...talk to your doctor. He or she will have a wealth of ideas about what to do about your medical problem.

Number two...don't brag about or even suggest that you have an "inside track" about dealing with your particular problem...be a consumer, find out the facts.

Number three...talk to your favorite lawyer. He or she will give you some good ideas about whether to respond to those television ads and how to deal with your doctor.

Be a smart consumer. In general, relax about the whole issue of class actions. They are useful and can reduce the number of lawsuits and the number of people involved in the legal system. Class actions have stopped price -fixing, have eliminated employment discrimination, have changed the way employers deal with their employees, and have made our legal system more responsive.

As always, thank you for reading my little column each month. If you have any questions or suggestions about this column, please feel free to contact me at tom.brown@lawbljs.com

Tom Brown

When should your lawyer send you to see someone else?

● ● ●

WITH ALL THE LAWYER ADVERTISING in the yellow pages and on television, people must think that lawyers are desperate to get new clients. It seems like lawyers are doing anything they can to get people into their offices.

In fact, one of the most difficult things that we lawyers face --particularly in small communities -- is the problem of telling our prospective clients when they should be seeing some other professional (accountant, clergyman, surveyor, etc.) or that they should be seeing another lawyer who is better equipped to handle their case.

Is true that in smaller communities, like our Garden of Eden here in Northwestern and coastal Washington, we lawyers tend to be what they used to call "generalists" -- lawyers who do a little bit of everything. The small town lawyer is somewhat of an iconic figure in our history... the caring, concerned, all-knowing, connected problem-solver who can straighten out almost anything.

He can keep little Joey out of Juvenile Hall; work out the problem of where the neighbor's fence should go; negotiate with the insurance company; straighten out Dad's business license with the City Council; put Grandma's will through probate; and head up the United Way campaign.

The truth of the preceding paragraph is what draws a lot of lawyers to "small law" (I just coined that phrase...like it?) for a lifetime. We enjoy the directness of what we do. We don't issue memos from a 30-story building to be read by insurance company executives. We get our hands dirty -- sometimes literally! -- When we help our clients deal with the crosswinds of life in small town America. We go to Court. We write wills. We collect debts. We walk property lines. We give advice.

We form small corporations. Some of us help people through difficult divorces (even divorce is getting so specialized that some lawyers won't touch it!). We serve on boards and committees.

We fight over unpaid bills, bad contractors, loud nuisances, biting dogs, and mean drunks.

But...back to the point of this month's column...it is true that the practice of law is becoming more and more specialized...even in the smaller communities. Many times over the last 40+ years, I have had good clients come to me for advice on patents and trademarks and copyrights...what we lawyers call "intellectual property." While I can mouth a few generalities about the law in this obscure area, the only safe tactic is to go to an expert. Accordingly, I have reluctantly sent quite a few good clients over the years to Seattle to a firm that I trust to give good advice in this area (...it's the same firm I went to with my invention!!). I think most of my colleagues here also refer these cases to lawyers who know what they are doing.

The same is true of other areas of the law. Generally speaking, I -- and many of my local colleagues -- won't touch a medical malpractice case... and I refer my clients to lawyers who understand this complex and sophisticated area of the law. (Not to mention the fact that I don't want to sue my Doctor friends or the local hospital...and not to mention the fact that I have to live with my wife who is an operating room nurse!!)

While we small-town lawyers create little corporations all the time, and create the stock for those corporations...those are what we lovingly call: "closely held corporations." That means that all the stock is "in the family" so to speak and nobody outside the "family" or group is ever going to want part of the corporation. But, if the company grew and thrived we wanted to sell that stock to the public, we would have a different "kettle of fish" (thanks, Grandma!). Yes, we would have to deal with acres of laws and regulations that would require the entrance of a lawyer or law firm that could navigate the choppy waters of "securities regulation" and prevent us -- and our clients -- from going to jail or to the poor house.

There are a number of other areas where we small town lawyers need to be careful and defer to our big-city brethren, who do nothing else but the single thing at issue...think about plane crashes, dangerous prescription drugs, building collapses, huge labor disputes, class actions...you get the idea.

So...it's still a good idea to go talk to your good friend and lifetime lawyer about whatever problem is facing you. But understand that part of the reason you trust that lawyer is that he or she will be honest with you and tell you when you need to drive down the road to the big city and talk to a lawyer that specializes in the issue you are facing. Perhaps even more importantly, that lifetime confidant will tell you when your problem is not a legal problem at all, but rather one that requires a counselor or an accountant or a priest or, maybe, even a psychiatrist.

EEK!

And if you see my picture on the front page of your next telephone book, and if that picture is removable to become a refrigerator magnet, you'll know that I have finally crossed the line.

Help!

As always, I welcome your comments, suggestions, criticisms and ideas. Thank you so much for the many wonderful comments I've received about this column.

There's absolutely nothing like being at the dump with your son-in-law, and have the guy next to you at the recycling station tell you how much he liked the last column...fabulous!

Tom Brown

Are you OK to drive home tonight? I doubt it!

• • •

A FEW WEEKS AGO, MY wife and I went back to Minnesota for her Mother's funeral.

Grandma Betty died peacefully on October 20, one month shy of her 96th birthday. She was a great Mother and a great person, and people came from all over the country to say good-bye to her. She had six children, 21 grandchildren, 33 great-grandchildren and a rich family history full of anecdotes and stories and memories that kept us all laughing and crying for days.

After the wake, the night before the funeral, many of the family and friends went to a local motel where most of the family was staying, to do what Grandma would have wanted us to do – have a good time with family and friends, celebrating her life.

Although I drove to the motel, I knew that I should not drive back to the next location for the end of the evening. I had some drinks, but I wasn't drunk, probably not even noticeably tipsy, but I knew it would be a mistake for me to drive. By consensus, we agreed that my wife's 49-year-old nephew – a very responsible guy – should be our designated driver. He was clearly not under the influence and had been keeping himself OK, knowing he would probably be required to drive our little group of 6 or 7 in my rental SUV.

The short trip of five miles or so was uneventful, the driving was fine, and the group was happy.

About one block from our destination, the blue lights came on behind us. The officer said that my nephew was exceeding the speed limit a few blocks back. We were surprised...but waited patiently as the officer went through the drill, ultimately asking if he had had anything to drink.

My nephew candidly told the officer that he had a beer or two earlier in the evening; but was not under the influence by any stretch of the imagination. To our shock, the officer went ahead with the physical tests and even administered a portable Breathalyzer, which showed him to be over the limit! Stunning! It was a close call; but the officer finally decided not to arrest him.

We spent the rest of the evening in shock, hardly believing that someone in his condition could even arguably be considered too "drunk" to drive. We had a marathon discussion of the "wisdom" of the DUI/DWI laws and where they were headed. Some of us in the group believed that the governmental goal across the country is to just completely stamp out drinking and driving altogether, no matter what the amount of alcohol in the system.

I can tell you, it was a huge lesson for me. I have always been pretty cavalier about the whole drinking and driving issue, believing that I know when I'm OK and when I'm not. C'mon...a couple of drinks with the boys after work on Friday. I should call a cab? I should have my wife come and pick me up? Ridiculous...right? Boy, have I been stupid.

What should we all know about drinking and driving? I conferred with my lawyer friends that handle DUI/DWI cases...here's what I learned:

1. It doesn't take very much alcohol to qualify you for a ticket.
2. The penalties are terrible, some even shocking.
3. The financial cost to the person charged is simply unbelievable.
4. The impact on the life of the person charged is incredible.

First of all, if you are charged with DUI, you need a lawyer. This is a serious crime, with serious penalties and you need representation. A lawyer is probably going to charge you somewhere between $3,000 and $5,000 for representing you. He or she will do everything possible to deflect or minimize the charge; but the law enforcement people are usually well trained and follow all the steps correctly. It's very difficult to "beat" a DUI charge.

If you refuse to take the Breathalyzer, your license can be suspended for a year. Your lawyer can challenge this, but the success rate of such challenges is very low.

In the case of an accident with an injury or death, a blood sample can be taken from you without your consent.

If you are convicted of DUI, you will be fined approximately $850.00 and will spend at least 24 hours in jail. You will lose your license to drive for 90 days (and then – if you do drive while your license is suspended – the consequences are terrible). You will also be required to have an interlock device on your car ignition for a year, at your expense. Your insurance will probably be canceled; and the only insurance you will be able to buy is very expensive – minimum limit – insurance that will probably cost you two or three thousand dollars per year. Also, you will have to be "evaluated" for an alcohol/drug problem and follow whatever recommendations are made by the evaluator. Of course, you will have to pay for all this...it's very expensive.

All of the preceding stuff is about what happens if you're just caught driving. If you get in an accident while you are under the influence, things are much worse. If you injure someone, you can be charged with a felony and actually do some serious jail time. If you kill someone, you will be charged with a very serious felony and go to a hard-core state prison.

You can't buy your way out of a serious alcohol-related charge. Just this year, a multimillionaire in Florida, who got into a wreck driving his $200,000 Bentley and killed the other driver, was sentenced to 16 years in prison and fined $10,000.00, even though he paid the parents of the deceased other driver $46 million dollars in settlement. Wow!

So, what should we take home from all this? Whatever you thought about drinking and driving before...trash it. Make a pact – in advance – with your spouse or partner that they will not cooperate in your stupid decision to drive. Put a big sign on the dash of your car. Sell your car. Buy an interlock device. Tattoo the taxicab number on your hand. Do your drinking at home. Do whatever it takes to stop you from getting behind the wheel when you've "...had a few."

Driving under the influence is a serious crime. It involves a lot of money. It involves a lot of disruption of your life. It can result in time in jail or even prison. A DUI arrest will change your life forever.

Let's face it...society has made a decision that it wants us to stop drinking and driving.

We'd better listen.

Tom Brown

There's a Whole Lot of
Swearing Goin' On!!

• • •

HAVE YOU EVER NOTICED HOW fixated the law and society are on swearing?

I don't mean the potty-mouth cursing and name-calling that we hear too much of these days.

No, I'm talking about the fact that every time someone blinks in a legal setting, you know there's going to be some swearing going on, in the sense of oaths or affirmations or vows, affidavits, testimony, etc., etc.

Every time we sign an important document or a deed or mortgage, we make oaths or affirmations or we get notarized or sworn.

What's the deal with all the swearing?

Well, first of all, it didn't start with the law. Our human history, and particularly our religious history is absolutely overflowing with the concept of taking an oath to show the truth and solemnity of what we are saying or signing. Actually, the religious connection has stuck around for quite some time, showing the underlying concept that we are asking a higher power to witness or approve or validate the thing that we are promising or saying. This is deeply entrenched in Judeo-Christian tradition and in other religions as well.

It is common for such religious oaths to be accompanied by the person holding or touching a sacred object. That endures even into modern day America, where we used to ask people to put their hand on the Bible when they were about to testify. The early Romans actually had an "Oath Stone" in the temple of the God Jupiter, where they would go to swear or take oaths.

Interestingly, the word "swear" has roots that emphasize the importance a weight of the act of swearing an oath. Across practically all language groups, the root word refers to something "heavy" or "hard" or even "difficult" – all showing how much weight we give to the act of swearing an oath. After all, we swear in voters, we swear in citizens, and – as noted above – we swear in presidents and mayors and judges and fire chiefs and lawyers.

An interesting side note: John Quincy Adams (a deeply religious man) refused to take his oath of office for the Presidency on a Bible. Instead, he took his oath on the Constitution of the United States and on a book of American laws…he said those were the things he was swearing allegiance to. And…showing again the religious background… Supreme Court Justice Arthur Goldberg, took his oath of office on the **Tanakh** (often referred to as the "Jewish Bible").

Theodore Roosevelt was the only President not sworn in on the Bible.

With all this history, it's not surprising that the law, which has to depend on people telling the truth, insists on using the rituals that society trusts. After all, when we install a mayor or a judge or a president, we insist that he or she must take an oath and swear to fulfill the duties of the office. This seems to comfort us and it adds gravity to the ceremony of taking over the office.

Over the years, the American legal system has gotten drunk on the concept of making people put it all on the line by taking an oath.

You have to swear to tell the truth when you're a witness; two people have to swear it was you that signed your will; a notary public has to swear that you actually signed the deed when you sold your house; if you're served with papers, the process server has to swear under oath about the details of serving you; if you give a power of attorney, your signature must be witnessed and sworn to. Even the court reporter that records the proceedings in Court has to swear that she wrote it all down and transcribed it truthfully.

In fact, there was so much swearing going on that Washington (and most states) finally decided to dispense with some of the rituals, and notarizations, and swearing for routine, everyday documents. In 1981, our state legislature adopted a law that said that most things that required a sworn statement, or declaration, or verification, or certificate, or oath, or affidavit could now be official with only a written certification by the signer, saying that: "I certify (or declare) under penalty of perjury under the laws of the State of Washington that the foregoing is true and correct." Pretty simple, huh?

Sure, it's sleek and functional...but maybe there's something missing when we take away the Bibles and take away the raised right hand. To some lovers of tradition, this trimming of the ceremonies takes away the "heaviness" (remember?) of the occasion. The raising of the right hand is historical as well as ceremonial...in medieval times convicted criminals would have their convictions marked on the palm side of their hand (on the fat part of the thumb) with a letter to designate their criminal history. When they entered Court, they would hold up their hand so the judge could see whether they were believable or not. (Another historical theory holds that the left hand was historically "unclean" and the right hand was the only one allowed to touch food or other persons...who knows?) Anyway, the raised right hand looks like it's here to stay.

"For so sworn good or evil an oath may not be broken and it shall pursue oath keeper and oath breaker to the world's end." J.R.R. Tolkien, The Silmarillion

Tom Brown

Love Thy Neighbor

● ● ●

OVER THE YEARS, I'VE OBSERVED that some of the nastiest, ugliest disputes are between neighbors, who can't work out their issues with boundary lines, noise, animals, parking, house colors, and the thousands of other things that get under people's skins.

Fortunately, most of these tempests stay in the teapot and don't find their way to a courtroom or a police station. However, because these dust-ups are so personal and so invasive to our way of life, they can sometimes end up in the comforting arms of the law.

My advice to my clients is always the same:
Work it out.
Don't fight about it.
Get along.

The worst of this group of problems is boundary disputes. For the most part, our world – at least here in the United States – is neatly divided into very clear and understandable parcels of land. In cities, they are usually "lots" in a "subdivision" which are numbered and appear very clearly on a map. You might own Lots 3 and 4 of Block 3 of the Lazy Estates Subdivision.

Most of these parcels have changed hands many times and there is little to bicker about.

Unfortunately, these parcels are owned by human beings, who have an almost infinite capacity for fighting over everything.

The most common problem is that one neighbor thinks that the other neighbor is doing something, or building something that encroaches on his property. Fences are one of the chief offenders here, but there are sheds, driveways, gardens, hedges, sidewalks, ...you get the idea: almost anything the mind of man can dream up.

Some of these epic battles between neighbors end up in Courtrooms, where the Judge or Jury is obligated to go back to the beginning, and look at what was done when Lazy Estates was surveyed and turned into a subdivision in 1910. That's when the lawyers and the surveyors and the neighbors all find out how imprecise and hazy things were back in 1910, when the line was drawn in the wrong place or improperly surveyed.

This kind of stuff drove the law and the lawyers and the surveyor nuts, so the law – in its infinite wisdom – came up with some rules to prevent or solve these disputes. These rules have different names in different states, but they're all basically the same. They say that if a certain condition has existed for a certain number of years, openly and without any agreement, the harmed person can't suddenly stand up after all those years (usually 7 or 10) and say: "Hey, your garage is on my property...move it!" Nope, it's probably too late then.

We have a cabin on the water. When the contractors built our cabin, they thought the lot was rectangular and was situated at a 90-degree angle to the shoreline. OOPS! Not so. Shorelines tend to curve and even change. So our property line was just a tiny bit off near the water...but as you went further away, the angle of the line increased the amount of property involved. So, even though we had clear lot lines and a clear old survey 80 or so years ago, that didn't stop our contractor from installing our well on our neighbor's property, where it sat quietly pumping away for the next 30 years. And, of course, the whole line was off by 10 feet or so, towards the back of the property. Just another nightmare in Paradise.

I've represented people in crazy, unbelievable property disputes, where the level of hatred and anger boils over. People get crazy about their property rights.

Many times, it's not so much the fence or the garage or the garden. Often, it is the activity. People drive across certain areas and get used to it. People let their animals go to the bathroom where there ain't no bathroom. People are sometimes noisy or rude. Sometimes the dogs bark every morning at 5:00 o'clock AM. People's kids play in the expensive garden. The new water trough that the neighbor installed is now pouring water directly into the neighbor's basement. All of these things can bubble over into the Courtroom if people can't work them out.

The one thing that is certain about legal disputes over property: it is grotesquely expensive. The amount of time involved for the lawyer is unbelievable. The lawyer has to interview his own clients in detail to get the facts. The lawyer has to go to the County Records and maybe to the old surveyor records to check the property lines. The lawyer has to interview neighbors and former property owners. The area has to be photographed, sometimes by a professional. Often, examination of existing aerial photographs can solve the case. The lawyer may have to hire a brand-new surveyor to start over from scratch. The lawyer has to take the testimony under oath (called a: "deposition") of everyone who knows anything about the situation. Then there's trial preparation... rehearsing everyone's testimony, researching the law, hiring an expert, writing a "brief" to educate the Judge about the case, etc. Sometimes, we lawyers figure that – for every day spent in the Courtroom, a case requires 2 or 3 days of preparation.

So, what should we do to protect ourselves from – or prevent – this kind of problem?

First, be flexible and cooperative. If reasonable people can work out the thing, try for that before going to the lawyer.

Second, if it is gnarly and difficult, spend the money to have a chat with your favorite lawyer. His or her advice will go a long toward letting you know what the alternatives are, what the lay of the land is (so to speak!), and what you can do to make things easier without an expensive lawsuit.

Finally, keep perspective in your life. If your neighbor's kids are driving you nuts, take a deep breath and see if it's you. Have a nice chat with the neighbor. Offer to cooperate in solving the problem and/or let them know how difficult it is making your life. Maybe they'll just solve it!

Thanks for reading my column and thanks for all the nice comments. (Boy, the column on drinking and driving really struck a chord!!!)

Tom Brown

Arbitration - Be Careful Before You Sign Up

● ● ●

IN THE PAST, WE'VE DISCUSSED in this column how the legal world is being turned upside down by the concepts of mediation and arbitration. The popularity of these procedures is almost unbelievable.

Remember the difference:

* Mediation is a process that is not binding, where the parties try to settle their dispute by using a trained mediator who is skilled in finding common ground and resolving disputes.
* Arbitration, on the other hand is usually binding. It is a process that replaces a long, expensive trial with a shorter, more informal process where a single lawyer acts as judge and jury.

Both of these have their place and can be terrific; but today we're going to talk about some of the hidden dangers in Arbitration.

Usually arbitration appears in a contract, where the seller has placed in the agreement or contracts a provision that any dispute will be resolved in Arbitration, rather than a lengthy and expensive lawsuit. On the face of it, that's not necessarily a bad thing; but -- as always -- the devil is in the details.

Who is going to pay for the Arbitration? How will the arbitrator be selected? Where will the Arbitration be held? What's the time limit for starting the arbitration?

The Supreme Court of the State of Washington just reminded us how tricky an arbitration agreement can be. In a case decided on February 7th of this year, our Supreme Court took a magnifying glass to an arbitration clause. A woman had signed a contract with an out of state company that had an Arbitration clause, providing that any disputes between them had to be decided by arbitration rather than a lawsuit. The Arbitration clause had many requirements, but the ones that grabbed the attention of our Supreme Court were:

1. The case had to be arbitrated in California;
2. The loser pays all costs;
3. The Arbitration had to be started within 30 days.

The Court held that these requirements were "unconscionable" and voided the arbitration clause. In ruling on this, the Supreme Court looked at its earlier cases on arbitration agreements and recounted the authority that an arbitration agreement will be held to be unconscionable when it is one-sided or overly harsh, or shocking to the conscience, "monstrously harsh" or "exceedingly callous." If the court finds that these problems pervade the entire agreement, the remedy is to throw out the agreement rather than try to fix it. (The case is GANDEE v. LDL FREEDOM ENTERPRISES, INC. and you can read it at http://www.courts.wa.gov/opinions/index.cfm?fa=opinions. showOpinion&filename=876746MAJ

An Internet search will reveal quite a few big time disputes over the use of Arbitration, including such giants as Subway and Meineke. It's a hot topic. And you might remember the squabble that broke out when cruise ship customers learned that their ticket included an agreement that any claims against the Cruise Ship company for disputes about the cruise had to be made in arbitration IN FLORIDA!! How convenient would that be??

Mandatory arbitration clauses are routinely used in contracts for phone service, employment, health insurance, nursing home care, medical services and credit cards, so you have probably agreed to Arbitration without even realizing it.

Now that you're all fired up over Arbitration, let's talk about the good side of it. When properly used and applied, Arbitration can be a useful, friendly tool. It's a way to have disputes resolved quickly and (relatively) inexpensively.

But you have to be good consumer to make sure it's going to be OK. Call your friendly lawyer and ask her or him what they think. Do your own homework: Who pays the arbitrator? How much? Who is in the pool of arbitrators? Does the arbitrator (or the arbitration company) have a deal with one of the parties? Do you need a lawyer to represent you in the arbitration? What are the rules of the Arbitration? (You have a right to read them).

And finally, let's talk about an interesting rule in our own Washington Superior Courts...it's called the "Mandatory Arbitration Rule." If a lawsuit is filed for money damages (as opposed to divorce or property division) and the parties agree that the amount at issue is $50,000.00 or less, then they have to go through an Arbitration proceeding paid for by the Courts using volunteer attorneys. The proceeding is fast, simple, and all takes place in a neutral location in the county of the parties. The Arbitrator/Attorney issues a decision. Either party can appeal the decision and have a full trial in Court on the same issue, but the penalties are harsh if they don't improve their position. It works very well and is used all the time!

As always, thanks for reading my little column and thanks for the wonderful comments. (P.S. My first column in this distinguished newspaper was in April of 2008, so this will be my 60th column covering five years...thanks, readers; thanks Lora; thanks to my bride and children and friends for all the great suggestions for topics!)

Tom Brown

The Pope's Lawyers

• • •

WITH THE ELECTION OF A new Pope (...good luck, Francis!), it seemed like a good time to talk about the law of religion and its legal system... and maybe some other legal systems.

I grew up going to Catholic School. All of us young boys were expected to "turn out " for training as altar boys (now, of course, they're called altar "servers", because girls are part of the deal). Anyway, at the insistence of my parents, I did the training and got on the regular schedule to serve Masses at our parish.

Like most things in life, there were good gigs and bad ones. The nastiest scheduling "opportunity" was the 7:00 o'clock AM weekday Mass. This was truly the bottom of the altar boy barrel. I had to get up early, and ride my bike the 1.12 hilly miles (thanks, MapQuest) from our house to the Church. The priest was often cranky at that hour and there were hardly any people in the huge church and there was only one altar boy...so the whole thing seemed kind of lame.

Anyway, on the morning I'm going to tell you about, I overslept a little bit, and was going to be late. I pedaled my bike like crazy; but I couldn't quite make up the time. I rushed in the back door of the Church, down the steps to the altar boys' locker room, grabbed a stinky cassock and surplus (they never washed them), and ran up the interior steps to the sacristy, which is the room off the altar where the Priest gets ready for Mass.

The bad news was that the Priest had already started the Mass with no altar boy; the good news was that it was Father Stewart, who was about as nice as they come, but was somewhat "mystical" and took the whole religion thing too seriously, in my view. Anyway, I crept out on to the altar as quietly as possible and took up my position kneeling on the marble stairs at the bottom of the altar.

As Father Stewart droned on, I realized that my cassock, a long, black, coat-like garment that had snaps all the way up the front, was not buttoned correctly when I threw it on. So, while the priest was reading the Epistle or the Gospel all in Latin, I was busy re-snapping all the snaps on my cassock. Suddenly, Father Stewart stopped the Mass and motioned for me to come up to the top of the altar where he was. He looked me right in my sleepy eyes and said: "Tommy, I think you'd better leave the altar."

There's no way that I can convey the horror of my situation. I knew that I had disturbed the mystical priest with all my snapping and re-snapping, after being late in the first place. I knew that this was the end of my life. I would have to confess what happened to my parents and suffer that punishment; plus I would be banned from ever serving Mass again; plus the priest and nuns would do whatever they do to martyrs... simply put, I thought it was the end of my life.

This fear was confirmed when I got out of school that afternoon and Father Stewart WAS OUTSIDE WAITING FOR ME!!! My first instinct was to run...but I knew that would make things worse, so I walked over to him. After explaining why he banished me from the altar, I got the biggest surprise of my life. He asked me if I had ever considered becoming a priest!! ...YIKES!

I told him that I had once thought that might be a possibility; but, as I got older, I had decided that I wanted to be a lawyer, which was true. From about 3rd grade on, I was sure that lawyering was for me. Was that the end of it? No...Father Stewart cut me off at the pass. He said: "That's wonderful...the Church needs lawyers to do all the Canon Law work and it would be perfect for you. WHAT????

I had never head of "Canon Law" and I had never thought that there was any such thing as a priest that was also a lawyer. I was thinking more of Perry Mason and James Whitmore and Abe Lincoln and Miracle on 34th Street. I excused myself and told Father Stewart that I would think about it.

Anyway, that's a long personal introduction to today's topic -- other legal systems that co-exist with our wonderful American legal system.

First of all, it's important to realize that the Catholic Church has what is claimed to be the oldest continuously functioning internal legal system in the Western world, much older than the evolution of modern European civil law traditions, and certainly centuries older than our own robust legal system. It has a code of laws (called "canons"). The legal system of the Catholic Church has courts, judges, lawyers and all the other dressings of a full-blown legal system, all based on the 1,752 Canons, some of which date back to the apostles.

As the oldest continuously functioning legal system in the western world, canon law affects virtually every aspect of the faith life of over one billion Catholic Christians around the world. All of the men who train for the Catholic priesthood study the Church's legal system, and some go on to be Canon lawyers and judges. . Canon lawyers spend three or four post-college academic years studying canon law, earning a licentiate (J.C.L.) degree. Some continue their education and earn a doctoral degree (J.C.D.). Most North American canonists attend one of the three Canon law schools in Canada, Mexico and the US, although some study abroad, often in Rome. In North America, four out of five canon lawyers are priests, but in recent years the number of religious men and women as well as laymen and women in canon law has been increasing.

Many canon lawyers have advanced degrees in theology. Still others have advanced degrees in related fields, such as Church history or civil law. It used to be that disagreements in the Catholic Church over a variety of things (like admission to Catholic schools, use of parish buildings, transfers of priests, etc.) would always be decided by the highest-ranking bishop or cardinal.

But, as we know, things have changed in the church after the abuse scandals, and Catholics are using the internal devices of the Canon Law; and, by God, they're even winning sometimes. It's changing the Church's legal system! There's even a group that posts a guide to using the Canon Law system called "Canonical Appeals for Dummies"!! (Download at http://www.futurechurch.org/downloads/sopc.htm) The willingness of Catholics to use these legal tools is a complex issue and reaches back decades, involving changes in the church and broader society.

Canon lawyers say the American concern for individual freedoms likely has played a role. So has the explosion of information on the Internet. But the change is also an unexpected consequence of the clergy molestation crisis, with the scandal exerting an influence far beyond cases that directly involve abusers. "The focus on canon law and penal procedures in the case of sexual misconduct has made people aware that the church has a law system, it can work and people can take advantage of it," said Michael Ritty, founder of Canon Law Professionals, a private practice in Feura Bush, N.Y. "For so long, especially in the United States, many of the lay people did not speak up and did not know how to speak up, and many people in the hierarchy did not know how to accept things when people did speak up. I think that is changing."

Ritty founded his private practice in 2000 to keep active after he retired and now employs three other canon lawyers. Abuse cases are a significant part of his work, along with marriage annulments, but Ritty also has many cases relating to everyday church issues, such as use of money.

All of the Catholic Church legal cases are guarded by pontifical secrecy, which bars advocates, judges and other parties from revealing details of the proceedings. So, no one knows the exact number of formal petitions before tribunals or agencies at the Vatican, or before church officials in the U.S. or in any country Even though we don't know the exact numbers, we know the Church's legal system is very, very busy -- and not just with divorce matters. U.S. canon lawyers say they have seen more widespread use of church law to resolve disputes.

Edward Peters, a canon lawyer and professor at Sacred Heart Major Seminary in Detroit, said the increase in canonical litigation is "indisputable." There is even the "Canon Law Society of America", a professional group for church lawyers. It held a workshop on the increased use of Canon Law called "Hierarchical Recourse: Can't We All Just Get Along?" "Most of us, when we were training, were preparing for marriage tribunals, marriage annulments," said Monsignor Patrick Lagges of Chicago, a canon lawyer for three decades who helped lead the canon law society workshop last year. "Now there's such a broad range of things. It's a much broader field."

Until recently, the only canon law most American Catholics knew related to annulments, church declarations that a marriage was never valid. (For years, the majority of annulment petitions to the Vatican have come from the United States.) The first complete code of canon law, published in 1917, was also the first to be translated from the Latin into English. Even then, the system remained obscure, considered the province of an educated clergy-elite who were fluent in Latin and could quote directly from centuries-old papal decrees. Obviously, that situation has changed!!

But, the Catholic Church's legal system is only one of many legal systems (or sub-systems) that are part of... or co-exist with, our main legal system.

Did you know that the State of Washington has a separate Court system that hears nothing but appeals from decisions of the Department of Labor & Industries? It has roughly 70 (yes!...70!) Judges, earning as high as $100,000.00 per year, not to mention the other well-paid 85 employees of that sub-system.

Did you know that the United States government and the governments of each of the states have administrative law systems that have many, many administrative law judges (or officers) that hear thousands and thousands of cases and appeals? Yes, the "administrative law" system in our country is a busy and expensive legal system that handles more types of matters than you can even imagine.

Even though it's technically part of the United States District Courts, our Bankruptcy Courts are virtually an independent Court system, with its own rules, its own judges, its own clerks, etc. Many court systems use "magistrate judges" or "commissioners" to handle a wide variety of judicial duties, often under a completely separate set of rules.

And, don't forget the U.S. Court of Appeals for Veterans' Claims; the U.S. Court of Federal Claims; the Court of International Trade; the Military Courts system; the State and Federal Tax Courts; etc.; etc.

Whew...it's too much! I think I'll unbutton my cassock and go to bed.

As always, thanks for reading my little column and thanks for all the nice comments and suggestions.

Tom Brown

Women in the Law...what's the score?

• • •

LIKE SO MANY PARTS OF our society, it was true for many years that the law was reserved for men.

Sure, a woman broke through every once in a while...but they were oddities, the exceptions, objects of amazement and wonder.

For people of my generation (I get a social security check now every month), to see a woman lawyer was an unusual event. In my 1970 law school class of 60 lawyers, there were two women...that's about 3%. But...by the year 2001, the national percentage had increased to just a hair under 50%. That's HALF! That is shocking! And...with a small statistical difference, it has remained true that women are still virtually half of the lawyers emerging from our country's law schools.

When I came to Grays Harbor in 1972, there was only one woman practicing law among a community of about 40 or 50 lawyers. She was Gladys Phillips, an iconic, amazing woman who showed men for generations that women were every bit as strong and powerful as the male lawyers. Gladys's father had been a Superior Court Judge and she served in t he State Legislature, as well as being a force among the barristers of Grays harbor County. She is a legend...Google her...she was amazing.

Now, of course, things have changed in Grays Harbor and the other smaller counties...women are an integral part of the fabric of the law... they are accepted, they are respected, they take on the hard jobs, they are part of the deal.

Things are also radically different in the larger counties of this state...women are integral parts of the private and public legal systems and are recognized as equals by most non-Neanderthal lawyers. Look around the state: Most of the members of our Supreme Court are women, including the Chief Justice. Many, many women serve on the Courts of Appeal in our State and many serve on the lower courts, ranging from municipal courts to Superior Courts and everything in between. They serve as administrative law Judges; they serve as Labor & Industries Judges, they serve as municipal Court Judges. Women have crossed the bar...they share with the men the heart and soul of the law.

Of course, this isn't just a phenomenon of Washington State or Grays Harbor and our fellow coastal communities. This is a national story...women have seized the law...with a passion. The Supreme Court of the United States finally had a woman 32 years ago when Sandra Day O'conner put on the robes. After graduation from law school, at least 40 firms refused to interview her for a position as an attorney because she was a woman. She eventually found employment as a deputy county attorney in San Mateo, California after she offered to work for no salary and without an office, sharing space with a secretary.

Now look at us! We have three fabulous women on the highest Court in the Land...isn't that refreshing?

I'd like to say that my experience with women has been perfect...but that would be a lie. Many of the women I have encountered in the law are difficult, cranky, obstinate...just like the men. There's a huge pool of women lawyers that I think are better than most men, better than me, and simply the best. On the other hand, there is a huge pool of women lawyers that drive me nuts...they're haughty, picky, difficult and impossible...just like many of the men.

But, you know, that's really what we want out of our lawyers. Of course we want them to be smart, quick, analytical, funny, driven, etc. ...but, on the other hand, we want them to be human, too. We want a little humanity, a little humor, a little imperfection, ...and we want someone we trust. If that's a woman, God bless you!

Thank you so much for reading and commenting on my column. This column depends on your support and your feedback (not to mention the incredible support of our editor Lora Malakoff). I truly listen to my readers and try to discuss issues that interest you and provoke your brain stems. Keep those ideas and comments coming.

Tom Brown

Guest Columnist

• • •

A FEW TIMES IN THE history of this column, we have stepped aside to showcase writers who have a special message or a new slant on an old problem or something witty or important to say.

When I read Judge Erik Rohrer's column in the Peninsula Daily News a few issues ago, I knew that his message was one that our readers need to hear. He speaks of problems in Clallam County that are mirrored in Grays Harbor County, Pacific County, Jefferson County, and throughout the rural counties of Washington State, east and west.

Judge Roher is a newly elected Superior Court judge in Clallam County; but he is no stranger to the Courtroom and is no stranger to the terrible inequalities that the poor and dis-enfranchised people of our state endure.

He was previously a District Court Judge for many years, serving the citizens of Clallam County in many ways that could not be measured by mere statistics. He was the classic country judge...accessible, friendly, understanding, wise and fair. By all reports, he has carried that demeanor to the Superior Court Bench and is serving there with distinction.

Judge Rohrer has served for years now on the Oversight Committee of the Washington State Office of Civil Legal Aid, an agency that fights for the funding to support programs that provide access to our Courts for people that don't have the resources to stand before the bar of justice, like the rest of us can. He is now the chair of that committee and he is in a unique position to see the terrible consequences of a system that does not extend its hand to those who need its protection the most.

Judge Rohrer and the Peninsula Daily News have graciously consented to let us run Judge Rohers' column as a guest columnist for "de minimis" this month.

What you read here will break your heart...but the stories need to be told. (To protect their privacy, the people cited in this column have been given pseudonyms by the author.)

● ● ●

Sophia, a domestic-violence victim, and her teenage son Jayden are about to lose their family home.

Her husband — who is facing domestic violence charges — left the home and has provided no financial support since then.

Sophia is behind on the bills, and their home is in foreclosure.

Where can she turn to resolve her legal issues?

Mia was severely injured as a teenager when she was struck in the head with a concrete block and has been in a wheelchair since the injury.

Mia currently suffers from serious dental issues and is also extremely sensitive to many chemicals.

She relocated to Sequim, in part, to access a dentist offering a chemical-free environment.

The state Department of Social and Health Services refused to pay the dentist's bills because he is not on the agency's approved-provider list.

The nearest dentist offering the services Mia needs is in Bremerton, and she has no way to get there.

What more can she do without being able to afford an attorney?

William lives in a federally subsidized apartment with his two sons, Noah and Ethan.

Ethan was recently accused of assaulting a classmate.

The housing authority served an eviction notice on William based on the allegations of assault against Ethan.

William receives limited SSI income, but does not receive child support. He and his sons have nowhere else to live.

What is he going to do?

Local resources for low-income individuals with civil (not criminal) legal needs are very limited.

While Clallam-Jefferson County Pro Bono Lawyers does an outstanding job coordinating lawyers who volunteer to handle civil cases, the need is simply too great for volunteers alone.

That's where the Northwest Justice Project, or NJP, comes in.

The Port Angeles NJP office opened in 2007 with three attorneys serving Clallam and Jefferson counties.

Since then, budget cuts have reduced staffing levels to a single attorney struggling to serve the indigent civil legal needs of both counties.

And it gets worse: a $3 million cut in funding for civil legal aid services under consideration in Olympia could force the outright closure of the North Olympic Peninsula's only NJP office as well as other offices serving rural communities across the state.

Any further reduction in state-funded civil legal aid would seriously impact the ability of indigent people to obtain access to justice — real people, like Sophia, Mia and William and their families.

As a result of NJP's intervention (including NJP's Foreclosure Prevention Unit), Sophia qualified for a loan she can afford to pay, Jayden will remain in the family home attending the same high school until he graduates and Sophia's former spouse will be required to pay child support.

Because of NJP's involvement, Mia has been approved to continue to see her dentist in Sequim.

William and his children are still in their home because of NJP's representation.

The court ruled that the housing authority did not have good cause to evict him.

The allegations against Ethan were ultimately dismissed as well.

It seems only fair that folks like Sophia, Mia and William — and so many others like them — have reasonable access to legal advice and representation in civil legal disputes that affect their most basic needs.

The state budget should not be balanced on the backs of our community's most vulnerable citizens.

Civil legal aid in our state should be fully funded.

● ● ●

Erik Rohrer is a Clallam County Superior Court Judge and serves as chair of the bipartisan Washington State Civil Legal Aid Oversight Committee.

Tom Brown

Are Law Schools Dying? ...Do We Care?

• • •

FOR THE LAST 30 YEARS or so, law schools have been riding a wave of popularity and demand that made it seem like everybody in America wanted to go to law school, and were willing to pay anything to do it, no matter how much they had to borrow.

The competition to get into the best law schools was brutal. The professors were the over-paid cream of the crop. The tuition and costs were off the chart...it could cost up to $200,000.00 to go to a top-notch law school. The law school admissions test (LSAT) was the" live or die" test for many budding law students. Graduates were coming out of law school with a debt load that would choke a dinosaur. New law schools were emerging everywhere.

...but the bubble wouldn't pop. The law schools got more expensive. Women were elbowing their way in to the law schools as never before. The demand for a seat in even mediocre law schools was fierce. It was like the economy in the early years of this century...it just kept expanding and it seemed like it would never stop.

For crying out loud, a respected University in Seattle *bought* a law school from Tacoma and moved it to Seattle!!! (...and now Tacoma has been working on starting a new one!!!)

The bubble seemed like it would never pop...until it did.

What happened? Well, let's talk about the symptoms first. The competition to get into law schools suddenly took a left turn. Going to law school was no longer seen as the Holy Grail of making a good life for yourself. The kids began to realize that the law was subject to the economic storms we've lived through, just like every other industry. Kids who were thinking about law school began to realize that the return on their investment was crappy. When they did the math, they realized that they were going to go $150,000.00 into debt in order to get a job that would not pay anywhere near enough to chop away at that debt. Economics is a brutal truth not usually taught in law school.

Law firms and law departments of companies were flooded with applicants in a stagnant economy...they couldn't afford to pay fresh-faced lawyers forty or fifty or sixty thousand dollars for their meager skills as starting lawyers. None of the positive economic factors that blessed those giddy years survived. Now the law schools actually had to go out there and compete for the students...and this at a time when salaries for professors and administrators had already gone through the roof and made the overhead crushing.

You'd think that all those bright minds could analyze the problem and re-shape the "industry" to make it work again. Hah! Fat chance! While the law schools were tinkering with the profit and loss issues, the pressure was on from many fronts to reform the educational process itself.

People were challenging the most fundamental elements of the legal education mystique, even asking: "Why three years of law school??" The faculties were making demands that would have seemed crazy a few years earlier. And...to put the cherry on the sundae, the Department of

Justice sued (yes, SUED!) the American Bar Association for its over-reaching requirements for accrediting law schools. Every aspect of the schools was put under the DOJ microscope...teacher salaries, library contents and sizes, teaching loads, tuition, etc.

In commenting on one book that outlined the problem, James Chen, the Dean of the University of Louisville Brandeis School of Law said: "Legal Education is a broken, failed, even corrupt enterprise. It exalts and enriches law professors at the expense of lawyers, the legal profession, and most of all the students whose tuition dollars finance the entire scheme." Wow, that's some sharp language!

So, legal education in America is re-organizing. It's becoming more human, more oriented to the students (rather than to the rich, fat professors. The advent of women as a dominant force in the law has contributed mightily to the change in the law schools. No longer are the law schools simply a money machine for the professors and the deans and the universities. The law schools now know that they are vulnerable. They must compete.

What will that competition do for you, the legal consumer? Hopefully, good things. If the law becomes less mysterious and more accessible to all of us, it's going to improve. It's not just in the law schools, but on the streets, in our workplaces, in our homes where the law is going to meet its toughest test.

If we all come to admire and respect the law and its managers, then we may have made this a better place to live.

As always, thanks to my readers for your wonderful comments and ideas...keep 'em coming!

Tom Brown

A Verdict In Florida

• • •

Maybe you've been watching the circus in Florida surrounding the sad shooting of Treyvon Martin by George Zimmerman.

After the verdict, the country erupted with demonstrations condemning the verdict, condemning the justice system, condemning the lawyers, etc., etc.

I've been troubled by all the passion and hatred that came out of this terrible event, and it made me fear for the future of our legal system.

The thing that troubles me is the unwillingness to see the result, the verdict, as the product of a fair and even-handed system that just wants to arrive at the truth.

I understand the pain and frustration of our black brothers and sisters, who see this as a racial issue; but that not how I see the case at all. It's about limits. It's about extremes. It's about how humans act in colossally stressful situations.

For many days, the protagonists and their lawyers went about their business in a Courtroom, with dignity, and politeness, and preparation and concern for the truth. Both sides bent the truth at times; but that's the nature of the beast. Both sides reared up at the rulings of the judge and tried to press her envelope to the breaking point. For crying out loud, she just walked off the bench once while the lawyer was arguing... now there's a message!

But that's what our system does...that's what it's supposed to do. It tests the limits. If Zimmerman's lawyers could have brought in a choir of angels to sing the praises of sweet little Georgie Zimmerman, they would have done it. If the prosecutors could have shown videos of Treyvon reading sweet poetry to first-graders, they would have done it.

Each side constructed a set of truths, a set of possibilities, a set of impossibilities, a set of hunches, a set of predispositions...and then let the facts wash over that landscape and flow towards a conclusion.

And then, with all that emotion flowing, with all those barbs hurled, with all the racial innuendoes flying like bats around a darkened room, then the Judge told the women of the jury what the law was and what it meant.

Gone was the possibility that they would rule on the basis of race. Gone was the possibility that they would rule on the basis of personalities, ...or hoodies...or mixed martial arts...or whatever.

No. It was about the law and the facts. Those jurors had to dig deep... even deeper when manslaughter was thrown into the pool...and sort out the facts, dismissing the poetry and the preening and the shock of a young man's death and decide if a crime was committed.

Being a juror is tough. People cry when they serve as jurors. Their lives change. Their perspective changes. They see things differently. It's not often in life that we truly control the outcome of a serious social event with terrible consequences. Life, death, jail, money, love, hate, beliefs, hatreds...the whole human experience is splayed out in front of 6 or 12 people who are trying to do their best under impossible circumstances.

If I were on that Jury, and someone demonstrating in the street told me afterwards that I was not being fair...or that I had been racially insensitive...or that I didn't try to do the right thing...I would be outraged. I would tell them to walk into that jury room and try to weigh every fact, every innuendo, and every piece of testimony and come out with a better decision.

I don't know if the verdict was "right" or "wrong." What I do know is that both sides did their absolute best to convince 6 strangers what the truth was. What I do know is that those six jurors felt the weight of thousands of independent facts; they felt the weight of the community; they felt the weight of the facts and the truth...and did the best they could...and tried to do the right thing.

We'll never see perfection from our juries...there's no such thing. Our juries are full of that extreme, difficult, elusive component called individualism that shapes our concepts of truth and justice and righteousness.

Sure, someone's going to be disappointed with every verdict in every trial, civil or criminal; but, rather than condemning the system or its personalities, we have to thank our forefathers and our guardians of the law that we have such an amazing system. It may not be exactly right all of the time...but it's usually fair and it usually represents what we as a national community think is right and just.

It sure beats the alternative.

Tom Brown

Should I Hire A Lawyer Who Advertises?

• • •

SHOULD YOU HIRE AN ATTORNEY based on a TV advertisement or a Phone Book advertisement?

Let's face it...we are constantly bombarded with advertising by lawyers.

They want you to hire them if you've been in a car accident; or if your doctor screwed up and hurt you; or if you got the wrong kind of artificial hip; or if your vaginal mesh implant went wrong; or if you're the member of a huge class action relating to some information that should have been provided to you about stock investments before you wrote the check to your stock broker; or whatever...

It's relentless.

They come at you from the front page of your local phone book; then they come at you from the back page of the same phone book; then they come at you from the yellow pages of the same phone book. Then they come at you in television commercials --short ones and long ones -- that promise all sorts of things. Then they are on the radio. Then they show up in advertising flyers. Then they show up in community newspapers like this.

What should you do? Can you trust them? Should you contact them? Are they any good?

Well, let's start with the basics: There's nothing intrinsically wrong with advertising by lawyers.

Many years ago, when I was a fledgling lawyer, it used to be against the ethical rules that lawyers operated under to advertise...but some serious lawyers took care of that by having the Supreme Court of the United States rule that it was against public policy to forbid lawyers from hawking their "wares" to the public, just like Chevrolet and Samsung and GE and everybody else that was trying to market their goods or services.

In 1976 the State of Virginia had rules that it was "unprofessional" for pharmacists to advertise different prices for prescriptions. The Supreme Court of the United States took care of this by pointing out that the public had a right to hear what the pharmacists had to say about the price of drugs, and ruled that this kind of restriction waqes against the constitution of the United States.

A few years later, a couple of young lawyers from Arizona, chafed at the idea that they could not advertise, and they went to the Supreme Court of the United States. They had the gall to place an ad for their services in a publication, seeking clients for divorce, bankruptcy and other legal services. The Supreme Court followed the course they had charted with the pharmacists in Virginia, and said that it was unconstitutional to prevent lawyers from telling the world what they do and how they do it.

Wow! What a difference! After that, the yellow pages exploded with advertising by lawyers.

Lawyers talked to us between episodes of weekly television shows. Lawyers were everywhere, hawking their abilities and expertise.

So, the stage is set. We are going to have lawyers barking at us about why we should use them for car accidents, wills, medical malpractice, DWIs, criminal defense, etc., etc. It's not going to stop. We are going to see pictures of them, of their office, of people bleeding after auto accidents, of people laying in hospitals with multiple fractures, etc., etc. Let's face it...this is the American way. People that want to sell their services to you are using every outlet, every opportunity, every avenue to get their message across to you

Should you use them? Should you trust them? Are they OK?

Well, like all things in life...it's not that easy. Many of the lawyers that advertise are excellent, ethical, professional, talented lawyers. Others are schmucks. Perhaps more to the point, almost all lawyers advertise in one way or another. We have websites; we are rated by rating services like Martindale-Hubbel and AVVO; our professional organizations tout us in articles; we give speeches to groups; we write columns for community newspapers -- OOPS! Anyway, you get the point. It's just damned difficult to figure out who are the good ones.

You, as a consumer, are challenged to sort out the riff-raff from the great ones.

Here's what I suggest when trying to find out who you should use as a lawyer:

1. Talk to your friends. Who have they used? Were they happy? Did they like the lawyer? Did they get good advice? How were they treated? Were the charges reasonable?

2. Google the lawyer. See if there's anything "out there" that you should know.

3. Check with the Washington State Bar Association. Their website will tell you if the lawyer is properly licensed and if he or she has had any ethical complaints or issues.

4. Check with the established websites, like Martindale Hubbel and AVVO...see what other people think of this lawyer.

5. See if the lawyer's firm has a website...take a look at it and see what useful information you can gather about the guy and his firm. Some of these websites are incredibly chatty and full of information.

6. If you have a friend "in the system" -- like someone who works in the Court clerk's office, or a sheriff's deputy, or someone who works at the Courthouse -- give them a call. Ask them what the reputation is. Ask them what they think.

7. Understand your needs. If you've never had a will, you probably need to talk to a lawyer. If you've been in an accident and you were hurt or someone else was hurt, you probably need to talk to a lawyer. If you think that your doctor screwed up and hurt you or a family member, you probably need to talk to a doctor. If you're nearing retirement age, you probably need to sit sown and "chew the fat" with a lawyer to discuss all of your life options.

8. Take the leap. Call a lawyer. Ask him/her what they think. Talk about your situation.

9. Ask if you need a lawyer.

Lawyers are human beings. Most of us want to help you solve your problem(s). Don't let today's advertising scare you off from talking to a lawyer. Chop through the receptionists and paralegals and have a chat with a lawyer...it's amazing what you can learn in a few minutes without spending a dime!

As always, thanks for your wonderful feedback on this column. I really enjoy hearing from you...both positive and negative. Please feel free to send along your comments and suggestions for future columns.

Tom Brown

Guest Columnist ~ Sarah Glorian

• • •

As my loyal readers know, I occasionally have a guest columnist weigh in with some wisdom that I think might interest and inform you. This month a column by my friend and fellow lawyer Sarah Glorian ran in the Daily World and caught my eye. She and the Daily World have graciously allowed us to reprint this for your enjoyment.

So, here is Sarah Glorian, the Senior Attorney of the Aberdeen Office of the Northwest Justice Project, with this month's column, discussing **"Common Scams to Avoid"**

Many people fall victim to scams. Those of you who have been scammed need to report it. There is no shame. Victims to scams are not dumb or naïve; these scammers (a.k.a. criminals) are just very good at what they do.

A few years back my mother and her husband (retired seniors with multiple graduate degrees between them) fell victim to a postcard they received that appeared to be from the federal government about changes in Medicare. They called the number and a very nice man and woman came to their home. Through fear tactics about not preparing for future uncertainties, these scammers successfully sold an insurance policy that would likely never provide any benefit. Thankfully, my mother woke up the next day and promptly stopped payment on the check and called and wrote the company to cancel the contract.

Seniors, in particular, are often targeted. The Consumer Financial Protection Board reports that for every reported case of elder financial exploitation, 43 cases are unreported. Seniors lose an estimated $2.9 billion annually. And sadly, many of these exploitations are perpetrated by family members or friends.

Here are common scams everyone should be aware of, as reported by the Washington State Office of the Attorney General:

Relative in Need Scam: A person posing as a family member calls and says they are in desperate need of money and asks you to wire funds.

Charity Scam: Telephone, email or mail solicitations for charitable causes—often based on a current tragic event or story.

Foreign Lottery Scam: Telephone call, email or mail stating you have won a foreign lottery.

Home Improvement Scam: (Usually unsolicited) offers to make home repairs.

Investment Scam: Stranger or known person might offer unsolicited investment advice and/or offer a free investment analysis of your finances.

Living Trust Scam: Telephone, email or mail solicitations to purchase a trust to protect your estate and avoid probate costs and taxes.

Sweepstakes Scam: Telephone call, email or mail stating you have won (or may have already won) a prize or sweepstakes.

Travel Scam: Telephone call, email or mail stating you have won an all-expenses-paid trip to someplace exotic.

In most scams, the scammer will request personal information, such as your full name, address, telephone number(s), social security number, place of employment, email, date of birth, credit card number, bank account number or where you bank, etc.

Especially if you did not initiate this first contact, STOP!

Do not provide any personal information! In all instances; do your homework—verify, verify, verify! Do NOT just write a check or give your financial information. Even when the information request seems fairly benign, like a telephone survey—trust your gut!

If you think the contact may be legitimate, ask the person to provide you with more information about who they are, such as their name, their company's name, address, and telephone number. Ask if they are licensed to do business in Washington; and if yes, request the business license number. Often, before you can complete these questions, the scammer will cease the contact, e.g., if it is a telephone call they will hang up on you.

If you get useful information, do your homework. If you cannot verify the organization is legitimate, you have your answer. You should also file a consumer complaint so state and federal databases of these criminals become more complete.

I promise you are neither the first nor the last to be scammed. The old adage "if it sounds too good to be true; it probably is" is still words of wisdom to live by.

For more information about the scams above, go to: http://www.atg.wa.gov/scam-alerts Also check out: http://www.fbi.gov/scams-safety/fraud/internet_fraud and http://www.consumer.ftc.gov/scam-alerts

To file a consumer complaint:
http://www.atg.wa.gov/file-complaint
www.consumerfinance.gov/complaint/
https://www.ftccomplaintassistant.gov

To find out if you are eligible for Northwest Justice Project services:

For cases including youth (Individualized Education Program and school discipline issues), debt collection cases and tenant evictions, please call for a local intake appointment Tuesdays and Thursdays from 9:00 a.m. to 1:00 p.m. at (360) 533-2282 or toll free (866) 402-5293. No walk-ins, please.

For all other legal issues, please call our toll-free intake and referral hotline commonly known as "CLEAR" (Coordinated Legal Education Advice and Referral) at 1-888-201-1014, Mondays through Fridays 9:10 a.m. to 12:25 p.m. If you are a senior, 60 and over, please call 1-888-387-7111; you may be eligible regardless of income. Language interpreters are available. You can also complete an application for services at http://nwjustice.org/get-legal-help. Be sure to also check out our law library at: www.washingtonlawhelp.org.

Tom Brown

After over 43 years as a lawyer...
what would I change?

• • •

I value this little column that Lora and I collaborate on every month. It's true that it's a pain in the degenerative hip sometimes...but what a great opportunity to talk to people about the law, and what a great opportunity to field the many questions and comments that I get every month.

The reaction to the recent column we did on what is happening with drinking and driving continues to amaze and shock me...so many stories...so many close calls...so many broken families.

So, as I came home today and chased the deer out of my yard...hilarious! They aren't scared...they just want a clean shot at the bird feeders...I began to think about what I could say this month...after 60 + columns!!... that could possibly be mildly interesting to you.

So, I said: "What's interesting to me about the law?" And, then, I thought: "What's wrong with the law after all these years? What would I change, from the point of view of a crusty old lawyer that thinks he's seen it all"?

OK, fair enough! Here's my laundry list:

1. Judges have to stop hiding in their chambers. The worst offend-
    ers here are the Federal judiciary. These judges act like gods...
    they can do whatever they want. They have decided that when
    lawyers have issues to be decided before trial, there will be no
    oral argument on those issues...it will all be on paper!! (...even
    this is wrong...it's not on paper...it's all digital...) So you e-mail in
    your arguments and you get a ruling by mail. The judge prob-
    ably has not seen the parties or the lawyers. C'mon...that's not
    what the law is all about!! Even the Supreme Court of the United
    States thinks it's important to see and hear what the lawyers (or
    their clients) have to say. I believe that Federal Judges and state
    court Judges should face the lawyers and their clients in open
    court and discuss and dissect and chew on the issues until they
    are resolved. Reading briefs in closed chambers doesn't cut it...
    our system values human interchange and argument and passion.
    Fortunately, the State Courts of our local counties recognize
    the value and importance of the exchange of ideas and welcome
    open argument in Court. But in some counties in Washington,
    the practice is drifting toward the Federal system...let's not let it
    happen.
2. The appellate system has grown out of its britches. It used to
    be a big deal to appeal a negative decision. Now, it seems like
    everything is appealed. We have three divisions of the first
    layer of appeals with 21 or so Judges cranking out opinions left
    and right. I know that the workload on the Supreme Court of
    our state is too much; but the solution to that is not to simply
    let the Intermediate Courts Crank out masses of opinions that
    the Supreme Court may have to review anyway to determine
    if the intermediate court screwed up. You may be shocked to
    hear that some of the appellate decisions are identified as "un-
    published" – meaning that they cannot be cited or relied on in

subsequent cases. In a nutshell...too many Courts, too many levels of appeal, too much judicial bureaucracy. I say tighten up the rules about how decisions are appealed...put some teeth into it and cut out this parade of cases to the appellate courts.

3. More women. Our system needs balance. It's been a male-centric system for zillion years. The influence of women (in my humble opinion) has been for the good. Are there bonehead, impossible women in the system? Yes. Are they worse than the ridiculous men? Nope. Are they smart? Yes. Do they have a different view of things than men? Hah! Do Judges give proper deference to womanhood? Yes (especially since so many of the judges are now women!). To the extent that our law schools and legal systems remain sexist, we need to change. Fortunately for all of us, the balance here is changing.

4. More and more "alternative dispute resolution". That's a clichéd, trendy phrase for a phenomenon that is sweeping the law. Nine times out of ten, we do not go to a jury (or judge) trial...we try to resolve the case with trained, experienced arbitrators and mediators who can settle or resolve the lawsuits cheaply, efficiently, and at incredibly less expense than a full-blown trial. It has the power to change our system of dispute resolution forever.

5. In my opinion, the criminal justice system is totally broken. We have to be tougher on crime with longer sentences (I know it's more expensive!!!), more intensive counseling and treatment, better monitoring of released criminals, and a totally revamped system of what happens to these folks when they get out of prison. If they are going to rob again, or molest again, or kill again, we can't let them out in our society. I don't fully know the answer to this...but we can't just continue to let these people poison our society. We have to take back the streets and make our streets safe and welcoming for our children and us. Stop and think...these people are dangerous. If it was a hurricane or a tornado or a tsunami, or a flood, we would mobilize and take care

of it...we have to stop accepting dangerous criminal conduct as a necessary part of our society...it has to stop. If we can't trust the system that deals with criminal behavior...

6. Make it easier to be a lawyer. The business of creating lawyers has turned into a multibillion-dollar enterprise. It's all about the best schools in the country, hundreds of thousands of dollars of tuition and student loans. Let's get back to the law schools that were founded on the principle of analysis, and evaluation, and classroom interchange. We don't need more Wall Street lawyers for the billionaires. We need more common sense lawyers for the streets of Aberdeen, Centralia, Omaha, Des Moines, Olympia and Cosmopolis. Replacing the law school in Tacoma would be a good start.

7. Finally, what we need, is a willingness of our lawyers to leave the books, leave the courtrooms, leave the boardrooms, and become society's enablers and tour guides. We lawyers have learned how the organs of this society function. We know how the lungs process air; we know how the digestive system processes fodder; we have learned how to adapt the world we see to the world we inhabit. We're not geniuses...but we do understand. We can push, pull, shove, and force. We're only human; but we can see the goal...our job is to bring us there. Lawyers owe a debt to our society to push, pull, shove, haul, squeeze and do whatever is necessary to make the system work.

The name of this column is "de minimis" which is Latin for "about little things."

I hope that these columns cause us to think or reflect or maybe even change our world.

Tom Brown

HAPPY NEW YEAR!!!!...Oh, and by the way...Merry Christmas!

• • •

EACH YEAR ABOUT THIS TIME I have given in to the pressure to write something cheery and sentimental about Christmas. Don't get me wrong; I love Christmas and all the baggage it hauls around.

Even we lawyers are as nutty as everybody else about the Spirit of Christmas.

But this year, while I was struggling to come up with an idea, and while our genius editor was whipping me to make the deadline, it struck me that our friend the New Year always gets short shrift at this time of year. It's all about Christmas...not the New Year. It's MERRY CHRISTMAS!...and Happy New Year.

It's gifts at Christmas, but hangovers at New Year's Day.

We make our Christmas lists in detail, but New Years generates only a couple of half-hearted resolutions about how much we're going to eat for the next year.

So this year...something different. We're going to stick with the legal theme, but I'm going to propose a short list of things we can do that might make that New Year safer, happier, more organized and just better. Here we go...

1. Get off your Lazy Boy and take care of your "estate planning" documents. If you already did this 20 years ago, it's time to have your lawyer look them over and see if they're still current. You don't have to be rich to need a simple set of documents, possibly including a Community Property Agreement (if you're married), a simple will, a durable power of attorney, a directive about keeping you alive if you're beyond hope, a power of attorney for medical care, and whatever else fits. This would also be an opportunity for you to mentally review and plan for your exit strategy. I think you'll find that a trip to your favorite lawyer to take care of this is surprisingly affordable and does wonders for your mental bucket list.

2. Review your auto insurance. Make sure that all of your cars and all of your houses are properly insured. Look closely at the amount of coverage you have on various things, and ask your insurance agent to tell you what's available at relatively low cost to increase your protection. As we have discussed several times in this column, it is critical these days to have Uninsured/Underinsured motorist coverage as part of your auto policy. This pays you as if the other driver did have insurance. There are so many uninsured and underinsured drivers out there, that this is absolutely mandatory...and make it as big as you can afford. DO NOT BE TALKED INTO DECLINING UNDERINSURED MOTORIST COVERAGE. Also be sure that your limits are sufficient. The minimum is $25K; but you need more protection than that. If you blow a red light and seriously injure someone, a $25K policy is a joke, and someone is going to be looking at your personal assets to pay for the accident.

3. Review your homeowner's insurance. Make sure that you have enough coverage to replace your home if disaster strikes. Ask

tough questions of your insurance agent about how much coverage you need. And don't forget that your homeowner's policy includes protection against someone being injured because of your negligence. For example, if you accidentally ran into someone with your grocery cart at the store, and they were badly injured, your homeowner's insurance would probably pay the damages and pay for the lawsuit against you. Check this coverage carefully and ask your insurance agent for advice.

4. Collect and protect your information. These days, we are loaded with critical information. We have passwords, combinations to safes, telephone numbers, credit card numbers, PIN numbers, and e-mail addresses. Unfortunately, this information is scattered all over hell and gone and we can never lay our hands on it when necessary (...and, let's face it, our memories aren't what they used to be). There are computer programs and cell phone apps that can keep all this information safe. Go to Google and type in "how to keep passwords safe"...you'll get an avalanche of advice. If you have a safe, wonderful...but never, never tell anybody that you have a safe at home.

5. Re-think drinking and driving. The column I wrote a few months ago generated an amazing response. Society has decided that it will not tolerate drinking and driving...even at very low levels of alcohol in the body. The penalties are breath-taking (pun intended) and the financial and personal risks are terrible. If you only had two beers when you plowed into the crowd of shoppers, it's not going to make any difference that your Breathalyzer score was borderline.

6. Take videos or still pictures of every room in your house and the contents and keep those images somewhere safe...away from the house.

7. Set up a reminder system that takes the guesswork out of remembering important dates and deadlines and things that need to be done. C'mon...we are getting a little older and we might forget a

thing or two. There are dozens of programs out there that will send you e-mail or call your cell phone or do other things to remind you of important things. I like one called MEMOTOME. It's at http://www.memotome.com/ The basic program is free, but you can upgrade for a fee. I've used this program for many years to remember everything from family birthdays to important deadlines at the office.

Of course, there are dozens, maybe hundreds, of good ideas that we could implement to improve our lives, which involve things like diet and exercise and relationships. Those are great goals for the New Year, but I'm not a psychologist or a weight trainer; so this is pretty much a "nuts and bolts" type of list.

What I've set out here are some things that might usually be forgotten or put off that can have a dramatic effect on our lives, and tend to be shoved to the back of our mental closet. But, as in all things, we do need to face this stuff.

What better time to square up and address our future than on the eve of the New Year?

As always, I appreciate the opportunity to talk about the law with our loyal readers. I very much enjoy your comments about the column and your suggestions for topics in the future. Happy New Year!

Tom Brown

What In The World Does The County's "Prosecuting Attorney" Do?

• • •

FOR THOSE OF YOU THAT live in Grays Harbor County, you already know that there is a titanic battle going on to claim the job of "Prosecuting Attorney" for the County.

The long-time prosecutor, Stew Menefee, recently resigned. His faithful and hard-working deputy, Jerry Fuller, was not interested in inheriting the job.

As we all know from the multiple, numbing stories in the newspapers and on the radio, a huge fight erupted over who *should* fill the job. The fracas involved the Democratic Central Committee of Grays Harbor; the Commissioners of the County Board of Commissioners (with a Republican majority); several interested candidates for the job; and some candidates that weren't interested in the job; and the whole brouhaha may ultimately make its way to the Governor's Office to make the disputed appointment.

I have my own ideas about who should be the Prosecuting Attorney... but this column (in its nearly six years of existence) is not here to make political statements...it's here to inform about the law and government, so we citizens can be more comfortable with the systems that sometimes govern our life.

I have always been bothered by the lack of understanding that we citizens have about the little bureaucracies --state, county, municipal, federal -- that have so much to do with our lives.

Today, then, let's talk about this "Prosecuting Attorney" job that everybody is tied in knots about. What in the world does the Prosecuting Attorney do?

Let's start with the basics. This is an elected position. Although someone may be initially appointed to the job, he or she will ultimately have to stand for election every four years. The person seeking the position must be admitted to the State Bar of Washington as an attorney.

Usually, the initial appointment to a vacant Prosecuting Attorney position is based on politics, or on relationships, or on inertia after the Prosecuting Attorney resigns, or dies, or simply decides not to run again. Very often, the appointment is political. Also, it is common that the appointment comes from within the office, and one of the deputies may be appointed. Sometimes, there's no binding appointment; and the whole thing is tossed in the laps of the voters.

The biggest source of misunderstanding about this position lies in the name of the job. The statutes of the State of Washington identify this position as the "Prosecuting Attorney" for such-and-such a county. To most of us, this would suggest that the job of this person and his office is strictly to prosecute criminals that are brought into the system by law enforcement. While a large portion of the work of the office is prosecuting crimes, the Office of Prosecuting Attorney is actually the Chief legal officer of the County, responsible for many, many aspects of the County's work. The Office of the Prosecuting Attorney is really the County's "law firm."

If the County is sued, a specialist in Civil Law in the Prosecutor's office will defend the County. If the Assessor's office needs a legal opinion on how to handle a certain situation, a specialist in the Prosecutor's office will respond, look up the law, and write an opinion. The Office will have a special section or a designated attorney to enforce child support obligations to protect the treasury of the county and of the state. If the County needs to sue a trucking company that ran into one of its bridges and destroyed it, a specialized attorney in the office will handle the lawsuit. A member of the Prosecuting Attorney's office is usually on hand for all of the meetings of the County Commissioners, to make sure they don't step in it; or to help with thorny legal issues that come up. Another attorney in the office might handle all of the tax foreclosures that the County has to pursue. If there is a question about how an election was handled (or should be handled), an attorney from the Prosecutor's office will examine the facts and advise the politicians, and -- if necessary -- handle any lawsuit arising out of the mess.

So, you can see that the name "Prosecuting Attorney" is more of an historical accident, than a description of what the office does. In fact, looking around the country, there are a blizzard of different names for legal offices that do exactly the same work as our Prosecuting Attorney Offices. Most states identify the office as the "County Attorney" or the "District Attorney" or the "State's Attorney." Actually, the whole thing is very similar to the concept of the Attorney General's office, which is the "law firm" for the State and handles hundreds of different kinds of legal problems. Well, that is the situation in our counties...the "Prosecuting Attorney" is really the Law firm for the County and all of its offices. To stretch the comparison, the "Prosecuting Attorney" for Grays Harbor County (or any County) is really the "Attorney General" for the County and for the County's business.

To give you some perspective on this, lets look around the state. When Stew Menefee resigned, Grays Harbor County's Prosecuting Attorney Office had a Chief Deputy, Seven Senior Deputies, and four deputies, along with highly trained staff to help them do their jobs. The Pacific County Prosecuting Attorney has the Prosecutor and two deputies; the Clallam County Prosecuting Attorney has the Prosecutor and twelve deputies; the Pierce County Prosecuting Attorney has approximately 217 lawyers to handle all their various legal responsibilities in a huge county. And then there's King County: well over 200 lawyers in a dizzying collection of divisions.

The elephant in the living room is the Office of the Attorney General for the State of Washington. This is the "law firm" for all of the State agencies, giving advice, drafting contracts, litigating cases, keeping state agencies on the straight and narrow, and literally doing hundreds or thousands of jobs as legal advisor for the state. This agency has over 500 lawyers and a total of over 1,100 employees...YIKES, that's a lot of lawyers!

In the Federal system, Each judicial district has an appointed "United States Attorney" with a huge staff of deputies that handles the prosecution of federal crimes in Federal Courts, and also handle all of the routine legal business and litigation of the United States of America...which is a truckload of work, believe me. This office in Seattle has about 70 lawyers.

So, anyway, to get back to our corner of the state...remember that the office of the "Prosecuting Attorney" is not just a bunch of lawyers trying to convict and sentence criminals. That's only one facet of their job. The rest of it is to act as the "law firm" for the county, doing what lawyers everywhere do: give advice; prepare and review contracts; prepare legal opinions for our elected officials; protect the county from lawsuits and claims; give guidance to county officials on what is "legal" and what is not; keep the elected officials out of trouble (if possible); and generally do anything necessary to maintain a smoothly functioning County government that is in compliance with all the laws and ready to defend itself in court, if necessary.

Tom Brown

Wouldn't it be great, if we could write the laws?

• • •

WOULDN'T IT BE GREAT, IF we could write the laws?

All of us, lawyers included, are prisoners of the body of laws that our legislators spin from their chambers in Olympia, Washington and Washington, D.C., and from the city halls of our towns and the chambers of our counties.

It's a big business that affects us in ways that we never imagined. They impact our lives in hundreds...hey, thousands of ways. They pass the laws...we obey them.

So, do you ever sit around and wonder what we would do, if we could take over those hallowed halls and craft our own laws.

Well, here's my list...one from a God-fearing, flag-loving, military-saluting child of the 50s.

1. Let's get rid of the Washington State Liquor Control Board. What are they doing anyway? We can buy vodka at Safeway, bourbon at Indian outlet stores, wine anywhere, and now they are pretending to regulate marijuana. Well we can only imagine

how many ways they are going to screw that up. Regulation of our sins is a tricky, ridiculous enterprise anyway. Let's save a few million or billion every year by throwing that agency on the trash heap, while we drive by and laugh at all those empty state liquor stores that drained us for years.

2. OK, I absolutely worship law enforcement. My dad was a State Trooper. I know they have to speed to terrible situations, talk on their cell phones for certain reasons, and make split second decisions. But, let's remember that we are all human and mistakes can happen. So I'm proposing a law that says that emergency personnel have to use their emergency equipment, when doing what we are forbidden to do. It's almost as dangerous for Officer Jones to speed as it is for me to speed. If he's going to speed, turn on the lights and siren. If he has to talk on the phone in emergencies, OK...but get a headset. He can make a stupid mistake as easily as I can. I don't want to drive on the highway at 100 miles per hour because I know it's crazy...but I don't want anyone else to, unless they have a loud siren and brightly flashing lights. Especially, I don't want a WSP Cadet passing me at 95 MPH because he or she can. Turn on the lights and siren unless there's a very compelling reason not to.

3. I grew up in Nebraska, the only state in the Union that has a unicameral legislature. Instead of two "houses" full of politicians, arguing, dickering, wheeling, dealing, and wasting our money on a ridiculously unruly process that produces the annual or bi-annual roster of laws, we could have just one! Do we need all those people in Olympia every time around? Nebraska seems to have perfected a system that gives everybody their say, allows plenty of citizen involvement. and nobody is the worse for wear. Do we really need that crazy ballet in Olympia every year or two? No, lets cut it down to one house with simple rules. And, what do we do -- you might ask -- with that other lovely chamber in Olympia where a similar group of people go over the same

ground, make the same arguments, hear the same citizen arguments...what do we do with that beautiful "chamber"? First, we quit spending money on cleaning it and decorating it every year and putting the latest and greatest electronic in every year and then we dedicate it as a museum to our fallen law enforcement heroes. I know that this would take a constitutional amendment to our State constitution; but the long-term savings would be terrific...not to mention economical. Unicameral...yes. We could save millions...maybe billions over the long haul.

4. As I write this column, I just heard about another random school shooting. I will tell you frankly that I hate to think or talk or write about school shootings. It makes me sick to my stomach, not only because of the terrible carnage, but because of the impact on all those innocent students who deserve better. A few years ago, I would have said that it was terrible to turn schools into safe zones by using TSA-style searching and evaluating. I don't want scanners in our schools...it creates a zone, a premise, a terrible kind of admission that we are scared. But now it's gone too far. We need to be sure our kids are safe. Hell, they know that it's scary out there...let's make it less scary by showing them that it's safe. Bring on the scanners and the wands. If we stop one whacko, one sick monster, then we win. I believe that our kids will understand and feel safer. I want the legislature and the teachers' union to address this squarely and bravely.

5. To go from the sublime to the ridiculous, I think we need to re-evaluate the whole concept of animal control in our world. I was a paperboy in my youth, and I spent my afternoons dodging aggressive animals whose owners didn't give a you-know-what about the conduct of their animals. i was chased, bitten, scared, and hospitalized by animals that were allowed to roam free and have their way. This last year, my wife -- while out for a walk -- was bitten by a random dog, whose owner was never found, so we had to go thru appropriate medical care. In our

present neighborhood, dogs are allowed to roam at night, bark-ing for hours on end, and visiting our yard to fertilize and dig. I clean up for them so we don't track their toilet into our house. It's really not fair. I love dogs...we had a Golden Retriever that enriched our lives for many years; but we didn't let her attack people or use people's yards as her bathroom or bark all night. I think it's a reasonable function of local government to make sure that people's dogs don't interfere with other people's lives.

The beauty of this column for me is the feedback I get from you readers.

I've made new friends and learned new lessons from the comments and suggestions of you readers. You readers are the actual authors of this column, because you inspire me to write about issues that are close to your hearts. I'm still reeling from the comments and issue arising out of the DWI column...it was a life changer for me and obviously for many of you.

Thank you for reading my column and thank you for your input. You are truly the authors.

Tom Brown

The Language Of The Law

• • •

WHEN I WAS A KID, my Mom used to have a bunch of "sayings" that she would repeat over and over again, to the dismay of my brother and me ...and even my Dad (who had to act like she was a genius).

One of her favorites was the Latin phrase for "Time Flies", which was "tempus Fugit." Of course, my Mom had to modify this every time she used it, by adding "...et non comebackibus." Pretty dumb, but we always got her pig Latin point, namely that the passage of time was fleeting and we would never get it back.

It's funny how the law has adopted many of these sayings and turned them into things that we use every day without really thinking about the underlying meaning of the phrase or word. Think "Guilty Plea" or "confession" or "Bless me Father, for I have sinned..."

We have a lot of those words in our legal vocabulary...but many of them ar so obscure that no one knows (or cares to know) what the heck we're talking about. Last week, I heard a news story about a businessman who entered a plea of what we lawyers call "nolo"...which is short for "Nolo Contedere."

This basically means: "Yeah...I did it, but I don't want to got to prison for a long time like other guys who were caught at the scene. Hah!"

My theory is that the law has attempted to soften the harsh meaning of legal phrases over the years, to keep a gentler image after all those years of bourbon-swilling, sloppy dress, rush-to-judgment solutions about things. When I was a young lawyer in Grays Harbor County, the day that all the motions were heard in court was Friday...which pretty much meant that all the lawyers in the County would show up in Court at 8:30 and most of the arguments would be heard in the morning, and then the lawyers would sidle down to the "Honeycomb Room" of the Beehive restaurant and take up a new set of arguments, fueled by a few beverages. This finally got out of hand and the judges changed the "Motion Day" to Monday...which tended to keep things on a more level-headed basis. (Unless, of course, you took into account the monthly "Bar meeting" at the then-elegant Oaksridge Country Club, where everybody transacted all the important business of the Grays harbor County Bar Association.)

But, back to the lingo of the law. I'm working on a case right now where everyone is talking about the rights of the parties to testify about what the "other guy" said. This is usually fair game, but we are a much more "sanitized" system now; and the judges are going to be particularly vigilant about letting a jury hear all of the bare-knuckles, angry, exchanges that mark so many of our contests these days.

Most of it is "fair game"...but a lot of it is merely "heat of the moment" overstepping. C'mon, we all know that sometimes: "I'm going to kill you..." has a meaning unrelated to homicide.

These are the hair-splittings that we deal with every day in the law. Lawyers are forever explaining to Judges and Juries that the defendant didn't really intend to burn down his neighbor's house and kill all his livestock...he was just annoyed at the new fence that he woke up to that morning.

Anyway, the law has to be the servant of all of us, not just the perfect citizens who never cause trouble; not just the priests and nuns, not just the quietly irritated citizens who quietly live their lives without violence. But it's a human institution that depends on the meanings of words and the context they were spoken in. It is wonderful that the language of the law has matured and ripened, so that every slight, every threat, every rant is no longer fodder for the heavy hand of the law...but the law stands by to wrestle with the real, serious threats.

As always thanks for reading my little column, and thank you for your suggestions and comments.

And thanks to you, Lora for your incredible devotion to this great little newspaper, and God bless you and your Mother at this difficult time.

Tom Brown

Lawyers In Trouble

• • •

C'MON...ADMIT IT...EVERYONE LIKES TO SEE a lawyer getting skewered by the system he or she works in.

We spend so much time hating lawyers for their apparent failure to be human, for their lofty dominance over the "system." It just feels good -- doesn't it? -- to see a lawyer get his or her due?

Most people don't understand that we lawyers live in a system that allows very few departures from the "straight and narrow." The lawyer code of ethics is rigid and sweeping. Let me expand on that -- it's more than rigid and sweeping. It is scary and powerful.

We have to report ourselves. We have to report our brethren. We cannot lie to the tribunals that govern our conduct.

Many people, even lawyers themselves, are shocked to find out how strict and demanding the system that governs lawyers' conduct is.

Lawyers in Washington (like most jurisdictions) live under a code of ethics that is as rigid and unforgiving as you can imagine.

Of course, there's the obvious stuff...if lawyers steal from their clients by taking money in their trust accounts, they are not only going to jail, but the Washington State Bar Association and the Supreme Court are going to take away their license to practice law...usually forever. If lawyers deliberately deceive the tribunal they are in front of, they will probably lose their livelihood forever. If lawyers lose control of their law practice, and repeatedly miss deadlines and court hearings and other obvious issues, there's a good chance that they will lose their "ticket" for a probationary period or forever, depending on the "grievousness" of the offense.

If you're interested in this sort of thing, you can go to the Washington State Bar Association website at http/wsba.com and particularly at http://www.wsba.org/Licensing-and-Lawyer-Conduct/Discipline and learn all about the discipline system that we lawyers labor under.

If you spend some time on that website, I think you will be amazed... even impressed...at how seriously the Washington State Bar Association takes its obligation to make sure that unscrupulous and deviant lawyers do not end up in he mainstream, representing and applying good, solid law.

The sad truth is that a small percentage of the lawyers admitted in this state are people who routinely violate those strict rules and routinely overlook the demands of their clients. Most of us normal lawyers wish that those scumbags would disappear from the radar...but it's simply not going to happen.

There are happy endings. I represented an individual whose family had come under the sway of a "sophisticated" family planning attorney who promised all sorts of easy solutions to complicated tax and IRS problems. None of his exotic ideas worked for the family or even offered hope for reasonable outcomes. We fought like hell, and the "expert" lawyer finally moved to Montana and his advice subsided. Our clients recognized the reality and absurdity of his advice and stayed "on the ranch." We saved our clients from lengthy and ridiculous battles with the IRS.

I don't discourage people from seeking "cutting edge" advice from responsible individuals. But we have to be very careful about late or supplemental advice or products.

As always, I enjoy and respect your feedback! Thanks for reading my little column.

Tom Brown

WHAT is your lawyer wearing?

• • •

Most of us have faint images of what lawyers used to look like in the early days of our judicial systems.

We see ancient pictures of powdered wigs and long coats and monocles and grey gloves, all adding up to a stereotype of what lawyer used to be.

It's true, in the early days of our English-American legal system, there were strict rules about what would and would not be worn while prowling the halls of justice.

Fortunately for us American lawyers, the waistcoats and powdered wigs of the English system faded early in our country's history, and lawyers were generally expected to appear in court in elaborate, three-piece suits, with monocles instead of glasses and with long chains to our timepieces. But, that too faded with time and the changes in our expectations of what we wanted our lawyers to look like.

For most of our American legal history, lawyers were expected to be fully decked out, not only in court, but also in their offices. If you came to a lawyer's office in the 50's or 60's or 70's, you would be shocked if the lawyer you dealt with wasn't at least in a blazer and tie, if not a three-piece suit.

But the influence of our changing times seeped inexorably into the offices of lawyers throughout the country, especially in small towns and close-knit communities. Usually the tie was the first to go, then the sport coat or suit, and finally the whole effort to maintain the "image" that people had in their heads about what lawyers should and should not be wearing to the office.

One time I remember years ago, I was working in my office in Aberdeen. I was strictly working in the "back room" researching cases and trying to put together a brief for an upcoming trial, when a woman dropped in unexpectedly to ask about her case. I'll never forget her shock and horror when she observed in a loud voice that I was wearing "dungarees." Of course, she meant jeans...but her shock was palpable and it taught me a lesson...namely, that peoples' expectations are part of the overall sense of what they expect from their professionals.

Nowadays, my clients (and the clients of most lawyer i know) expect to meet their lawyers in slacks and sweater and sport shirts when the meeting is in the office and it's one-on-one with the lawyer. If it's a group meeting or a deposition, that may be different, but the expectation of fancy, expensive lawyer-clothes is gone forever.

I'll have to confess that my beautiful bride was a difficult case to convert. She never really got over the fact that I should go to work every day in a coat and tie, just like the old days. She grits her teeth, but she accepts it now.

But, everything I've said so far ignores the tsunami of lawyer dress, the hand grenade of what lawyers wear, the parting of the waves...yes -- you guessed it -- the advent of women lawyers.

When I was a young lawyer, there were really no women lawyers to speak of, except for one or two icons in each small community.

In Aberdeen, it was the legendary Gladys Phillips, who could wear whatever she damn well pleased to Court or in her office and no judge or lawyer or client dared challenge her taste in lawyer duds. She stood alone.

But, inexorably, the tide shifted, and shifted again, and shifted again. Now, we are inundated with women lawyers. There are more women than men in law school. Many of our Judges are women. Women are part and parcel of the fabric of the law in our country. Our docket day in Court features as many women as men...all in an incredibly diverse range of clothing tastes and styles that would have sent Judge Kirkwood or Judge Schumacher of 30 years ago scrambling back to his chambers to figure out what to say or do.

The idea of controlling what women wear in Court is a laugh. The same Judge that chastised a male lawyer for his dress 30 years ago would now get a serious ethical complaint for "dressing down" a woman lawyer for "unprofessional" dress in Court.

My experience is that clients are now used to the fact that lawyers don't dress up in three-piece suits every day while they wander around the office. The casual dress of lawyers in slacks and a nice shirt is more likely to produce a comfortable relationship between lawyer and client, without any pretension about who is "superior" to whom.

Most of us lawyers still strongly believe in the importance of formality in the Courtroom as part of the respect and honor that we give the law and its activities. You'll never see a trial -- either to the Court or to a jury -- where the lawyer doesn't wear a suit and tie. The female lawyers honor that tradition with tasteful and dignified apparel that reflects the gravity and honor that we afford to our legal system, while the Judges continue the ages old practice of wearing a judicial robe while presiding over legal proceedings. (That part of the deal is so important that it is covered by a State Law...a judge (male or female) must wear the judicial robe when presiding in the Courtroom.

What do we take away from all this? As the song says..."the times they are a-changing..." and we have to accommodate those winds of change. The forces of the 60s and 70s made changes in our system. The advent of women as lawyers and judges swept in changes that will never be reversed.

It truly doesn't make any difference whether your lawyer wears a suit in his office. If he honors the system by wearing proper attire in the Courtroom and/or she dresses with dignity in the courtroom, the system will honor and respect the traditions that have grown up and will continue to grow up in the future.

Who knows what we will be wearing in the Courtrooms of the future? We can only hope that the quality of the justice that is dealt remains as strong and honorable, no matter whether there's a tie or a vest or a cuff that's been shot.

So...the next time you visit your lawyer, and he (or she) is wearing jeans at the office, remember that it's not the clothes that makes the lawyer...it's the brain, the imagination, the resourcefulness, the moxie, and the good, old-fashioned guts.

Tom Brown

What in the world does a "paralegal" do?

● ● ●

IT'S FASHIONABLE THESE DAYS FOR lawyers to make a point of telling their clients or other lawyers that a particular task has been assigned to a "paralegal." This has a lot of ripples...some good, some not so good. One of the negative ripples is that my clients sometimes tell me to give something to my paralegal, when they don't know what a paralegal is, or whether we have one, or whether the task at hand would even be suitable for a paralegal.

But, any discussion of the role of paralegals in the law today requires us to start with the basics...what is a paralegal?

Well, like most things, it's not a simple, easily answered question. If you went out to observe a number of paralegals, and you carefully documented what they do, you would ultimately throw up your hands in confusion at the wide variety of tasks that they perform and how far they have come in complementing the full skills of a lawyer. Basically put, a paralegal is a person (many are men now) who performs certain defined legal tasks under the supervision of a practicing lawyer that is admitted to the bar.

Many of these tasks were historically done by "secretaries" before the advent of the term "paralegal." Many of the people that were traditionally identified as "secretaries" now want to be known as paralegals.

Other former secretaries reject the re-branding of their job" and remain known as secretaries. To complicate things even further, many legal office workers are now identified as "legal assistants"!!...go figure!

At this stage, it does not appear that there is a formal rule or license, authorizing a paralegal to "practice" ...but it is clear that any such practice must be under the supervision of a practicing attorney. There is simply no denying that paralegal/legal assistant practice is a wave that is transforming the practice of law. Effective September 1, 2001, the Washington State Supreme Court adopted General Rule 25 (GR25) which established the Practice of Law Board (POLB).

GR 25 provides that the purpose of the Board is to:

* promote expanded access to affordable and reliable legal and law-related services
* expand public confidence in the administration of justice
* make recommendations regarding the circumstances under which non-lawyers may be involved in the delivery of certain types of legal and law-related services
* enforce rules prohibiting individual sand organizations from engaging in unauthorized legal and law-related services that post a threat to the general public
* ensure that those engaged in the delivery of legal services in the state of Washington have the requisite skill and competencies necessary to serve the public.

The POLB is composed of 13 members, at least four of whom are non-lawyers. The Board of Governors of the Washington State Bar Association believes that it is important that the POLB represent the broad public interest in the delivery of legal services. Also, the Board of Governors is concerned that the POLB reflect the broad range of diversity of individuals who are part of or who use the legal system.

All of this means that the State of Washington and our State Supreme Court are committed to the principle that our system is going to take seriously the movement toward allowing non-lawyers to deliver legal services under controlled and regulated supervision.

The Washington State Paralegal Association has a fine website at www.wspaonline.org that discusses the training, education and certification of paralegals.

There is also a National Association of Paralegal groups that appears to be quite active and supports the state groups. As defined by the National Federation of Paralegal Associations, paralegal is a person qualified through education, training or work experience to perform substantive legal work that requires knowledge of legal concepts and is customarily, but not exclusively, performed by a lawyer. This person may be retained or employed by a lawyer, law office, governmental agency or other entity or may be authorized by administrative, statutory or court authority to perform this work.

Gone are the days when lawyer had to "start from scratch" on a new project, and develop every word, every phrase, every comma, and every supporting document to perform a relatively simple task. Now, a smart secretary/legal assistant/paralegal knows what document is going to be important in a particular situation, and can tailor it for the attorney's review, along with a set of comments and warnings about the peculiarities of the immediate matter.

The truth is that competent secretaries and paralegals and legal assistants...whatever they are called...are a critical part of the day-to-day operation of law offices of all sizes. They identify information that is critical for the lawyer to have; they serve as a buffer between the attorney and the "world at large" so the attorney can devote himself to the project or projects at hand; they identify issues that the lawyer needs to know and recognize while addressing a particular issue, and – finally – they put another brain to work on the thorny problems that every lawyer faces every day.

This movement can only make lawyers better servants of our clients' needs.

Tom Brown

Law and Medicine...oil and water?

• • •

IT'S A FACT OF LIFE...WE senior citizens are likely to encounter the world of medicine as we glide into our "Golden Years."

I had that encounter this last month, in the form of a hip replacement at Grays Harbor Community Hospital (GHCH) in Aberdeen.

My previous serious encounter with medicine was at a major metropolitan medical center, a huge, multi-layered facility with all the bells and whistles that were available at that time in history.

Could a little hospital in Grays Harbor compete with a "big-box" metropolitan facility?

The lawyer side of me was curious to see how medicine had aged with respect to the law, since my last serious medical encounter 14 years ago; and how our local hospital stacked up against the mega-center of the last decade.

On the other hand, the author side of me wanted to let our readers in on some of the expectations they might have in our local medical community.

I'll begin by saying that the lawyer side of me was very impressed with one thing that I had not seen in my earlier experience with a big hospital; namely: that they follow their own rules. I know that hospitals are tightly regulated and are subject to review by agencies that can judge them very harshly. But, way too often, medical facilities recognize but only give lip service to the hundreds (thousands?) of rules and directives that they are supposed to follow.

In my recent experience at Grays Harbor Community Hospital, the supervisors and nurses and nurse assistants and aides ---and even the dietary aides that bring your food and drink -- all religiously repeated the things required by those rules, as if their lives (not just yours!) depended on it. They are stringent about identifying the patient each time, communicating with the patient about the issues being faced, and explaining clearly to the patient what is going to happen. This was in sharp contrast to my earlier experience at a regional mega-hospital, which treated the patient like an idiot that should just shut up and let big time medicine do its workl

In my four days at Grays Harbor Community Hospital, no drug was prepared and offered without an explanation to the patient; no change in the care was made without consultation with the patient. My roommate at the hospital had some personal and medical issues that challenged the staff...but they unfailingly responded with professionalism and firm direction and a smile.

And...how crazy is this?...in each room on a big board, each day, the staff writes out what the goal and program is for the day and identifies in big block letters the names and titles of the persons who will be delivering the care. On the same board they identify the special issues that each patient in the room may have...what's the danger of this patient falling? ...who is the patient's doctor? ...are there dietary restrictions? If you're just practicing defensive medicine, you don't write that stuff on a big board for the patient and all the world to see.

In my mind, the true test of a medical facility is how the institution and its people respond if something goes wrong. In my case at GHCH something did go wrong post-surgery that challenged the staff and could have been very serious. Fortunately for me (...and for all the other patients that fall into their hands...), they responded "by the book" and protected me from unnecessary and unanticipated harm. What's more, they not only averted the immediate danger, but they added the issue to their "menu" of treatment options and made the rest of my stay relatively benign. I was impressed!

The biggest contrast between my experience at GHCH and the mega facility years earlier, was the collaborative, team approach from the very beginning. When I was in the pre-operative suite at GHCH, I was in the hands of a skilled nurse who followed a "menu" of all the crazy things that can be presented by an incoming patient. They made doubly sure I didn't have certain diseases or conditions or other issues that could be dangerous -- or even worse -- to a surgery patient.

Even more impressive was the presence of the principal actors during the preoperative phase.

The surgeon checked in and reviewed all the possible problems; the anesthesiologist carefully and openly charted the ways I could be anesthetized and the dangers and pluses of each alternative. Even more reassuring, other professionals involved themselves in my situation to make sure that every "t" was crossed, before I was wheeled down the hall.

Although my earlier experience at the major facility involved a lot of people, the intimate, individualized type of attention to the needs and concerns of the patient was not even close to the excellence of individual care that I experienced here in Grays Harbor County.

Another facet of medicine that is often not discussed or even evaluated relates to how the patient and the patient's family are treated by the staff, from the top of the pyramid down to the workers who are in contact with the patients. My experience with the major medical facility was filled with long waits, incomplete explanations of what was going to happen or what had already happened, lack of detail about the treatment, and lack of general regard for the patient who feels helpless. At GHCH, to the contrary, the patients seemed to me to be the focus of the work of the staff. I saw incredible, hands-on patient care and attention that was not even on the horizon in the larger hospital.

I will credit my profession, the law, with some of what we see in competent modern hospitals.

The expansion of medical malpractice litigation has helped create an atmosphere of carefulness and attention to detail. But the excellent care I witnessed and experienced at Grays Harbor Community Hospital was based in the organizational strength of the hospital and its employees, who want to do the right thing...as opposed to being afraid of doing the wrong thing.

In no way was it the classic case of "defensive medicine"...rather, it was institutional attention to quality patient care.

So...what did I conclude as a lawyer?...as a patient? ...as a potential future user of medical care?

Well, as a lawyer, I concluded that this hospital was a safe, competent medical facility that met the very stringent requirements of a modern hospital; but also had a heart. As a patient, I concluded that the medical care in a small, quality hospital can be every bit the equal of the big-box, mega-buck hospitals of the last decade and probably this decade as well.

We know that there aren't going to be any heart transplants in Grays Harbor County; but we have the comfort of knowing that our medical facility can handle a broad variety of medical procedures and care, that is every bit the equal of the big boys. Further, we know that the patients are going to be treated with dignity and respect; and that the hospital meets the very stringent standards imposed by the regulators, by the law, and by the facility itself.

Tom Brown

Should I Sign Up For A Reverse Mortgage??

● ● ●

LOTS OF PEOPLE ARE ASKING me (and other lawyers) whether it's a good idea to get a reverse mortgage.

My first response is always the same: "Be careful!"

I don't tell people that it's always a bad idea to get a reverse mortgage; but it is a complicated, sophisticated transaction that can have an impact on your "later in life" planning. It is important that you clearly understand what you are doing and what the consequences are.

The first step is to get a grip on what the transaction means. You are borrowing money, and putting up your house as equity. It's like every other home loan with one main difference...you don't have to make monthly payments on the loan. Instead, the bank or mortgage company makes monthly payments to you...and charges those payments to your loan balance.

...and here's the rub: that money has to be paid back sometime, with interest.

One of the first steps is to get a clear idea of the cost (or costs) of the transaction. Very often, the loan fees can be much higher than you would normally see for a home loan. Check and compare. Don't be afraid to ask the person who is trying to sell you the loan what the fees are and when they are due. Another cost of the transaction is the interest rate. The interest rate on a reverse mortgage can be much higher than a traditional home loan mortgage. Remember, the fees and the interest rate cut into the actual amount of money you will receive each month.

The basic idea of a reverse mortgage is that you will continue to receive monthly payments until you die. When you die, the idea is that the home will be sold to pay back the reverse mortgage. If your family wants to keep the house, they have to pay back the reverse mortgage out of your estate or out of their pockets. This can interfere with your desires relating to gifts of money or property that you set up in your will.

If you are thinking about a reverse mortgage, ask your lawyer how it will inter-act with any will or other estate planning that you have set up. You want to avoid conflicts between the reverse mortgage and your overall plan for transferring your property and money to your family.

It is also important to remember that most or all reverse mortgages require that you continue to live in the house most of the time. If you move out, or if you are out of the house for over a year or so, you have to start re-paying the mortgage. This could come at a difficult time for you, particularly if you have to move in with a family member or move to a nursing home or move to some other type of long-term care facility.

Most people who sign up for a reverse mortgage are surprised to find out that they still have all the normal costs associated with owning a home, like insurance, taxes, repairs, maintenance, utilities, etc. These are not automatically covered by the reverse mortgage, unless you arrange to borrow more in order to provide for those expenses.

On the good side, you do retain ownership of the home, and the repayment of the loan is not due as long as the home is your primary residence and you maintain it and pay your taxes and insurance.

You can even use the reverse government mortgage to pay off your mortgage and eliminate mortgage payments altogether. In fact, there is no restriction on the use of the funds from a reverse mortgage. You can use it as the source of your regular income, or pay off debts, or whatever. Also, it may affect benefits, like Social Security or Veterans benefits, etc.

The program does require that the homeowner be at least 62 years of age and that there be a certain amount of equity already built up in the home.

Also, don't forget that you can just get a loan on your home, if you have enough equity. If you are concerned about a short-term need for money, that may be the best choice.

Whatever your situation, be sure to talk to your lawyer or financial planner before you take the step. Don't let the slick commercials with friendly guys be the basis for your decision. They don't need a reverse mortgage and they get paid a lot of money on the backs of people who choose a reverse mortgage without full knowledge and due diligence.

Tom Brown

Everything you never wanted to know about Hung Juries.

● ● ●

A "HUNG JURY"...SOUNDS KIND OF gruesome, doesn't it?

Actually, the phrase refers to a deadlocked jury.

In Washington State, as in most states, if all the jurors in a criminal case cannot agree to convict or acquit, the case is a nullity and the parties have to either settle or start over with a new trial. In a civil case, ten of the twelve jurors must agree, or that case has to settle or start over.

This is actually a pretty obscure topic; but I'm interested in it this month (and I hope you are, too), because my wife served on a jury in a criminal case last week, and it ended with a hung (or deadlocked) jury. A very rare situation indeed!

In the case where my wife sat as a juror, the defendant was charged with being a felon in possession of a firearm, which – in itself – is a felony. (A felony is any serious crime that can result in imprisonment in a state prison, as opposed to a misdemeanor, which has much less serious consequences.)

In this case, the defendant had been convicted of eluding a police officer at some time in the past and therefore was a felon. He never was seen with a gun; but there was a hunting rifle with his name and his father's name on the case. This rifle was in the garage of a neighbor of the defendant. The prosecution admitted that the evidence that he actually possessed the rifle at any time was circumstantial. Even though it was circumstantial, the prosecution said that was enough and he should be convicted.

Obviously, the defense disagreed, and argued to the jury that he should not be convicted on such feeble evidence. The defense made a strong case for the proposition that a man should not be convicted of a felony on circumstantial evidence.

Unlike the classic situation where there is a single holdout, in this case five of the jurors refused to vote for conviction, while seven thought that the prosecution had proved their case. They worked and worked at it, with the encouragement and help of the Judge, but they could not reach a unanimous verdict.

This case is a great illustration of how seriously our society takes the presumption of innocence and the unwillingness of our society to hang the label of criminal on someone without very, very strong proof; or, as we all know, *proof beyond a reasonable doubt.*

This all got me interested in the whole area of deadlocked – or hung – juries, so I did a little research to see what was going on in this area.

It turns out that there are studies on this subject. The National Center for State Courts commissioned an exhaustive study of the issue in 2002.

A jury expert –Kathy Kellerman, PhD – also studied the issue, relying on the 2002 study and on a 1966 study of American juries. She concluded that the rate of hung juries in criminal cases has remained fairly steady for the last fifty years, at approximately 5% of trials, or one in every twenty trials. This is an average, and the numbers in different jurisdictions can vary wildly. It's more likely to happen in state court rather than Federal Court. It's way more likely to happen in Los Angeles County, California than in Pierce County Washington.

Her study highlighted three issues that cause juries to deadlock in criminal cases:

* The evidence in the case is ambiguous or close.
* The prosecution is charging multiple counts or crimes.
* The case is very complex.

She concluded that: "Hung juries signal weaknesses in a case rather than weaknesses in the jury system. Hung juries are the result of case characteristics, not juror characteristics. Higher rates of hung juries in particular practice areas and jurisdictions signal more cases tried with ambiguous evidence, complex facts, and extensive charging."

In short, it's more proof that our legal system bends over backwards to protect the innocent and come to the correct decision.

As always, thank you for your wonderful comments about this column and your ideas and suggestions for topics!

Tom Brown

Should I Fight That Traffic Ticket??

● ● ●

MANY TIMES IN MY CAREER as a small town lawyer, my clients have asked me what they should do about a traffic ticket. What should I do? Should I just pay it? Should I go to court? What should I do in court?

Like all things, it's not an easy answer. Like lawyers like to say: "… it depends".

The first thing to think about is the gravity of the ticket and the gravity of the situation.

If the charge is serious, like Driving under the Influence of alcohol or drugs, or driving while suspended, then there is no choice…you have to talk to an attorney and you are facing serious consequences. Both the attorney and the charges are going to be expensive, but you have to accept these consequences, because it will affect your life for months and years to come.

On the other hand, if the charge is simple…like running a red light or speeding, you have some choices to make.

In Washington, you basically have three choices:

1. You can just pay the ticket without contesting what happened or the circumstances, and not even appear in court or explain what happened;

2. You can ask for a trial before the Court describing what happened and attempt to prove that you did not commit that offense.

3. You can plead "guilty" to the ticket and explain to the judge what the circumstances were that caused this situation.

This is where insurance comes in…if you plead guilty or are found guilty, this "conviction" becomes part of your record and your insurance company will see it and act accordingly…usually by raising your rates.

In addition, it is important to understand human nature. Municipal Court judges are usually lawyers who practice law like the rest of us and deal with clients all the time who have good defenses to traffic tickets. They like to see something different or something interesting or something they can "get their teeth into." If your situation is not routine, or, if your situation involves some issues that may have influenced the ticketing officer; or if you have something important to say, then – by all means go to court and tell the judge about this ticket.

The worst thing you can do is go to Court and rail against the police and the system and whatever. Judges are protective of the police and the municipality and don't like cheap shots against the police.

Whatever, you do, don't be a jerk or a smart-ass to the judge. Judges like to see nice citizens come to court and explain what happened. They don't like to have people come in and bad-mouth the police and bad-mouth the system, and hear all the complaints that the person has against the "system."

Truth be told, probably the best thing you can do if the ticket is righteous, is to go to court and tell the judge what happened, throwing in all the good things, like you've never had a ticket; you're a law abiding citizen; you didn't realize that the speed limit had been changed at that location; you only want to do the right thing; etc. That is what judges like to hear.

Again, if the ticket is serious (DUI, DWI, Driving while suspended, or someone was hurt), you absolutely must call an attorney to assist you because the consequences can be terrible.

If you do appear in Court on your own behalf…be courteous; don't criticize the officer; don't give a political rant about the "system"; don't lie; be yourself (unless yourself is a jerk); and, above all, be courteous and respectful to the judge.

As always, thanks for your great comments about this column and thanks for your suggestions for topics.

You readers are the soul of this newspaper and this column.

Tom Brown

Here comes the Judge!

$\bullet \bullet \bullet$

THE APPOINTMENT AND RETENTION OF Judges is a very important corner-stone of our judicial/political system. As you know, the knotty/difficult/quasi-impossible problems that confront our society and our political system usually end up before a Judge or a group of Judges on appeal. That makes it critically important that the men and women that sit on our judicial benches be wise and honorable.

Further, our judges are the "front line" in dealing with property disputes, marital disputes, employment issues, adoption battles and ever sort of societal problem that we citizens manage to come up with...so they have to be realistic and practical in dispensing justice. Every state has its own system for selecting judges.

Some have outright elections for people who are candidates; some states have a system where the governor appoints the judges and they then go before the voters at the end of their term to see if they should be retained; some states have the bar association provide a "slate" of candidates for appointment.

Most states do have a way of making the judges responsible to the people...after all, that is that they serve. The process in most states is then complicated by the system of endorsements. No matter how the judge is elevated to the bench, the public usually wants to know what their qualifications are and whether they have any serious blemishes on their record.

Usually, the state and local bar associations get in on the fun by polling their members on the qualifications of judges and releasing that information to the public.

Here in Grays Harbor and Pacific counties, the citizens have been blessed with a high quality of judges over the years. Grays Harbor has three Superior Court judges who have been in place for a long time and served honorably. (The Superior Court is the court of general jurisdiction that handles the larger and most common civil and criminal cases.)

Also, many of the readers of this fine publication are in Clallam County, which also has a strong and effective judiciary. What prompted this subject for our monthly column is the fact that one of those three Grays Harbor County Judges is retiring after a long and distinguished career on the bench.

Gordon Godfrey has been serving (and entertaining) the citizens of Grays Harbor County for over 22 years; but has decided to hang up the robe and enjoy life as a normal citizen. Our system of filling judicial seats is strictly in the hands of the citizens by election. We vote for our Judges, who put their names on the ballot. They have to be admitted to the bar as lawyers and they have to have a clean record. But what happens if the Judge retires and there is no election pending?

In that case, candidates submit their names to the Bar Association and to the Governor. The Governor asks the Bar Association for its recommendation and then considers all the information, and then makes an appointment that lasts until the next election. In our county, two candidates have announced their intention to seek this Judgeship, so their names have been submitted to the Governor for appointment until the general election. The two candidates are Stephen Brown and Jean Cotton.

Both are highly qualified and have significant judicial and legal experience. Stephen Brown is currently serving as a Judge of the District Court, a court that handles a wide variety of "smaller" cases that are not in the Superior Court, but present many of the same or similar issues.

Judge Brown has been serving in that position for many years, with distinction.

Jean Cotton is a practicing lawyer in Eastern Grays Harbor County, who has been a front-line practitioner for many years. She also regularly serves as a Court Commissioner and as a "pro-tem" Superior Court Judge on many occasions when our regular Superior Court Judges are not available or are over loaded.

Fortunately, the Governor faces a "win-win" situation here, with two outstanding candidates offering to serve in this important position. Whoever he appoints, the next election will decide who takes the bench for the next full term, with the voters of Grays Harbor County evaluating the qualities of the candidates.

The message that is really important here is for the citizens of Washington to understand that the process of filling judicial vacancies is not willy-nilly, is not capricious, is not overtly political, and is not corrupt.

It is a careful, open, and serious procedure that calls on the judicial branch of government and the executive branch of government, and on the lawyers and their Bar Associations, and on the people themselves, to participate.

If you have thoughts or ideas on who should hold this important Judgeship, you should contact the Governor's office and let them know what you think.

Thanks for reading my column and thanks for all the great comments!

Tom Brown

Merry Christmas

● ● ●

I READ AN ARTICLE THIS week about how the French and the Dutch and the English and the Italians and other European people take the opportunity of Christmas to honor our United States servicemen who died on their soil to protect freedom for all of us.

This was especially moving for me because I just got back from a small family gathering (just three of us!) to go over the relics of our family's recently departed. The tone was heavily weighted toward military matters.

My family is infused with threads of military history, from World War I, World War II, Korea, Bosnia. We visited the national cemetery at Fort Sam Houston, Texas to say goodbye to the most recently departed, a father and a son who were both army officers.

One only needs to visit a National Military cemetery to understand the toll that military service has taken on our families. The headstones stretch for as far as you can see. The reports of rifles are constant, as additional soldiers are laid to rest. Earth moving machines with huge augurs dig graves at a furious rate, trying to keep up with the influx of brave Americans qualified to rest in a national cemetery. Many of these were not active warriors on the battlefield... but many were.

But, now, at Christmas time...it is right and honorable for us to say "thank you" to our brave soldiers, just as the Europeans thank us for saving their countries.

But, hey! This is a column about lawyers and judges and laws and statutes and trials and appeals and other boring stuff about the law. What does that have to do with our military history?

Answer? Everything.

At the root of this country and its incredible system, lies a strong military history that has enforced our will to be a free, productive people.

But, let us never forget that our strong military stands guard over our commitment to the rule of law. Every day in our courtrooms, in our legislatures, in our city councils, in our tribal conclaves, in our appellate courts, in our city councils, in our neighborhood meetings...we wrestle with those issues that our nation relies on to keep us free.

We hope and pray that our brave soldiers will never have to march into those meetings in Aberdeen, Washington or Olympia, or Montesano to enforce the rule of law, as they had to do in the South in the 50s and 60s. But we cheer them in parades, honor them in their glory, and stand behind them always.

Christmas is the time to say that we will never wander from the rule of law. We will always trust our judges to rule with wisdom and care. We will trust our lawyers to stand before the bar of justice and seek fairness and honor for their clients. We will trust our politicians to preserve the system that allows us to worship and celebrate at Christmas, no matter whether we are Christians or Jews or simple children of the earth.

Merry Christmas!

Tom Brown

Happy New Year

• • •

By the time you are reading this, it will probably be the year 2015!!

How can that be? When I was a kid growing up in the 50s and 60s, the years beginning with 2000 seemed an eternity away...surely we wouldn't live that long!

But here we are...the Baby Boom Generation...bones creaking; artificial hips and knees gliding; pills in little daily boxes of plastic, so we take the right ones every day; reading a newspaper designed for "Seniors" – but bearing the ominous word "Sunset"!

So we are embarking on a new year. And this column is supposed to help us deal with (or understand) our legal issues. What should we do to eliminate or at least moderate our legal problems? Since the New Year is a time for resolutions and checklists, let's see what is on our legal agenda.

1. It's time to get those dusty estate planning documents out and see if changes are in order. I had some long-time friends contact me the other day about their old wills and we were amazed at how many things had changed. Children were married. Grandchildren were born. People had died. So take a look at your estate planning

documents and sees what doesn't make sense anymore. Be sure that you and your spouse have a Community Property Agreement and Powers of attorney for each other. Check to see if your will still makes sense. How about medical Powers of Attorney? How about being kept alive if you are terminal? Look them over and call the lawyer for an appointment if necessary.

2. While we still have our marbles, it's a good idea to consider giving things away. If there's a cabin or a camping property that you own, and you intend for it to stay in the family; maybe it's a good time to make the transfer now to your kids. You should have competent legal and accounting advice before a big move like this...but it can certainly ease things down the line. There are wonderful books out there on what to do with the family "place" if you have one. It's not just real estate...my son thinks my garage-queen classic car should go to the kids in California, but I'm not quite ready for that. Look around the house. Is it time for the books to be donated to the library? Is it time for the pool table to move to the kids' house?

3. Take a good hard look at your house and yard? Is it safe? I've read that most of the injuries to seniors occur right in the home, where we take things for granted. One powerful item is grab bars. Falling is a serious problem for us old folks and it is important to lessen that risk. In the bathroom, along the steps, ... anywhere where we might slip or trip and fall. Have your kids or a contractor put in some smart grab bars to keep you dancing. At the same time, identify other hazards in the house: Extension cords need to be out of the way. Loose carpeting and throw rugs are dangerous to older folks...get rid of them. Slippery spots in the home are scary. Get some lights on those dark stairs. Move the clutter away from walkways.

4. At our age, we've encountered all kinds of insurance and we pretty much just pay the premiums and hope we're doing the

right thing. This is an area where you can take control. Sit down with your lawyer or your insurance agent and "go to school" on your insurance policies. If you don't know what something means, then ask...or research it. Every one of those paragraphs means something. In the past, I've written about how important UIM automobile coverage is these days; but most people still ignore it or avoid it. Some people decline it to save a few bucks! Review your entire insurance package and make sure you understand it and change it if necessary.

5. Money. It's a pain in the billfold! But, as we ease into those golden years, it's very important for us to be smart about money. I thought I was pretty smart about investing until the stock market tanked a couple of times and interest rates went into the dumpster. So...professional financial advice can be critical at our ages. If nothing else, it forces us to collect all our information in one place and take a good hard look at it with a professional at our side. Stockbrokers can be fine...but I went for many years thinking they were primarily looking out for me.

6. Senior resources. It is flat amazing how many resources there are out there for us "seniors." Go to the senior center and see what's offered. Check the curriculum at the community college to see if there are courses designed for seniors. Use the Google search function every time you have a question...or an idea. It's shocking what's out there for us.

OK, that's my little collection of ideas that we should think about as we tiptoe into 2015.

As always, I want to thank Lora for this great little newspaper and for giving me the opportunity to share some legal thoughts with you over the years.

Please feel free to forward comments or suggestions or ideas or criticisms to the paper and Lora will get them to me.

Have a wonderful New Year!!!

Tom Brown

Who Would Sue Man's Best Friend?

• • •

I CAME FROM A FAMILY where hard work was a daily, unrelenting theme. My father was military, so he had strong opinions about what children should be doing...and it wasn't usually just playing in the yard.

In my case, it resulted in me having newspaper delivery routes for years in late grade school and in high school. If you think that cuts into your social/sports/fun life...you're right.

Anyway, one of the many drawbacks to having a paper route back in the 50s and 60s was that nobody gave a lick about the paperboy's relationship with their dog (...or dogs). The dogs were left free to bark, attack, bite, snarl, jump, etc., etc. and the paperboy was just supposed to deal with it.

Fortunately, things have changed. As we have matured as a society, we have come to recognize that it is not a good thing for people to be bitten or attacked or mauled by people's pets. In fact, the law has come to recognize that if you let your dog roam free, you are responsible for what it does. The range of possibilities -- like most things in life -- is huge. A dog might just bite without breaking the skin or it might scar a young woman's face forever.

The law's view of this is simple: If your dog causes damage to another person, you are probably responsible for the result. If it's a serious mauling that results in hospital treatment and subsequent plastic surgery, the bill could be astronomical. Even worse, the person mauled is entitled to be compensated for the pain and suffering experienced at the jaws of the dog, even if it goes on for years.

My wife was bitten in our neighborhood, but the people would not own up to it. It wasn't a terribly serious bite, but she had to have shots and medical follow-up and she has a scar on one of those fabulous legs.

Like everything connected with the law, it all depends on the facts. If you have a group of angry pit bulls that are on the attack constantly, the law is going to frown on your position. On the other hand, if your fabulous golden retriever is tortured by the neighborhood idiot into biting, it's a different story.

If you have a dog or dogs (or other animals), what should you do?

First of all, if you have animals, talk to your insurance agent and find out what your Homeowner's policy says about liability for attacks by your animals. If necessary, talk about a rider. Again, if you have pit bulls or other scary breeds, talk at length and in detail with your insurance person. Find out what your coverage is...and get it in writing.

Next, understand that the duty is on the owner of the animals... that's YOU! Your job is to make sure that your animals do not attack the usual group of people that are exposed: like service people who come to your house; like your neighbors who like to walk down the street in the evening; like your houseguests; like the mailman.

We've been mostly talking dogs here; but the same rules apply to other animals. In fact, if the animal is particularly hostile and scary, the rules may be even more rigid. If you have an eleven-foot anaconda roaming the house or yard, you have a particular duty to monitor the activity and whereabouts of that animal. The same is true of other "exotic" animals that can hurt people or other animals.

Remember, your neighbors have the right to live and enjoy their neighborhood without being bitten or killed or scared to death by your cute little animals. If neighbors or visitors or workmen are injured or killed by your pets, the law will support their claim against you for medical bills, lost wages and pain and suffering.

In some cases, relentless barking throughout the night has been the basis of a lawsuit for pain and suffering experienced by the neighbors who can't sleep.

What should you do?

1. Assess your situation. Do you have an animal that is having an impact on the world outside your house?
2. Talk to your insurance agent about your situation and take his/her advice about your animal(s).
3. If you have an extreme situation, (exotic animals, fierce animals, many animals), make an appointment with your lawyer and ask him/her what steps you should take.
4. Remember...the most common situation is a dog or multiple dogs. Figure out if you are a scary neighbor. Figure out if your animals are scary or noisy or are crapping on everyone's yard or are biting people...so immediately do something about it.
5. If you think your animals are a problem, address it immediately...if you sit around and let it boil, you will find yourself

on the ugly end of a letter from a lawyer or a visit from the police.

As always, I thank you for taking the time to read my little column. I also thank Lora for the opportunity to talk to you for all these years about how the law works...and sometimes doesn't work!!

Tom Brown

How should I act in court?

● ● ●

THE TEMPTATION IS TO THINK that the real actors in the Courtroom drama are the lawyers.

They do all the talking to the judge and/or jury.

They prepare and show the exhibits to the Judge and/or Jury and/or witnesses.

They shout out the objections at various times.

They argue the facts and law to the Judge and Jury.

They write the briefs for the Judge to read before and during the case.

They are surrounded by piles of papers and briefcases

They must be the most important persons in the Courtroom, right?

Totally and absolutely wrong! The most important and pivotal person or persons in the Courtroom are the clients themselves, the Plaintiff...the Defendant...the parties.

Jurors and Judges are smart. They are looking for those clues that give them insight into what makes the person(s) that they are judging..."tick."

It's about *demeanor*, that great neon marquee that we all carry around, whether we are in a bar, in a church, or in a courtroom. Judges and jurors are looking at every twitch, every raised eyebrow, every snicker, and every offshoot of our demeanor that tells the viewer what kind of person is being judged.

In fact, the concept of something that *tells* the juror or judge what they are dealing with, is what it is all about. We all have tells. We raise an eyebrow, we cough, we snicker, we smile, and we elbow our lawyer. These are all "tells" and the wise judge and the sharp juror will watch those tells throughout the proceeding, and measure what each activity means.

When I think of what a client can do -- inadvertently -- to screw up his or her own case, I shudder.

The one that immediately comes to mind is the woman who was suing for damages for the tragic death of her child. The Judge had given the usual stern warning to everyone (jurors, lawyers, witnesses, parties) about the evils of cell phones in the courtroom, with the usual warnings of confiscation and other horrors. The mood during the trial was somber. The subject matter was terrible. And yet, at a critical time in the trial, the mother's cell phone started chirping away...loudly! It was one of those situations where you wish you had the power to transport everyone to another planet. In that case, the result wasn't terrible; but it certainly impacted the case.

Another crazed situation is when an "expert witness" testifies. Experts are often used to help the jurors understand some really obscure issue that affects the case...like the effect of heat or cold on the effectiveness of a car's brakes. Experts too often take the title of "expert" too seriously.

Most jurors and judges are pretty smart and have a pretty good idea about the issues in the case. Way too often, the expert doesn't realize how pompous and dorky he or she sounds when lecturing the Judge or jury on the effect of temperature. Jurors and judges hate pompous asses.

The best experts are the ones that honestly want to transmit information and act like human beings. The worst experts are the ones that think they are God's gift to the legal system.

The thing that it is important for witnesses and lawyers to remember is that the judges and jurors are not as bored and detached, as they may seem. They are *riveted* by what is going on before their eyes. They want to get it straight. They want to do the right thing. If they sense phoniness or falsity or game playing, that person's case is going to suffer.

Jurors and Judges want to do "justice." They want their decision to be the correct one. They want to go home and tell their spouse that justice was served and the "right" thing was done.

So...as part of that, they are suspicious and wary. They watch every move of every witness. They interpret every gesture. They can smell lies. They can see exaggeration. They can feel falsity. Their view of the lawyers is important, of course, ...but it pales in comparison to what they read on the faces and lips and gestures of the witnesses.

So...how should we act in Court? My routine answer to that question for my clients is pretty easy...act like we are in a bar, or in church, or at the bowling alley. Be normal. Don't try to be someone else. That someone else is probably not going to be someone that the jurors and judge respect. If they smell that you are acting like someone else, they are not going to believe you or trust you. Take a deep breath and do what your lawyer tells you to do. Don't try to be a star...you'll end up as a fallen meteor. Don't try to be cool...you'll come across as cold. Don't try to be smart...you'll come across as a smartass.

Remember that the courtroom is a place for truth...not a place for actors, or smartasses, or one-upmanship, or liars. The jurors will know. The Judge will know. You will know. The result will reflect the truth. Usually.

Tom Brown

Don't Wait Until Your Loved One Dies

• • •

I REALLY HATE THE TRENDY, over-the-top lingo that is so prevalent these days. Included in my wrath is the word "pro-active" which has attached itself to everything from child raising to dealing with your banker.

It just means "everything"!

Anyway, I sort of had my mind changed this morning, driving from our cabin (...what a glorious day!!!) to Aberdeen. One of my favorite guys was on the radio...a lawyer who has been handing out advice on the air for many years.

Robert Pittman was a hero of mine. He would patiently field all callers on KIRO radio for many years on a show called "Legal Line." He was so patient, so friendly, so helpful...as people called in with all sorts of fabulous (...and goofy) legal issues. I loved Robert Pittman's "Legal Line" show for many years.

Anyway, as Bob started to wind down, his chair was taken over by Rajiv Nagaich, who has a show (and a website), called "Aging Options." If you can raise KIRO down here in God's country, he's worth listening to. In the meantime, spend some time exploring Nagaich's website ("Aging Options") and also Google Robert Pittman and I think you can listen to old versions of his show with all kinds of great advice.

So, back to my "proactive"point. Bob Pittman was sitting in today for Nagaich, advocating something I have never encouraged. Not because I disagree with him...but because I never thought of it!! What a dummy we lawyers can be!

Bob was advocating a process called a "family meeting" to go over the game plan for the declining members of the family, before a death or before a crisis.

Who is going to call the lawyer?

Where are the wills?

What if Mom loses it...what do we do about the Durable Power of Attorney that Dad has?

Should we see the lawyer?

Maybe we should call the lawyer? Most people are afraid of this avenue, because they think it is going to generate some huge bill. Actually, that is usually not true. Most lawyers that I know (including me) are happy to spend a few minutes with the family on the phone or in person without any charge to discuss what all those papers we generated years ago actually mean today...when it counts.

Even more important, the "family meeting" is the opportunity to face reality and maybe do something about it. Is Dad still driving? Should he be? What legal documents exist and where are they? Do we need the lawyer to look at them?

Usually, the situation of Mom or Dad dying or failing has been pretty well covered by a Community Property Agreement (in Washington) and a Durable Power of Attorney. But those are legal solutions...the family solutions can be tougher. Who is going to talk to Dad about letting Mom do the driving? (I have a friend whose Dad is a semi-famous lawyer who wouldn't think of letting his bride Mary do the driving... he's 96, she's 93...finally the family had to step in and put an end to the driving for both of them...their driving exploits were the stuff of family legends!)

Anyway, I was totally knocked over today by the concept of a family meeting to sort out what's going on and what needs to be done. It's a great, healthy, smart idea. It gives us a chance to look each other in the eye and say, "What's best for Mom & Dad? What's best for our sister Mary who can't cope? Do we need more attention from a lawyer? Have we talked like this in the last 10 years?

Most families I know have smart, caring people who want to do the right thing. They just don't know how to put together the moment, the opportunity of getting together and facing these issues.

I hope our kids do it for us.

Tom Brown

de minimis

• • •

I HAVEN'T REMINDED MY LOYAL readers in many months (or years) what the name of this column ("*de minimis*") means.

It is shorthand for a famous Latin phrase: "De minimis non curat lex," which translates to "...the law does not concern itself with little things."

...but the best thing about it -- like many idioms and slang of our speech -- is that it's simply not always true. The law does indeed concern itself with all kinds of little things and little ideas and little gestures that inhabit our day-to-day world.

The law is an amoeba, an octopus, a squid that tries to cover and envelop every human experience, and give us understanding and realization about what is meant or caused by this particular phenomenon. The law is not evil or vindictive...it just wants to KNOW, and to UNDERSTAND what is in its salty folds. Once it understands, that knowledge will be indexed and evaluated and stored in the bowels of the law.

Those of us that have gone to law school have caressed those willowy, salty folds of understanding and tried to reconcile the rule of law with the day-to-day dealing of being a human being in a crazy world.

De Minimis

We come to the law for certainty and guidance and history. Usually the law can respond and say: "Here is what has happened before...good or bad...do you want to follow that path?"

The law does not want conflict. Shocking? Unbelievable? ...of course. We tend to think of the law as a system that generates and preserves ancient, ridiculous forms of combat that have survived today as lawsuits and terrible conflict. In truth, the law actually seeks to de-fuse those conflicts. If a man dies and leaves assets (things) behind, the law wants to make sure that those things are preserved and honored and sent to the proper person in the next generation, without litigation or conflict.

If a man dies and leaves a will, directing the distribution of his assets, the law steps in and says this direction will be honored and insulated from outside attackers.

Trouble is...when there is no will, no statement, no scribbling, no responsible legend of what the deceased left behind, to show us the way. Then we reach into the bowels of history and look for guidance. Hopefully we find in the law the guideposts to help us figure out what is right.

When neighbors fight over a property line, the law forces us to look into the history of the properties, look at the usages of the property, look at what the parties said or did in the past, and then arrive at a just and reasonable result that hopefully serves the best interests of both parties.

When there is a dispute over the value of an item, the law forces us to measure that value against the known value of similar items; or the law may require us to have an expert look at the item and offer an expert opinion on the value of that item. Again, the law will take those matters into account and try to render a result that is reasonable and fair.

It is when the law treads in the really nasty areas that people see the harsher, sharp edges of the law that cut through the falsity and lies and deception that often accompany criminal cases or bitter divorces or similar difficult cases.

So, when you go to your lawyer, you may be asked dozens of questions that seem irrelevant or intrusive or unnecessary or even stupid. Remember that the lawyer certainly wants to know the big, obvious stuff that seems plain to you. But, he or she also has a wider agenda.

The lawyer is concerned with the tiny, seemingly irrelevant remarks or letters or photos that seemed *de minimis* to you; but may make all the difference in the world to a Judge or a jury.

So, in the bigger picture, it is true that the law does not concern itself with little, inconsequential things, like a dispute over fifty cents... that is *de minimis*.

But, in resolving a multi-million dollar divorce or determining the value of exotic real estate, the law will look at all the factors that bear on the truth, even if those factors may seem *de minimis*, to arrive at a fair and just resolution of the dispute.

As always, I hope these little columns make the law more understandable, more fun, less scary and somewhat interesting. Please feel free to share any comments with me at tom.brown@lawbljs.com

Tom Brown

www.ingramcontent.com/pod-product-compliance
Lightning Source LLC
Chambersburg PA
CBHW060540200326
41521CB00007B/428